Watercourse Co-operation in Northern Europe

– A Model for the Future –

Norwegian Sea
Barents Sea
Finnmark
NORWAY
Alta
Tana/
Teno
L. Inari
Pasvik
Tuloma
Voron'ya
Lotta
Ivalo
Murmansk Oblast
Iokanga
L. Lovozero
Kola Peninsula
L. Umbozero
Ponoy
L. Imandra
Lokan Res.
Muonio
Torneträsk
Lainio
Lapland
Luiro
Torne
Ounas
Varzuga
Stora
Lulevatten
Kalix
Kemi
L. Kovdozero
Norrbotten
Torne/
Tornio
L. Pyaozero
White Sea
Kemi
L. Kitka
L. Topozero
Lule
Pite
Kem'
Vindel
Ii
L. Kianta
L. Kuyto
Skellefte
Oulu
Ume
Onega
L. Oulu
Ångerman
L. Vygozero
Pyhä
FINLAND
SWEDEN
L. Segozero
L. Pielinen
L. Vodlozero
Indals
L. Keitelä
Kallavesi
L. Höytiäinen
Ljungan
Gulf of Bothnia
Orivesi
L. Syamozero
Haukivesi
L. Onega
Puruvesi
L. Näsi
L. Puula
Päijänne L.
Svir
L. Saimaa
Ljusnan
Kokemäen
Vuoksi
L. Ladoga
L. Beloye
Kymi
RUSSIA
Dal
Gulf of Finland
Volkhov
Mälaren
Narva Res.
Mologa
ESTONIA

Watercourse Co-operation in Northern Europe

– A Model for the Future –

Malgosia Fitzmaurice
&
Olufemi Elias

with the co-operation of

Vaughan Lowe

T·M·C· Asser Press
The Hague

Published by T·M·C·Asser press
P.O.Box 16163, 2500 BD The Hague, The Netherlands
<www.asserpress.nl>

T·M·C·Asser press' English language books are distributed exclusively by:

Cambridge University Press, The Edinburgh Building, Shaftesbury Road,
Cambridge CB2 2RU, UK,
or
for customers in the USA, Canada and Mexico:
Cambridge University Press, 40 West 20th Street, New York, NY 10011-4211, USA
<www.cambridge.org>

ISBN 978-90-6704-172-0

PREFACE AND ACKNOWLEDGEMENTS

This book has been written with the aim of making a contribution to the ongoing debate on global water scarcity in general and on the equitable sharing of watercourses in particular. It examines relevant aspects of the practice of Finland, Norway and Sweden and, to a lesser extent, Russia against the background of relevant principles and rules of international environmental law. Chapter Four, written by Professor Vaughan Lowe, demonstrates the extent of co-operation in respect of the use of watercourses between the countries in question, underlining the basis for their selection as the focus of the book.

The authors would like to express their appreciation for the useful comments by Dr Rene Lefeber on earlier drafts of the manuscript and for the invaluable assistance of Dr Maria Vogiatzi during the preparation of the book. They are also grateful to Beites Amund and Ovind Seather of the Norwegian Ministry of the Environment, and to officials of the Finnish Ministry of the Environment for their assistance in providing useful documentation. The authors are also grateful to the Finnish Yearbook of International Law, published by Martinus Nijhoff Publishers, for permission to use, in Chapter 3, some material previously published in Volume VIII (1997) of the Yearbook. Finally, the authors would like to thank the staff of T.M.C. Asser Press for their assistance and professionalism in the preparation of the book.

London, March 2004

MALGOSIA FITZMAURICE
Professor of International Law,
Department of Law, Queen Mary,
University of London

OLUFEMI ELIAS
Legal Adviser,
UN Compensation Commission,
Geneva

TABLE OF CONTENTS

ABBREVIATIONS

AJIL	American Journal of International Law
ATS	Australian Treaty Series
AYIL	Australian Yearbook of International Law
BYIL	British Yearbook of International Law
CJTL	Columbia Journal of Transnational Law
CLR	Canterbury Law Review
CYIL	Canadian Yearbook of International Law
CWRJIL	Case Western Reserve Journal of International Law
EC	European Community
ECOSOC	United Nations Economic and Social Council
EPL	Environmental Policy and Law
EU	European Union
GIELR	Georgia International Environmental Law Review
GYIL	German Yearbook of International Law
HHRJ	Harvard Human Rights Journal
HRQ	Human Rights Quarterly
ICLQ	International and Comparative Law Quarterly
ICJ	International Court of Justice
ICJ Rep	Reports of Judgments, Advisory Opinions and Orders of the International Court of Justice
ILA	International Law Association
ILC	International Law Commission
ILO	International Labour Organization
ILR	International Law Reports
ILM	International Legal Materials
IUCN	IUCN – The World Conservation Union
LNTS	League of Nations Treaty Series
LJIL	Leiden Journal of International Law
MLJ	McGill Law Journal
NGO	Non-Governmental Organization
NJIL	Nordic Journal of International Law

NRF	Natural Resources Forum
NRJ	Natural Resources Journal
NSAIL	Non-State Actors and International Law
OECD	Organization for Economic Co-operation and Development
OJ	Official Journal of the European Communities
PCIJ	Permanent Court of International Justice
PYIL	Polish Yearbook of International Law
RBDI	Revue Belge du Droit International
RCADI	Receuil des Cours de Droit International
RECIEL	Review of European Community and International Environmental Law
SALJ	South African Law Journal
UKTS	United Kingdom Treaty Series
UNCED	United Nations Conference on Environment and Development
UNECE	United Nations Economic Commission for Europe
UNESCO	United Nations Educational, Scientific and Cultural Organization
UNGA	United Nations General Assembly
UNRIAA	United Nations Reports of International Arbitral Awards
UNTS	United Nations Treaty Series
VJIL	Virginia Journal of International Law
WCED	World Commission on Environment and Development
YILC	Yearbook of the International Law Commission
YIEL	Yearbook of International Environmental Law

Chapter 1
INTRODUCTION

1. The Problem[1]

The current and anticipated global problems in relation to the adequacy of the world's water supply have been widely discussed. According to one source,[2] the availability of more than 5,000 m^3 of water per person is comfortable, while less than 2,000 m^3 per person is cause for serious concern, and 1,000 m^3 is the viability threshold for a community. The average amount of water available per person worldwide has dropped from nearly 4,500 m^3 in 1965 and is expected to be less than half of that by 2015. This is due to a number of factors. Geographical factors, in particular the extremely uneven distribution of water in the world, contribute to this. Ninety-eight per cent of world water is salt water, and only 2% fresh water. Ice covered areas constitute 87% of world water, rivers and lakes 2% and ground water 12%. Of the world's fresh water, less than 0.5% is in the form of useable fresh water. Desertification is also another phenomenon that has deleterious consequences on water supplies. The problem is worst in equatorial Africa and Central Asia, but severe water shortages are expected to affect the world's population well beyond these areas.

Apart from the geographical, there are other factors that contribute to the situation. Economic and demographic factors also play a part. The use of water has greatly increased in the course of this century; the total use at the beginning of the century was approximately 500 km^3, and this has risen to over 5,000 km^3 in 2000, and is still rising. The problems abound. Over-extraction has made the already difficult situation worse. Pollution has affected the amount of potable water available. Agricultural practices, such as irrigation, account for up to 80% of water usage in many develop-

[1] See, further, Section 1 of Chapter 6 below.

[2] See *Shared Water Systems and Transboundary Issues with Special Emphasis on the Iberian Peninsula*, Proceedings of the Conference held at the Luso-American Development Foundation, Lisbon, 2000, pp. 23-28.

ing countries, but is known to be uneconomical and eventually weakens the usability of soil for agricultural purposes. Population growth and higher standards of living also take their toll on water supply, and many natural sources are increasingly depleted as a result of diversion of water. This itself has deleterious effects on the environment, as ecosystems suffer. The construction of dams for hydro-electric and/or water management purposes has also resulted in movement of populations, with the poorer and indigenous peoples generally suffering the most.[3]

The amount of fresh water in lakes and rivers being replenished by precipitation does not amount to more than 0.01% of the liquid water available on earth. In absolute figures, there are approximately 11 million km^3 of liquid fresh water on earth. It is to be borne in mind that this figure does not indicate that this is the amount of water available to the human race. The use of water is limited by the requirements of sustainability. Sustainable use of fresh water should not exceed the amount by which these reserves are replenished through precipitation. Over half of the precipitation falling on earth every year is lost through evaporation. Therefore, from the point of view of sustainability, the absolute maximum available annually is only about 45,000 km^3. The supply of fresh water through precipitation is unequally distributed within and between continents. Approximately 33% of Europe, 60% of Asia, 85% of Africa and most of Australia and the western section of North America consist of arid regions.

The majority of countries with limited available water are in the Middle East, North Africa and Sub-Saharan Africa. In other countries shortage of water affects only a part of the country, such as for example, in the north of China, and the south west of India, the western regions of South America and much of Pakistan and Mexico. Dams and reservoirs have been built on most rivers of the world. The arguments for their building were better distribution of water, the generation of energy and

[3] H.L.F. Saeijs and M.J. van Berkel, "The Global Water Crisis: The Major Issue of the Twenty-first Century, a Growing and Explosive Problem", in *The Scarcity of Water, Emerging Legal and Policy Responses,* E.H.P. Brans, E.J. de Haan, A. Nollkaemper, J. Rinzema (eds.), Kluwer Law International London, The Hague, Boston (1997), p. 5. See also P. Birnie and A. Boyle, *International Law and the Environment* (2nd edn. 2002), p. 299.

safety. However, excessive construction of dams and reservoirs resulted in biomass being destroyed and dislocated and animals and plants disappearing. In reservoirs, rotting vegetation causes uncontrollable problems of oxygen depletion and toxic substances in the water and toxic gases above it. Reservoirs are filled with pollutants from cities and upstream industry or with sediment. The usual practice is to build dams for reasons justified at the local level: for urban water supplies, irrigation in agriculture, shipping, energy and safety. However, the problem is that these local interests are not weighed against global effects on the ecosystem and on people living elsewhere in the river basin. It is a matter of the utmost importance that this should be subject to proper water management.[4]

But if the water problems facing our world are sometimes a cause of tension and concern, they can also be a catalyst for co-operation. Two thirds of the world's major rivers are shared by several states. More than 300 rivers cross national boundaries. Increasingly, countries with expertise in the management of watersheds and flood plains, or with experience in efficient irrigation, share that knowledge and technology with others. Scientists from many nations and disciplines are pooling their efforts, assessing risks and working to bring about a much needed "blue revolution" in agricultural productivity. Policy-makers can and should draw on this body of experience, which has generated a rich inventory of best practice.

2. The Aim of the Book

From the foregoing, it should be apparent that it is of fundamental importance to develop a set of acceptable rules to govern the co-operation between states in management of international watercourses. Such a system should take account of developmental needs and of environmental concerns in such a way as to minimise disputes and conflicts over water. The

[4] H.L.F. Saeijs and M.J. van Berkel, *ibid.*, pp. 6-9. The Sadar Sarovar Project in India is a good example of such unsustainable construction of dams. See, e.g., J.D. Werksman, "Greening Bretton Woods", in *Greening International Law*, P. Sands (ed.), 1993, in particular pp. 73-74; P. Cullet, "Human Rights and Displacement; The Indian Supreme Court Decision on Sadar Sarovar in International Perspective", 50 *ICLQ*, (2001), pp. 973-987.

aim of this book is to contribute to the development of such a set of rules by considering the situation in certain northern European countries, namely Finland, Norway, Sweden and Russia, with a view to seeing how such co-operation works. It is hoped that this will shed some light on the possibilities that exist for a generalizable model for the development of the needed legal regulation.

Why focus on these countries? There are a number of reasons for this. In the first place, these neighbouring countries have a long history of activity and co-operation in the use and regulation of the many watercourses under their jurisdiction. As will be seen, this co-operation is reflected in the large network of multilateral and bilateral treaties on the issue, some dating back to the nineteenth century. Also, Finland, Norway and Sweden offer a perspective of the possibilities of co-operation and the practical application of the principle of good neighbourliness given the relative similarity between their legal and social systems. This may be contrasted with the position in Russia, in which the national legal system, at least for the most part of this century, is founded on a different political, economic and social vision. By examining co-operation between countries with more homogeneous as well as those with divergent foundations, it is hoped that some difficulties to be faced in implementing principles of good neighbourliness in this regard will be brought out.

3. The Structure of the Book

The book contains a number of discrete essays. Each essay has been written with focus on its particular subject-matter, and not necessarily as a part of a unified sequence of parts of a monograph. The idea is to provide a view of the subjects discussed in each chapter independently, even though there is some cross-reference between the chapters. As a result there is some overlap between the issues considered in the different chapters.

Chapter 2 provides a general introduction and overview of the international law relating to the navigational and non-navigational uses of international watercourses, as a backdrop for the consideration of the practice of the Nordic states regarding the principles and rules of international environmental law. It also examines the practice of these states in their relations inter se as well as their national legislation. Chapter 3 is an examination of the position of indigenous peoples living in these countries, *in casu* the Saami of Lapland and Finnmark, whose lifestyle is dependent on the use of watercourses, with a view to seeing the extent to which the practice of the states reflects international standards concerning the rights of groups in general and their application to the use of watercourses in these states in particular. Chapter 4 provides a broad look at the history, nature and extent of co-operation between these countries regarding the use of watercourses, underscoring the basis of the selection of these states as the subject of consideration. It provides insights into how the principle of good neighbourliness, fundamental in the law governing the use of shared resources, has been put into effect in the rules procedures and mechanisms in place in these countries. Chapter 5 considers the institutional dimension – if legal regulation of watercourses is to be based on a holistic approach aimed at sustainability, the importance of joint management cannot be overestimated. Finally, in view of the problem of water scarcity, which places a premium on sustainability, Chapter 6 examines the place of the fundamental concept of sustainable development in the regulation of the uses of international watercourses.

It is hoped that the various issues considered in the following chapters will offer some useful insights for efforts aimed at dealing with the fundamental problem of water scarcity and the achievement of the ultimate goal of ensuring the availability of water for present and future generations.

Chapter 2
THE LAW OF THE NAVIGATIONAL AND NON-NAVIGATIONAL USE OF INTERNATIONAL WATERCOURSES

1. Introduction

This chapter will provide an introduction to the regulation of the uses of international watercourses under general international law. The main legal issues arising in this context, including the different doctrinal approaches to the problem and their practical implementation, have been the subject of a considerable amount of academic writing, particularly since the adoption of the 1992 UNECE Convention on the Protection and Use of Transboundary Watercourses and International Lakes (1992 UNECE Watercourse Convention) and the 1997 UN Convention on the Law of the Non-Navigational Uses of International Watercourses by the UN General Assembly (1997 UN Watercourse Convention).[1] The 1997 UN Watercourse Convention in particular is a milestone in the development of the law on the non-navigational uses of international watercourses,[2] and is expected to have a significant impact on the development

[1] See, for the text of the 1992 UNECE Watercourse Convention, Convention on the Protection and Use of Transboundary Watercourses and International Lakes, which was signed on 17 March 1992 and entered into force on 6 October 1996, 31 *ILM* 1312 (1992). Finland signed on 18 March and ratified on 21 February 1996; Norway signed on 18 September and ratified on 1 April 1993; Russia signed on 18 March and ratified on 2 November 1993; Sweden signed on 18 March 1992 and ratified on 5 August 1993. For the text of the 1997 UN Convention on the Law of Non-Navigable Uses of International Watercourses, see 36 *ILM* 700 (1997), signed on 21 May 1997, not yet in force. Sweden acceded to the 1997 Convention on 15 June 2000; Finland signed on 31 October 1997 and accepted on 23 January 1998; Norway signed and ratified on 30 September 1998; Russia is not a party.

[2] There are numerous publications on this subject. See in particular, on this convention, in particular two in depth studies: S. McCaffrey, *The Law of International Watercourses Non-Navigational Uses* (2001), and A. Tanzi and M. Arcari, *The United Nations Convention on the Law of International Watercourses*, (2001). See also S. McCaffrey and M.

of new agreements and the amendment of existing ones relating to particular international watercourses. Article 3(1) of the 1997 Convention provides that "nothing in the present Convention shall affect the rights and obligations of a watercourse State arising from agreements in force for it on the date on which it becomes a party to the present Convention". Thus the Convention does not affect the rights and obligations arising from existing agreements and is residual in character. A fundamental question that arises, for present purposes, is the relationship between existing treaties on watercourse co-operation between Nordic States and the 1997 Convention. As for the 1992 UNECE Watercourse Convention, a close link exists between this Convention and the existing treaties on watercourse co-operation between Nordic States. This Convention, which was a blueprint for the 1997 UN Watercourse Convention, was the first to codify, on a regional basis, the rules governing the protection and use of international watercourses. It is based to a certain degree on existing international law and on the ILC's draft articles on the non-navigational uses of international watercourses. In fact, as all Nordic States and Russia are parties to the 1992 UNECE Watercourse Convention, the recommendations of that Convention are regularly applied on the level of bilateral co-operation between the above-mentioned states (for example, between Finland and Russia in relation to setting up the joint monitoring programmes envisaged under the 1992 Environmental Co-operation Convention, discussed in Chapter 6 below). Thus, it may be said that the 1992 UNECE Watercourses Convention is part and a parcel of the common network of watercourse treaties linking these states.

2. The Definition of "International Watercourse"

One of the most controversial problems relating to the law of the non-navigational uses of international watercourses has been the definition of

---

Sinjela, "The 1997 United Nations Convention on International Watercourses", 92 *AJIL* (1998), pp. 97-107; A. Tanzi, "The UN Convention on International Watercourses as a Framework for the Avoidance and Settlement of Water Law Disputes", 11 *LJIL* (1998), pp. 441-472; X. Fuentes, "Sustainable Development and the Equitable Utilization of International Watercourses", 69 *BYIL* (1998), p. 120; M. Fitzmaurice, "General Principles Governing the Co-operation between States in Relation to Non-Navigational Uses of Watercourses', 13 *YIEL* (2002) (forthcoming)".

"international watercourse". The classic definition of an international watercourse, for long regarded as international customary law, was included in Articles 1 and 2 of the Regulation of 24 March 1815 concerning the free navigation of rivers and in Articles 108 and 109 of the Final Act of the Congress of Vienna of 8 June 1815.[3] These limited definitions referred to international watercourses as being those which separate or cut across the territory of two or more states. The meaning of the term "watercourse" could be limited in this way to flowing waters, i.e. the river and tributaries, lakes and canals, but could however also be considered more widely, to include for example "the material portion of land contained in the *divortium aquarium* or the limits of the watershed draining into the international river".[4] This wider approach, which takes account of the so-called drainage basin, was adopted in Article 11 of the 1966 ILA Helsinki Rules.[5] The ILC also initially considered such an approach, but it proved to be very unpopular with states and was abandoned by the ILC. The adoption of such an approach would have meant that it was possible that vast expanses of territory might be governed by a regime of multiple sovereignty in regarding different matters relating to the management of rivers.[6] Accordingly, the 1997 UN Watercourse Convention defines a "watercourse" as "a system of surface waters and groundwaters constituting by virtue of their physical relationship a unitary whole and normally flowing into a common terminus" (Article 2(a)).[7] An international water-

[3] L. Hertslet (ed.), A Collection of Treaties and Conventions between Great Britain and Foreign Powers, Vol. I, p. 3.

[4] J. Sette-Camara, "Pollution of International Rivers", 186 *RCADI* (1984), p. 128.

[5] International Law Association, *Report of the Fifty-Second Conference*, Helsinki, (1966), p. 484. See, on the negotiating history of the 1966 ILA Helsinki Rules, C. Bourne, "The International Law Association's Contribution to International Resources Law", 36 *NRJ* (1996), pp. 170-173.

[6] See Sette-Camara, *supra* note 4, at p. 130.

[7] Both the 1994 ILC Draft Articles and the 1997 UN Watercourse Convention exclude confined groundwater. The ILC, however, passed a separate resolution on confined transboundary ground water, which, in the view of the ILC, is also a natural resource of vital importance for "sustaining life, health and the integrity of ecosystems"; see the preamble to its "Resolution on Confined Transboundary Groundwater", in "Report of the ILC on the work of its Forty-sixth Session", UN Doc. A/49/10, *YILC* (1994), Vol. II, (Part Two), p. 135. The ILC commended "States to be guided by the principles contained in the draft articles on the law of the non-navigational uses of international watercourses, where appropriate, in regulating transboundary groundwater".

course is defined as a "watercourse, parts of which are situated in different States" (Article 2(b)). The definition also encompasses tributaries of cross-frontier rivers, frontier straddling lakes, and ground water that is connected with other parts of an international watercourse independently of the ground water. The Convention does not differentiate between contiguous watercourses, which form a boundary, and successive watercourses, which cross a boundary.[8]

A number of issues arise from this definition. One is the use of the term "common terminus", which was controversial because it constituted one of the elements of the definition of "international drainage basin" in the 1966 ILA Helsinki Rules. The ILC, however, explained in its commentary to the 1994 ILC Draft Articles on the Law of the Non-Navigational Uses of International Watercourses (1994 ILC Draft Articles)[9] that the term was included to impose certain limitations on the geographic scope of the definition.[10] Also, the word "normally" was added as a compromise between the proponents of the enlargement of the definition of "watercourse" and those who wanted to limit it.[11] The ILC's Special Rapporteur on the law of the non-navigational uses, Stephen McCaffrey, has stated that "[a]part from its compromise function, the word 'normally' is a convenient way of dealing with hydrological conditions that are well-known but not generally present, and that would not strictly satisfy the 'common terminus' requirement".[12]

Opinion is also divided on the question whether international watercourses belong to the category of "shared resources", a concept that many writers regard as underlying the principle of prevention of transboundary water pollution.[13] The ILC, having initially included the concept of "shared resources" in its draft articles on the law of the non-navigational

[8] See S. McCaffrey, "The International Law Commission Adopts Draft Articles on International Watercourses", 89 *AJIL* (1995), p. 398.

[9] See "1994 Draft Articles on the Law of the Non-Navigational Uses of International Watercourses", in "Report of the ILC on the work of its Forty-sixth Session", *supra* note 7, p. 89.

[10] *Ibid.*

[11] *Ibid.*

[12] S. McCaffrey, *supra* note 8, p. 399.

[13] For a general view of the problem, see G. Handl, "National Uses of Transboundary Air Resources: The International Entitlement Issue Reconsidered", 26 *NRJ* (1986), pp. 405-467. See also UNEP, 1978 Principles of Conduct on Shared Natural Resources, Offi-

uses of international watercourses, subsequently abandoned it in the 1980s, explicitly recognising the minimal value of the use of the "shared resources" doctrine in relation to international watercourses.[14] The reasons for abandoning this theory were in principle its new and imprecise character and the lack of certainty as to its legal consequences. In doctrine, as in the ILC, the concept of "shared resources" is regarded as too novel and ill-defined to be relied upon by states.[15] Nonetheless, despite all the theoretical and practical uncertainties, some writers include international watercourses in the category of shared resources, together with fish, oil, gas, and atmospheric resources.[16] This view finds support in the qualification of the Danube as a "shared resource" by the International Court of Justice in the *Gabcíkovo-Nagymaros* case.[17]

3. Main Theories on the Use of International Watercourses[18]

The legal regime of international watercourses is based on the general international law relating to territorial sovereignty.[19] There are three main legal theories[20] that deal with the relationship between the utilization of

cial Records of the General Assembly, Thirty-third Session, Supplement No. 25, (A/33/25), pp. 154-155; A. Nollkaemper, *The Legal Regime for Transboundary Water Pollution: Between Discretion and Constraint*, (1994), pp. 26-28.

[14] On the discussion within the ILC see *YILC*, (1983), Vol. I, pp. 70-71.

[15] See, e.g., P. Birnie and A. Boyle, *International Law and the Environment* 220 (1st edn., 1992); A. Nollkaemper, *supra* note 13, pp. 26-28.

[16] See, e.g., N. Schrijver, *Sovereignty over Natural Resources: Balancing Rights and Duties in an Interdependent World* (1997), pp. 336-339.

[17] Judgment of 25 September 1997, *ICJ Rep* (1997), paragraph 85.

[18] See P. Birnie and A. Boyle, *International Law and the Environment* (2nd edn. 2002), pp. 298-447.

[19] On the relationship between state sovereignty and the environment, see, e.g., G. Handl, "Territorial Sovereignty and the Problem of Transnational Pollution", 69 *AJIL* (1975), pp. 50-77; and J.D. Van Der Vyver, "State Sovereignty and the Environment in International Law", 109 *SALJ* (1992), p. 472

[20] P. Birnie and A. Boyle include equitable utilization as one of the theories. In our view, however, this is a principle underlying the use of international watercourses rather than a theory that explains the utilization of an international drainage basin by states. See P. Birnie and A. Boyle, *supra* note 18, pp. 302-304.

international watercourses, on the one hand, and the concept of territorial sovereignty, on the other.[21]

3.1 The Theory of Absolute Sovereignty (the Harmon Doctrine)

The first of the above-mentioned theories is the so-called "Harmon Doctrine". The underlying premise of this theory is that a state exercises full, unlimited sovereignty over its national territory. Attorney-General Harmon of the United States first formulated this opinion in 1895 in connection with the diversion of the river Rio Grande. The doctrine, which would vest in the United States the right to divert the river unilaterally, was based on the premise that the jurisdiction of the United States over the part of the river located on its territory is absolute and exclusive.[22] The Harmon Doctrine is now of no more than historic value. It has been criticised for its unjust and egoistic character, focusing, as it does, exclusively on the rights of upper riparian states.[23] In the practice of states, international jurisprudence and doctrine, there has been little or no support for the theory of absolute territorial sovereignty.[24]

---

[21] The terminology used in various publications to describe the theories on the subject is not uniform, and this should be bone in mind in the discussion. Nevertheless the general gist of the terms is nearly the same. Differing terminology is used by J. Lipper in "Equitable Utilization", in A.H. Garretson and C.J. Olmstead (eds.), *The Law of International Drainage Basins* (1967), p. 18; P. Birnie and A. Boyle, *supra* note 18, p. 302, refer to the problem of territorial sovereignty in relation to the principle of allocation of water resources; J. Bruchacs presents the concepts of extreme territorial sovereignty, absolute territorial sovereignty and absolute territorial integrity in *The Law of Non-navigational uses of International Watercourses* (1993), p. 43; and B.R. Chauhan, in *Settlement of International Water Law Disputes in International Drainage Basins* (1981), p. 136, uses the expression "conflicting interests and theories in international water law disputes".

[22] See 21 Official Opinions of the Attorneys-General of the United States (1895), p. 274.

[23] See, e.g., J. Lammers, *Pollution of International Watercourses* (1984), p. 557.

[24] In a rare example, the Austrian Government, in a dispute with Bavaria, relied on this theory; see "Austrian Statement of Principles regarding Successive Rivers", in *Legal aspects of Hydro-Electric Development of Rivers and Lakes of Common Interest*, UN Doc. E.ECE/136 (1952), p. 51.

3.2 The Theory of Absolute Territorial Integrity

The theory of absolute territorial integrity – the obverse of the above-mentioned theory – is based on the principle that, since water forms part of a state's territory, lower riparian states have an absolute right to the continuation of the flow of water from upper riparian states. Upstream states must refrain from obstructing the flow of water to downstream states.[25] Criticism, similar to the theory of absolute sovereignty discussed above, has been expressed towards the theory of absolute territorial integrity, on the basis that the relative rights and interests of the upper and lower riparian states are not treated in a fair or even manner.[26]

3.3 The Theory of Community of Interest

The theory of "community of interest" was adopted by the PCIJ in the *River Oder* case.[27] In this case, the Court supported the view that limited sovereignty represents the rule of law. Although the dispute before the Court related to navigational rights, its fundamental statement that the community of interest of riparian states "becomes the basis of a common legal right, the essential features of which are the perfect equality of all riparian States in the use of the whole course of the river and the exclusion of any preferential privilege of any one riparian State in relation to the others" is applicable in respect of other uses of international watercourses.[28] This link has also been made by the ICJ in the *Gabcíkovo-Nagymaros* case where it said that "[m]odern development of international law has strengthened this principle for non-navigational use of international watercourses".[29]

The theory of community of interest is linked to the so-called "common management" theory, which is also based on the premise that an international watercourse constitutes an integrated whole. Accordingly,

[25] See, e.g., J. Lipper, *supra* note 21, p. 18.

[26] See, e.g., B.R. Chauhan, *supra* note 21, p. 137; J. Lammers, *supra* note 23, p. 562.

[27] *Territorial Limits of the Jurisdiction of the International Commission of the River Oder* (1929), PCIJ Rep, Series A, No. 23, and Series C, No. 17.

[28] *Ibid.*, pp. 26-27.

[29] *Supra* note 17, paragraph 85.

optimum results can only be achieved through joint management.[30] Such joint management would include, for example, joint planning and/or joint construction. This approach usually involves the establishment of a joint control body.[31] However, the theory of community of interest should be distinguished from this so-called theory of common management. The latter is supported by some state practice,[32] but the narrowness of this practice puts in doubt the possibility that the theory of community of interest or common management has entered the body of customary international law. The establishment of a common regime was supported by the ICJ in the *Gabcíkovo-Nagymaros* case where the Court acknowledged that the establishment of a joint regime reflected "in an optimal way the concept of common utilization of shared water resources for the achievement of several objectives mentioned in the Treaty..."[33] However, Article 24 of the 1997 UN Watercourses Convention contains only a procedural rule on the management of international watercourses. Watercourse states are required, at the request of any of them, to enter into consultations concerning the management of an international watercourse, including the establishment of a joint management mechanism; but the Convention does not clearly require joint management of international watercourses. The management of international watercourses by northern European states, however, clearly follows the theory of common management. As discussed in Chapters 3 and 4 below, there are joint management bodies – frontier river commissions – which regulate all uses of international watercourse in the region.

The contemporary law regarding the use of international watercourses is oriented towards respect for the sovereign rights of individual states, albeit that the exercise of such rights is limited by the theory of community of interest. This doctrine of "equitable consideration" or, as it is also called, the doctrine of "limited territorial sovereignty", has gained the

---

[30] See, e.g., S. Schwebel, *YILC* 1982, Vol. II, (Part One), p. 76, paragraph 70.

[31] On the difficulties arising from joint management, see, e.g., B.R. Chauhan, *supra* note 21, p. 137.

[32] See, e.g., the 1969 Treaty Between Argentina, Bolivia, Brazil, Paraguay, Uruguay on the River Plata Basin, on the River Plata Basin, 8 *ILM* (1969), p. 905; 1961 Treaty Between the United States and Canada relating to the Columbia River Basin, 542 *UNTS* 244; 1978 Treaty for Amazonian Cooperation, 17 *ILM* 1045.

[33] *Gabcíkovo-Nagymaros* case, *supra* note 17, paragraph 147.

overwhelming support of the international community, particularly, as will be seen below, in the context of the non-navigational uses of international watercourses.[34]

4. The Navigational Use of International Watercourses

4.1 The Right of Free Navigation

The law relating to the navigational use of international watercourses is more firmly established and more straightforward than the law relating to their non-navigational use.[35] In fact, navigation constitutes the classical example of the use of international watercourses. As long ago as the eighteenth century, states concluded treaties with respect to navigation on what were called "common rivers" or "watercourses".[36] The primary aim of these treaties is the establishment of the right of free navigation. For example, the 1815 Final Act of the Vienna Congress provides with respect to "international rivers and lakes" that

---

[34] See, e.g., H.L. Dickstein, "International Lake and River Pollution Control: A Question of Method", 12 *CJTL* (1973), p. 492. The same views were expressed by the ILC. The Special Rapporteur said as follows: "all available evidence of general practice of states, accepted as law, in respect of non-navigational uses of international watercourses – evidence including treaty provisions, positions taken by states on specific disputes, decisions of international tribunals, statements of law prepared by intergovernmental and non-governmental bodies, the views of learned commentators, and decisions of municipal courts in cognate cases – demonstrate that there is overwhelming support for the doctrine of equitable utilization as a general guiding principle of law for the determination of the rights of states in respect of the non-navigational uses of international watercourses"; see S. McCaffrey, "Second Report on the Law of Non-navigational Watercourses", *YILC* (1986), Vol. II (Part One), p. 130.

[35] On the history of navigation, see L.A. Teclaff, "Fiat or Custom: The Chequered Development of International Water Law", 31 *NRJ* (1991), pp. 45-73; see also L. Caflisch, "Règles Générales du droit des cours d'eau internationaux", 219 *RCADI* (1989), pp. 4-226, esp. pp. 37-42.

[36] See, e.g., 1804 Convention between France and Elector of Mainz, in G.F. von Martens, *Nouveau Receuil General des Traités*, (1843-1875), Vol. VII, p. 261.

> "[t]he navigation of the rivers, along their whole course, [...] from the point where each of them becomes navigable, to its mouth, shall be entirely free, and shall not in respect to commerce, be prohibited to anyone; it being understood that the regulations established with regard to the police of this navigation, shall be respected; as they will be framed alike for all, and as favourable as possible to the commerce of all nations" (Article 109).[37]

The right of free navigation on international watercourses is also included in the 1921 Barcelona Convention and Statute on the Regime of Navigable Waterways of International Concern (1921 Barcelona Convention).[38] This Convention, including the Statute which is an integral part of it, is the only instance of the codification of the rules concerning navigation on international watercourses. The Preamble to the Convention recognises

> "in particular that a fresh confirmation of the principle of Freedom of Navigation in a Statute elaborated by forty-one States belonging to different portions of the world constitutes a new and significant stage towards the establishment of co-operation among States without in any way prejudicing their rights of sovereignty or authority".

The 1966 ILA Helsinki Rules also provide, in principle, for rights of free navigation on the entire course of a "river or lake" (Article XIII). Article XIV defines free navigation means as follows:

> "(a) freedom of movement on the entire navigable course of the river or lake;
> (b) freedom to enter the ports and to make use of plants and docks; and
> (c) freedom to transport goods an passengers, either directly or through transhipment, between the territory of one riparian State and the territory of another riparian State and the territory of a riparian State and the open sea".

It is interesting to note that although not expressly stated, it is understood that this use is (together with non-navigational uses) subject to and consistent with the principle of equitable utilization. The commentary to Articles XIII and XVII of the Helsinki Rules states that "the principle of

---

[37] See 1815 Final Act of the Congress of Vienna, note 3.
[38] See VII *LNTS* 37.

free navigation [...] does not assure navigation any priority over conflicting non-navigational uses".[39]

The scope of the right of free navigation of international watercourses – and, for that matter, national watercourses – is controversial. Evidently, the right of free navigation can only exist if the watercourse is "navigable".[40] The difficulties have been more legal than geophysical, and they include the following:

(a) what constitutes an international watercourse for the purposes of the right of free navigation and, in particular, whether tributaries of such a watercourse are also subject to the right of free navigation;
(b) what is the legal basis of the right of free navigation and, in particular, whether such right must originate in a specific treaty or a unilateral act of a state, or whether a general right can be derived from customary international law;
(c) which states are entitled to exercise the right of free navigation on an international watercourse and, in particular, whether this right only extends to riparian states or also to non-riparian states;
(d) what limitations may be imposed on the right of free navigation and by whom.

4.2 The Meaning of "International Watercourse" for the Purposes of the Right of Free Navigation

It appears from treaties with respect to navigation that the right of free navigation exists on watercourses that are "international". Therefore, it is relevant to determine what constitutes an "international watercourse" for the purposes of the freedom of navigation and, in particular, whether tributaries of such watercourses are also subject to the right of free navigation.

Some general principles concerning navigation on international watercourses were enshrined in the 1815 Final Act of the Congress of Vienna. Article 108 of the 1815 Final Act uses the expression "international rivers and lakes", which refers to navigable watercourses of interest to two or

[39] *Supra* note 5.
[40] See, e.g., Article 109 of the 1815 Final Act of the Congress of Vienna, *supra* note 3.

more states. These international watercourses were divided into two categories: "successive international rivers", i.e. rivers that cross those states, and "contiguous international rivers", i.e. frontier rivers. The rules of the 1815 Final Act of the Vienna Congress also applied to lakes that were crossed by a frontier or surrounded by several riparian states.[41]

The navigability of a river, together with its geographical characteristics and the potential of its other uses, such as irrigation or the production of hydroelectric power, was also one of the criteria of its international character according to the 1885 Act of Berlin.[42] The peace treaties that were concluded after the end of the First World War expanded the right of free navigation of international watercourses. It applied not only to international waterways, but also to national waterways crossing the territories of the defeated powers, and, later, it was extended to include tributaries, canals, and secondary courses as well as lakes connected to rivers. The phrase "international navigable river" as developed in practice became so broad as to include internal surface waters of lakes, seas, and other river systems having an outlet to the sea.

The 1921 Barcelona Convention uses the term "navigable waterways of international concern" and stipulates that it does not affect the rights and obligations arising from the provisions of the 1919 Treaty of Versailles and related treaties (Article 2). The 1921 Barcelona Statute applies a geographical criterion to define what constitutes "navigable waterways of international concern":

> "[a]ll parts which are naturally navigable to and from the sea of a waterway which in its course, naturally navigable to and from the sea, separates or traverses different States, and also any part of any other waterway naturally navigable to and from the sea which connects with the sea a waterway naturally navigable which separates or traverses different states" (Article 1(1)).

---

[41] Note 3. The Final Act of the Congress of Vienna related mainly to the rivers Main, Neckar, Moselle, Meuse and Scheldt. See D. Caponera, "The Law of International Watercourses, Some General Conventions, Declarations and Resolutions adopted by Governments, International Legal Institutions and International Organisations", in the *Water Management of International Water Resources*, (Food and Agriculture Organisation, 1980), p. 4.

[42] See 1885 Act of Berlin, *ATS* (1920) No. 17, concerning the Congo and Niger. See D. Caponera, *supra* note 41.

The Statute explains the use of terms in the following manner (Article 1(1)):

(a) transhipment from one vessel to another is not excluded by the words "navigable to and from the sea";
(b) any natural waterway or part thereof is termed "naturally navigable" if now used for ordinary commercial navigation, or capable by reason of its natural conditions of being so used, "ordinary commercial navigation" being understood as navigation which, in view of the economic condition of the riparian countries, is commercial and normally practicable;
(c) tributaries are to be considered as separate waterways;
(d) lateral canals constructed in order to remedy the defects of waterway included in the above definition are assimilated thereto;
(e) the different states separated or traversed by a navigable waterway of international concern, including its tributaries of international concern, are deemed to be "riparian states".

In the Barcelona Convention, canals are treated in the same manner as waterways. On "internationalized canals", all states have the right of free navigation. The canals, however, remain under the sovereignty of the state on whose territory they are situated.

For its part, the 1966 ILA Helsinki Rules deals with "rivers and lakes" portions of which are both navigable and either separate or traverse the territories of two or more states. The Helsinki Rules give a definition of what constitutes a navigable river or lake: they must be in their natural or canalised state used for commercial navigation or be "capable by reason of their natural condition of being so used" (Article XII(1)).

The definitions in all these various instruments confirm the existence of the right of free navigation on international watercourses. One issue that has been the subject of controversy relates to tributaries. It is generally thought that the right of free navigation exists in respect of tributaries of a river on which states enjoy the right of free navigation.[43] For

[43] The 1948 Belgrade Convention concerning the Regime of Navigation on the Danube, however, in Articles 2 and 8, excludes tributaries from its compass. This Convention was a product of the Cold War and concluded under the auspices of the Soviet

example, the Institute of International Law's non-binding 1887 Heidelberg Regulation on River Navigation (the "Heidelberg Regulation")[44] provides that "[t]he navigable affluents of international rivers are, in every respect, subject to the same regime as the rivers whose tributaries they are, in conformity with the agreement concluded between the riparian states, and with the present Regulation".[45]

The uniform legal status of a watercourse and its tributaries was also recognised by the PCIJ in the *River Oder* case. Under Articles 331 and 338 of the 1919 Peace Treaty of Versailles certain rivers, including the Oder, and such other parts of navigable river systems which naturally provide more than one state with access to the sea, together with lateral canals and channels constructed to improve navigation, were placed under an international regime. Under Article 341 of the Treaty, the Oder was placed under the administration of an international commission comprised of representatives of Poland, Prussia, Czechoslovakia, Great Britain, France, Denmark, and Sweden. One of the tasks of the Commission was to define the sections of the river or its tributaries to which an international regime was applicable. The Commission encountered difficulties in determining what portions of tributaries should be internationalized. Poland claimed that the Warthe and Netze had to be under an international navigation regime only as far as the Polish frontier. The other members of the Commission maintained that in order to achieve internationalization of tributaries, an integral approach had to be adopted, and this meant inclusion of tributaries situated in Polish territory.

The question before the PCIJ was the following:

> "[d]oes the jurisdiction of the International Commission of the Oder extend, under the provisions of the Treaty of Versailles to the sections of the tributaries of the Oder, Warthe (Warta) and Netze (Notec) which are situated in Pol-

---

Union. France, the UK and the US were excluded from participation in regulating of the traffic on the Danube thus leading to non-recognition of the new Danube Commission by these states (reconstructed after replacing of the 1921 Definite Statute of Danube by the 1948 Convention).

[44] Annuaire de l'Institute de Droit International, Session de Heidelberg 1887 <http://www.idi-iil.org/idiF/resolutionsF/1887_hei_01_fr.pdf>; see D. Caponera, *supra* note 41, p. 535.

[45] *Supra* note 44, Article 2.

> ish territory, and if so, what is the principle laid down which must be adopted for the purpose of determining the upstream limits of the Commission's jurisdiction?"[46]

The claimant states in this case argued that the jurisdiction of the Commission extended to sections of the rivers in question situated on Polish territory if these sections were "navigable waterways of international concern" according to the 1921 Barcelona Convention or, alternatively, if these sections fulfilled the conditions of navigability under Article 331 of the 1919 Peace Treaty of Versailles. The argument of the Polish Government was based mainly on the premise that Article 331 provides that only those parts of the River Oder system that provide more than one state with access to the sea are international, and that it consequently excludes from this definition those parts of the tributaries of the river above the Polish frontier.

Since Poland had not ratified the 1921 Barcelona Convention, the Court relied on Article 338 of the 1919 Peace Treaty of Versailles. The Court made an important statement to the effect that the wording of Article 331 indicated that the internationalization of a watercourse is subject to two conditions, namely that the watercourse must be navigable and it must naturally provide more than one state with access to the sea. These two characteristics distinguished international watercourses from national ones. The Court then examined whether the expression "all navigable parts of these river systems which naturally provide more than one state with access to the sea" referred to tributaries and sub-tributaries in such a way that, if a tributary or sub-tributary in its natural navigable course traverses or separates different states, it falls as a whole within the definition of an international watercourse; or whether they refer rather to that part of such tributary or sub-tributary which provides more than one state with access to the sea, in such a way that the upstream portion of a tributary is not under an international regime above the last frontier crossing its natural course. The Court rejected the idea that the case in question should be looked upon from the perspective of the interests of upstream states and found a proper justification of inclusion of tributaries to the

[46] *Supra* note 27, p. 6.

whole navigational system on the basis of a community of interests of riparian states. The PCIJ observed that

> "[t]he community of interests in a navigable river becomes the basis of a common legal right, the essential features of which are the perfect equality of all riparian States in the user of the whole course of the river and the exclusion of any preferential privilege of any one riparian State in relation to others".[47]

From this, it followed that that this common right extended to the whole navigable course of the river and did not stop at the last frontier. The Court also confirmed the rights and interests of non-riparian states in navigation. The Court said that

> "[i]t would be difficult to understand why that interest should not be recognised where the question of reaching the ports of the last upstream State is involved. The interests of all States is in liberty of navigation in both directions".[48]

In the light of all these principles, Article 331 was interpreted as meaning that the internationalization of a watercourse does not stop short at any political frontier, but extends to the whole navigable watercourse. Accordingly, the Court found in the *River Oder* case that the jurisdiction of the Commission includes all navigable parts of the river systems that naturally provide more than one state with access to the sea, with or without transhipment from one vessel to another; together with lateral canals and special channels. Thus, the jurisdiction of Commission did not extend beyond navigable points of the rivers in question. This finding of the Court was reiterated in the *Gabcíkovo-Nagymaros* case.[49]

The decision of the PCIJ in the *River Oder* case clarified that tributaries are part of an international watercourse. The 1921 Barcelona Statute is far from clear on this point, providing in Article 1(c) that "[t]ributaries are to be considered as separate waterways". This provision may be assessed from geophysical and legal points of view. From a geophysical

---

[47] *Ibid.*, p. 27.
[48] *Ibid.*, p. 28.
[49] *Gabcíkovo-Nagymaros* case, *supra* note 17, paragraph 84.

point of view, a tributary may constitute a separate entity. However, as the PCIJ elaborated, from a legal point of view (freedom of navigation), the river and its tributaries constitute one integral whole and all riparian states form a community of interests based on the principle of perfect equality of all states.

4.3 The Legal Basis of the Right of Free Navigation on International Watercourses

There is no automatic right of access to a watercourse situated in the territory of a state, even if this watercourse is geographically of "international concern", i.e. is navigable and provides more than one state with access to the sea. According to Article 1(2) of the 1921 Barcelona Statute, this requires either a unilateral act of the state under whose sovereignty or authority a waterway or parts of a waterway are situated, or an agreement made with the consent, in particular, of that state. It also appears from state practice that there is no general right of freedom of navigation for either riparian or non-riparian states on international (or national) watercourses absent the conclusion of an agreement granting such a right.[50] When such a right is granted, however, all states, riparian and non-riparian alike, are on a footing of perfect equality. This was also confirmed by the above-mentioned Heidelberg Regulation, Article 4 of which provides that "[t]he subjects and flags of all nations are in every respect on the footing of perfect equality. No distinction shall be made between the subjects of riparian States and those of non-riparian States". It may be noted that the 1921 Barcelona Convention does not exclude the possibility of any riparian state granting a right of navigation to a non-party to the Convention, unless such a right would be contrary to its provisions.

4.4 The Subjects of the Right of Free Navigation on International Watercourses

In the 1815 Final Act of the Congress of Vienna, the right of free navigation was provided for the benefit of all riparian states. In later treaties,

[50] See R.R. Churchill and A.V. Lowe, *The Law of the Sea*, (2nd edn., 1999), p. 65.

such as the 1856 Treaty of Paris (on the Danube), the 1885 Treaty of Berlin (on the Congo and Niger) and the 1919 Peace Treaty of Versailles (on the Oder, the Elbe and the Niemen rivers, among others) – it was granted in favour of all states in relation to the particular watercourses that were the subject of the treaty regulations.

The 1921 Barcelona Statute is also based on the principle of "perfect equality" of all parties to the 1921 Barcelona Convention. Accordingly, no distinction may be made between the nationals, the property, and the flags of different riparian states, including the riparian states exercising sovereignty or authority over the portions of the navigable waterway in question. Furthermore, no distinction may be made between the nationals, the property, and the flags of riparian and non-riparian states. This equal treatment means that no exclusive right of navigation is to be accorded on a navigable waterway to companies or to private persons (Article 4). The freedom of navigation of riparian states is only restricted by the right of cabotage (Article 5).

Similarly the main principle of the 1966 ILA Helsinki Rules is the attribution of rights of free navigation to riparian states (Article XIII). Of great importance is Article XVII which provides that a riparian state may grant rights of navigation to non-riparian states on rivers and lakes within its territory. Thus, the Helsinki Rules clearly indicate that riparian states have the freedom of navigation. It may be vested in a non-riparian state, but only if it relates to the portion of a navigable watercourse under the authority of the riparian state granting that right.

4.5 The Regulation of Navigation on International Watercourses

Agreements dealing with the navigation of international watercourses also contain provisions that harmonise substantive and financial regulations with respect to navigation on watercourses. For example, the 1815 Final Act of the Vienna Congress provides that

> "[t]he system that shall be established both for collection of the duties and for the maintenance of the police shall be, as nearly as possible the same along the whole course of the river; and shall also extend, unless particular circumstances prevent it, to those of its branches and junctions which, in their navigable course, separate or traverse different states" (Article 110).

The Final Act also contains provisions on duties and tariffs. It also stated that regulation of the river has to be settled by a general agreement which can only be changed with the consent of all the states bordering the river.

The 1921 Barcelona Convention also regulates matters relating to duties and tariffs and other problems related to the operation of "waterways of international concern". Article 14 of the 1921 Barcelona Statute provides for the establishment of an international body, the Commission, which may also consist of representatives of states other than riparian states. The Commission is required to have "exclusive regard" to the interests of navigation. The Statute provides a non-exhaustive list of the powers and functions of the Commission:

(a) it is entitled to draw up such navigation regulations as it thinks itself necessary to draw up, whereas all other navigation regulations must be communicated to it;
(b) it indicates to the riparian states the action advisable for the upkeep of works and the maintenance of the navigability of the waterway;
(c) each state has the duty to furnish official information as to all schemes for the improvement of the waterway; and
(d) it is, in principle, entitled to levy dues and charges in accordance with the provisions of Article 7 of the Statute.

According to the 1966 ILA Helsinki Rules, the right of free navigation of riparian states are subject to an exhaustive list of limitations (Article XIII). One example is the right of police, which may include – but is not limited to – the protection of public health and safety, provided that the exercise of such rights does not interfere with the right of free navigation (Article XV).

In his important book, McCaffrey investigates the difficult relationship between navigational and non-navigational uses.[51] He is of the view that navigational uses have an impact on non-navigational uses; for example they may result in a foreclosure of non-navigational uses and restriction or even cessation of irrigation in order to preserve water levels indispens-

[51] S. McCaffrey, *The Law of International Watercourses, supra* note 2, pp. 46-50. On the relationship between different uses under the 1997 Convention. See also A. Tanzi and M. Arcari, *supra* note 2, pp. 133-142.

able for navigation. The same author observes that historically navigational uses had priority over other uses. However, at present, non-navigational uses have grown in importance. McCaffrey refers to Article 10 of the 1997 Watercourse Convention, which provides that:

> "1. In the absence of agreement or custom to the contrary, no use of an international watercourse enjoys inherent priority over other uses.
> 2. In the event of a conflict between uses of an international watercourse, it shall be resolved with reference to Articles 5 to 7, with special regard being given to the requirements of vital human needs".

This Article, of course, would be very difficult to apply, due to inherent problems with the underlying concept of equitable utilization, which are discussed in Section 5 of this chapter.

4.6 The Navigational Use of Northern European Watercourses: An Overview

As for Nordic co-operation, it should first be noted that Finland, Norway, and Sweden have ratified the 1921 Barcelona Convention. Russia has not. Evidently, the parties to the Convention may not act in a manner contrary to its provisions when entering into other treaty obligations on the same subject with other states. From this, it follows that other conventions concerning internal navigation to which they are party should conform with the provisions of the Convention. Article 18 of the 1921 Barcelona Statute is explicit in stating that:

> "[e]ach of the Contracting States undertakes not to grant, either by agreement or in any other way, to a non-Contracting State treatment with regard to navigation over a navigable waterway of international concern which, as between contracting states, would be contrary to the provisions of this Statute".

With respect to navigation, the Nordic states are connected by a network of bilateral treaties concluded in the 1920s.[52] In addition, they concluded

[52] See, e.g., 1923 Navigation Convention Between Finland and Sweden and Final Protocol, XVIII *LNTS* 59; 1925 Navigation Convention Between Finland and Norway, LVI *LNTS* 185; 1923 Convention between Finland and Russia With Regard to Navigation by Finnish Merchant Cargo Vessels on the Neva Between Lake Ladoga and the Gulf of Fin-

in 1962 a multilateral agreement on the marking of navigable waters.[53] The network of bilateral treaties, with the exception of a treaty between Russia and Finland referred to below, primarily concerns "maritime" navigation. Pursuant to the bilateral treaties between Finland and Sweden, and Finland and Norway, the national treatment standard applies to "maritime" navigation and, accordingly, Swedish or Norwegian vessels and their cargoes in Finland, and Finnish vessels and their cargoes in Norway or Sweden, are entitled to be treated as national vessels and their cargoes. However, the national treatment standard does not apply to navigation on natural or artificial inland watercourses. In this case, Swedish or Norwegian vessels and their cargoes in Finland, and Finnish vessels and their cargoes in Norway or Sweden, are subject to the same conditions as the vessels of the most favoured nation and their cargoes. However, the duties leviable on such vessels and their cargoes may not exceed the rate applicable to national vessels and their cargoes.

In some regions, however, inland navigation is subject to different regulations. For example, the lower part of the River Pasvik is regulated by a special memorandum that is attached to the 1925 Navigation Convention between Norway and Finland. Under this special regime, the national treatment is extended to Finnish vessels transporting goods and passengers to Finnish territory in the Pasvik Valley. In addition, barges, boats, and other small craft that are used for the transport of goods and passengers in transit to Finnish territory in the Pasvik Valley benefit from exemption from the payment of duties other than the ordinary duties for the use of harbour, quays and other port installations.

The 1923 Convention between Finland and Russia with Regard to Navigation by Finnish Merchant and Cargo Vessels on the Neva between Lake Ladoga and the Gulf of Finland is a follow-up to the 1920 Peace Treaty between the two countries. The provisions of this Convention

land, XVIII *LNTS* 217; 1928 Convention between Finland and The Union of Soviet Socialist Republics, Modifying Article 7 of the Convention of June 5, 1923, Regarding Navigation by Finnish Merchant and Cargo Vessels of the Neva between Lake Ladoga and the Gulf of Finland, LXXX *LNTS* 159.

[53] See 1962 Agreement between Finland, Denmark, Norway, and Sweden Concerning Uniform Rules for the Marking of Navigable Waters, 442 *UNTS* 217.

regulate the status of Finnish vessels and crews while navigating in Russian waters on the River Neva between Lake Ladoga and the Gulf of Finland. Article 6 sets out the main principle that Finnish merchant and cargo vessels within the boundaries of Russia are not liable for any income or capital tax or for any other higher duties or charges of whatever kind or description than levied on Russian private vessels of a corresponding nature. The national treatment standard also applies to goods in transit.

A different, although related, problem from navigation in inland watercourses is that of navigation in frontier waters. Navigation in such waters is usually regulated by a frontier agreement, such as the 1960 Frontier Agreement between Finland and the Soviet Union.[54] The Agreement states that in the case of all rivers intersected by the frontier line and lakes and coastal bays along which the frontier line runs, a strip of water 100 metres on either side of the frontier line is deemed to be frontier waters (Article 11). On lakes and rivers intersected by the frontier line, ships of a party to the Agreement are entitled to navigate only on the side of the frontier line in the territory of that party. Only situations of distress justify the tying up or anchoring of ships of one party on the banks on the territory of the other party (Article 13).

5. The Non-Navigational Use of International Watercourses

5.1 The Principle of Equitable Utilization

The principle of "equitable utilization" features in many legal instruments, such as the 1992 UNECE Watercourse Convention (Article 2(2.c)) and the 1997 UN Watercourse Convention (Article 5(1)). According to the ILC, "[t]he basic principles underlying the doctrine of equitable utilisation are reflected, explicitly or implicitly, in numerous international agreements between States in all parts of the world".[55] As further

---

[54] 1960 Agreement Concerning the Regime of the Finnish-Soviet State Frontier and the Procedure for the Settlement of Frontier Incidents, 379 *UNTS* 277.

[55] See the ILC's commentary to Draft Article 5, in "Report of the ILC to the General Assembly on the work of its Forty-sixth Session", *supra* note 7, p. 96

examples of state practice, the ILC cites a plethora of declarations, statements of law prepared by governmental and non-governmental bodies and decisions of various judicial bodies, both international and national.[56] It is beyond any doubt that the ILC considers the principle of equitable utilization as a part of the body of international customary law as it stands at present. The ICJ gave support to the ILC's view in the *Gabcíkovo-Nagymaros* case.[57] Referring to the 1997 UN Watercourse Convention, the Court concluded that Czechoslovakia, by *unilaterally* assuming control of a "resource", deprived Hungary of its "right to an equitable and reasonable share of the natural resources" of the watercourse concerned (the Danube).[58] Also, Judge Kooijmans, in his Separate Opinion in *Kasikili/Sedudu* case, expressed the view that this principle was part of international law; "in doctrine there was already overwhelming support for the principle of the equitable utilisation of shared water resources when in 1971 the International Law Commission included the topic 'The Non-Navigational Uses of International Watercourses' in its general

[56] *Id.*, paragraph 10.

[57] The *Gabcíkovo-Nagymaros* case, *supra* note 17. On the case, see, e.g., C. Cepelka, "The Dispute over Gabcíkovo-Nagymaros System of Locks is Drawing to a Close", 20 *PYIL* (1993), pp. 63-73; M. Fitzmaurice, "Environmental Protection and the International Court of Justice", in V. Lowe and M. Fitzmaurice (eds.), *Fifty years of the International Court of Justice, Essays in Honour of Sir R.. Jennings*, 308-315 (1995); E. Hoenderkamp, "The Danube: Damned or Dammed? The Dispute Between Hungary and Slovakia Concerning the Gabcíkovo-Nagymaros Project", 8 *LJIL*, 287-309 (1995); J.G. Lammers, "The Gabcíkovo-Nagymaros case Seen in Particular From the Perspective of the Law of International Watercourses and the Protection of the Environment", 11 *LJIL* 287-320 (1998).

[58] See the *Gabcíkovo-Nagymaros* case, *supra* note 17 paragraphs 85 and 147. See also the views of A. Boyle in "The *Gabcíkovo-Nagymaros* Case: New law in Old Bottles", 8 *YIEL* (1997), pp. 13-20. The Court referred to "sustainable" utilization of international watercourses, a concept that appears to be different from equitable utilization. The former concept belongs to the broader realm of sustainable development. The author states that "[i]f this conclusion is correct, it will stand as perhaps the most radical re-writing of the law relating to international watercourses since the *River Oder* case". For a different view, see C. Bourne, "The *Case Concerning the Gabcíkovo-Nagymaros Project:* An Important Milestone in International Water Law", pp. 6-13, at 11, who was of the view that the case "... marks a milestone in the evolution of international water law and international environmental law. It establishes that the protection of the environment has no absolute priority over other considerations, particularly the case of the developments involving the utilization of international watercourses".

programme of work."[59] It may be said that the doctrine of equitable utilization is the fundamental rule governing the use of international watercourses, notwithstanding some certain ill-defined or unclear aspects.[60]

Equitable utilization is at the core, and is one of the guiding principles, of the 1997 UN Watercourse Convention, Article 5 of which provides that:

> "1. Watercourse States shall in their respective territories utilize an international watercourse in an equitable and reasonable manner. In particular, an international watercourse shall be used and developed by watercourse States with a view to attaining optimal and sustainable utilization thereof and benefits therefrom, taking into account the interests of the watercourse States concerned, consistent with the adequate protection of the watercourse.
> 2. Watercourse States shall participate in the use, development and protection of an international watercourse in an equitable and reasonable manner. Such participation includes both the right to utilize the watercourse and the duty to cooperate in the protection and development thereof, as approved in the present Convention".

The meaning of the principle of "equitable utilization" is not easy to grasp. This principle, like all principles, purports to be applicable to a wide variety of situations. International watercourses, however, differ from each other in their natural and economic make-up. Therefore, in practice, the application of the principle of equitable utilization has to be determined on a case-by-case basis through a process of balancing of interests, during which all relevant factors and circumstances "pertaining to the international watercourse in question, as well as to the needs and uses of the watercourse States concerned" must be taken into consideration.[61] Article 6(1) of the 1997 UN Watercourse Convention sets out a non-exhaustive list of such factors and circumstances:

> "Utilization of an international watercourse in an equitable and reasonable manner within the meaning of article 5 requires taking into account all relevant factors and circumstances, including:

[59] Separate Opinion of Judge Kooijmans, *Case Concerning Kasikili/Sedudu Island, (Botswana/Namibia)*, Judgment of 13 December 1999, *ICJ Rep* (1999), Vol. 3, p. 1149, paragraph 28.

[60] S. McCaffrey, *supra* note 2, pp. 343-344.

[61] See the ILC's commentary to Draft Article 6, *supra* note 55, p. 101, paragraph 1.

(a) Geographic, hydrographic, hydrological, climatic, ecological and other factors of a natural character;
(b) The social and economic needs of the watercourse States concerned;
(c) The population dependent on the watercourse in each watercourse State;
(d) The effects of the use or uses of the watercourse in one watercourse State on other watercourse States;
(e) Existing and potential uses of the watercourse;
(f) Conservation, protection, development and economy of use of the water resources of the watercourse and the costs of measures taken to that effect;
(g) The availability of alternatives, of comparable value, to a particular planned or existing use."

These factors and circumstances will, amongst other things, dictate the extent of the legitimacy of a watercourse state's demands in any consultations and negotiations on the equitable and reasonable use of a specific watercourse.[62] The International Law Association has viewed these objectives of equitable utilization in a more general manner, i.e. as the achievement of the maximum benefit to each basin state from the uses of the waters with the minimum detriment to each.[63] The 1997 UN Watercourse Convention focuses on the general benefits for all the riparian states and on meeting all their needs. Nonetheless, the ILC has emphasised that an "[o]ptimal use of finite water resources of an international watercourse is considered in light of the interests of each watercourse State concerned".[64]

The view has been expressed that equitable utilization is conditioned by the economic and social needs of the riparian states and should involve "beneficial use".[65] Equitable utilization presupposes "equality of rights" which is based on all relevant factors and circumstances. By "equality of rights" is meant equality of the right of *utilization* of water rather than equality of *division* of water.[66] The notion of equitable utilization entails the right to a reasonable and equitable share or portion of the

[62] See also A. Nollkaemper, *supra* note 13, pp. 61-64.
[63] *Supra* note 5, at p. 487
[64] See the ILC's commentary to Draft Article 7, *supra* note 55, p. 102, paragraph 1.
[65] J. Lipper, *supra* note 21, p. 63.
[66] *Ibid.*, p. 44.

uses of an international watercourse within a state's territory and the correlative obligation not to exceed its right of equitable utilization and not to deprive other watercourse states of this right.[67]

The principle of equitable participation, contained in Article 5(2) of the 1997 UN Convention, seems to be a rather broad concept. According to Lammers, its scope is comprehensive and entails more than just the concept of equitable utilization. It not only embraces a duty to co-operate but also a duty to adopt an integrated approach which is founded on a premise of "comprehensive consideration and accommodation of great variety of water uses and other related water concerns such as flood control and nature conservation".[68] This concept entails a duty to co-operate in relation to disasters caused by human activities and nature. Last but not least, it requires states to attain optimum utilization of the water of an international watercourse system.[69]

Article 10 establishes relationship between different kinds of uses. The main principle, stated in paragraph 1, is that "in the absence of an agreement to the contrary, no use of an international watercourse enjoys inherent priority over other uses". Paragraph 2 provides that in case of any conflict between the uses of an international watercourse, recourse is to be had to principles and factors contained in Articles 5 (equitable and reasonable utilization and participation), 6 (factors relevant to equitable and reasonable utilization) and 7 (obligation not to cause significant harm), with special regard to "the requirements of vital human needs". It is a difficult and controversial matter to define the content and extent of these needs in the context of conflicting situations. Furthermore, the Convention does not clarify whether vital human needs factor are to be considered in balancing of interests process. It would appear that they should be shielded from that process.[70] It also appears that in the case of conflict between uses, navigational uses are also subject to the principle of equitable utilization.

A practical approach to the doctrine of equitable utilization is to treat it as a process that would involve an active pursuit by a riparian state of en-

---

[67] See ILC commentary to Draft Article 5, *supra* note 55, p. 97, paragraph 2.

[68] See J. Lammers, *supra* note 23, p. 548.

[69] *Id.*

[70] A. Nollkaemper, *supra* note 13, pp. 61-62

vironmentally sound procedures, such as environment impact assessment, sharing of information with other riparian states and following the obligations of consultation and notification. On this view, the implementation of the obligation of equitable and reasonable use requires from riparian states good faith and on-going co-operation.[71]

5.2 The Obligation not to Cause Significant Harm

5.2.1 *The General Obligation not to Cause Significant Harm*

Together with the principle of equitable utilization, the obligation not to cause significant harm is the second pillar of the law of the non-navigational uses of international watercourses. The two general principles form the foundation for all uses of international watercourses, but the obligation not to cause significant harm aims at the protection and preservation of the ecosystems of international watercourses in particular.[72]

The obligation not to cause significant harm is rooted in general international law, but has especially become a corner stone of international environmental law. It is embodied in many international conventions, international jurisprudence, as well as in governmental and non-governmental declarations.[73] In relation to international watercourses, it has been

---

[71] The relationship between equitable utilization and sustainable development should also be noted. It has been said that equitable utilization will not be sustainable if it does not take into account environmental, developmental and intergenerational issues; see P. Birnie and A. Boyle, *supra* note 18, p. 316.

[72] For the origins, general features, and sources of the obligation not to cause significant harm, see J. Lammers, *supra* note 23, pp. 361-377 (in relation to watercourses), and R. Lefeber, *Transboundary Environmental Interference and the Origin of State Liability* (1996), p. 34 (in relation to the protection of the environment).

[73] See, e.g., the 1971 Finnish Swedish Frontier River Commission (see Chapter 5). For case law, see, e.g., the *Trail Smelter* case, III *UNRIAA* 1905, at 1965-1866; and the *Corfu Channel* case, Judgment of 9 April 1949, *ICJ Rep* (1949), p. 4 at 22. For governmental declarations, see, e.g., the 1972 UN Declaration on the Human Environment (Principle 21); the 1992 UNCED Declaration on Environment and Development (Principle 2); and several resolutions of the UN General Assembly, e.g., UN Doc. A/Res/2995 (1972) on Co-operation between States in the Field of the Environment; UN Doc. A/Res/3129 (1973) on Co-operation in the Field of Environment concerning Natural Resources Shared by Two or More States; and UN Doc. A/Res/3281 (1974) on the Charter of Economic

incorporated in the 1997 UN Watercourse Convention. Article 7(1) provides that

> "[w]atercourse States shall, in utilising an international watercourse in their territories, take all appropriate measures to prevent the causing of significant harm to other watercourse States".

It is said that the obligation not to cause significant harm has developed as a follow up to the principles *sic utero tuo alienum non laedas* and good neighbourliness. In practical terms, these principles mean that each and every state must take into consideration the interests of other states,[74] and allow a certain degree of harm, resulting from lawful activities from adjacent states.[75] The lack of a precise definition and of any clear specification in relation to these principles limits their utility in practice. They are best seen as the background to the obligation not to cause significant harm than as providing practical guidance in the definition of the precise threshold of permissible harm.

The term "harm", as used in Article 7 of the 1997 UN Watercourse Convention, is to be understood in a factual sense.[76] It covers actual harm to the environment, such as impairment of use, injury to health or property, or a detrimental effect upon the ecology of the watercourse. It is well established that the obligation not to cause significant harm does not prohibit all harm – a certain level of nuisance is permitted. Difficulties arise, however, in relation to the establishment of the permissible threshold of harm. Several qualifications have been employed in legal texts, such as "serious",[77] "appreciable",[78] and "significant"[79] or "having signifi-

---

Rights and Duties. For non-governmental declarations, see, e.g., the 1982 ILA Rules of International Law Applicable to Transfrontier Pollution, *Report of the Sixtieth Conference*, Montreal, (1982), pp. 531-552, (Article 3(1)).

[74] See J. Lammers, *supra* note 23, at 571.

[75] *Ibid.*, p. 568.

[76] See "Report of the International Law Commission on the Work of its Fortieth Session", *YILC* (1988), Vol. II, (Part Two), p. 22 at 36.

[77] See, e.g., *Trail Smelter* case, *supra* note 73.

[78] See, e.g., the 1991 ILC Draft Articles (Article 7), in "Report of the ILC on the work of its Forty-third Session", Doc. A/46/10, *YILC* (1991), Vol. II, (Part Two), p. 67

[79] See, e.g., the 1997 UN Watercourse Convention (Article 7(1)); and the 1994 ILC Draft Articles (Article 7(1)), *supra* note 7, p. 102.

cant adverse effects".[80] Whatever qualification is used, it is generally acknowledged that the threshold of harm has been considerably lowered over time. The changes in the threshold of harm reflect the growing level of environmental awareness coupled with the expanding level of economic development. A very low threshold has been formulated by the UNECE Task Force on Responsibility and Liability Regarding Transboundary Water Pollution. This threshold is meant to be applicable in the absence of a universally or regionally agreed level. According to the Task Force's guidelines, harm must be deemed significant, if an affected, or potentially affected, state is required, as the result of an activity within the jurisdiction or control of another state, to take preventive and/or restoration measures in the interest of the protection of the environment or population.[81] This definition would provide a practical test; yet, in order to be acceptable at all, a test of reasonableness will have to be applied in order to avoid the adoption of unnecessary measures by the affected, or potentially affected, state.

The question of the threshold of harm, particularly the supposed differences between different qualifications, was the subject of extensive discussion within the ILC. The ILC, in its previous drafts, had referred to "substantial" or "appreciable" harm. In its view, however, these terms might have a variety of meanings and this ambiguity made it undesirable for use in its draft articles. In the final draft, ILC replaced the qualification "appreciable" with the qualification "significant", in order to bring the terminology of the 1994 ILC Draft Articles in line with the ILC's work on International Liability for Injurious Consequences Arising out of Acts not Prohibited by International Law (ILC Draft Articles on State Liability).[82] The second reason for the change, according to the ILC, is that the qualification "appreciable" could mean both "measurable" and "significant", and is therefore not sufficiently precise.[83]

---

[80] See, e.g., the 1992 UNECE Watercourse Convention, *supra* note 1, Article 1(2).

[81] See the 1990 UNECE Guidelines on Responsibility and Liability Regarding Transboundary Water Pollution (paragraph 16.2). See also R. Lefeber, *supra* note 72, p. 88.

[82] See S. McCaffrey, "Non-Navigational Uses of International Watercourses", in R. Lefeber (ed.), *Contemporary International Legal Issues: Opportunities at the Time of Momentous Change*, (1994), p. 380.

[83] See "Report of the ILC on the work of its Forty-sixth Session", *supra* note 55, p. 103.

It is generally accepted that the obligation not to cause significant harm embodies a due diligence obligation. The 1991 ILC Draft Articles on the Law of the Non-Navigational Uses of International Watercourses (1991 ILC Draft Articles)[84] do not contain an explicit reference to due diligence. However, it became apparent from the discussion in the ILC that the obligation not to cause significant harm was presumed to be an obligation of due diligence. Hence, a lack of due diligence would be required for a finding that the obligation not to cause significant harm has been violated. The 1994 ILC Draft Articles were more clear in this respect by providing that "[w]atercourse States shall exercise due diligence to utilise an international watercourse in such a way as not to cause significant harm to other watercourse States" (Article 7(1)). However, this article was not included in the final text of the 1997 UN Watercourse Convention. Article 7(1) of the Convention merely states that watercourse states shall "take all appropriate measures to prevent the causing of significant harm to other watercourse States". An obligation of this kind is, however, tantamount to an obligation of due diligence. Although the mere failure to adopt appropriate measures amounts to a violation of an international obligation irrespective of lack of due diligence, obligations of this kind concentrate on the action to be taken rather than the result of such action, i.e. the prevention of actual harm, even though the latter is the ultimate objective of the obligation.[85] In other words, an obligation that requires a state to adopt appropriate measures also requires that state to act diligently in order not to cause significant harm.[86]

Quoting from the *Alabama* case, the ILC has defined the concept of "due diligence" as "a diligence proportioned to the magnitude of the subject and to the dignity and strength of the power which is exercising it" or "such care as governments ordinarily employ in their domestic affairs".[87]

---

[84] 1991 Draft Articles on the Law of the Non-Navigational Uses of International Watercourses, in "Report of the ILC on the work its Forty-third Session", *supra* note 78, p. 63.

[85] See also R. Lefeber, *supra* note 72, pp. 65-69.

[86] See S. McCaffrey and M. Sinjela, *supra* note 2, p. 100.

[87] See *Alabama Claims* arbitration, in J.B. Moore, *A Digest of International Law*, Vol. 7, (1906), p. 1059. On the content of the concept of "due diligence", see R. Lefeber, *supra* note 72, pp. 65-69.

The ILC has qualified the obligation of due diligence as an obligation of conduct and not as an obligation of result, i.e. the application of the due diligence standard does not guarantee that harm will not occur.[88] According to the ILC, "[a] watercourse State can be deemed to have violated its due diligence obligation only if it knew or ought to have known that the particular use of an international watercourse would cause significant harm to other watercourse States".[89]

5.2.2 *The Obligation to Prevent, Reduce, and Control the Pollution of an International Watercourse that may Cause Significant Harm*

The obligation not to cause significant harm has particular relevance for the protection and preservation of the environment. This is also reflected in special provisions on the protection and preservation of the environment in the 1997 UN Watercourse Convention. Article 20 of the 1997 UN Watercourse Convention calls upon watercourse states to protect and preserve the ecosystems of international watercourses. According to the ILC, the term "ecosystems" refers to an ecological unit consisting of "living and non-living components that are independent and functions as a community".[90] The ILC has further explained that the term "protection" includes "the duty to protect those ecosystems from a significant threat of harm" and the term "preservation" applies in particular "to freshwater ecosystems that are in a pristine or unspoiled condition".[91] This general provision is elaborated in subsequent articles. In Article 21(2), the Convention establishes an explicit link between the principle of equitable utilization and the obligation not to cause significant harm, on the one hand, and the protection and preservation of ecosystems, on the other:

> "[w]atercourse States shall, individually and, where appropriate, jointly, prevent, reduce and control the pollution of an international watercourse that may cause significant harm to other watercourse States or to their environ-

[88] See commentary to Draft Article 7, *supra* note 55, p. 103, paragraph 4.

[89] *Ibid.*, p. 104, paragraph 8.

[90] See the ILC's commentary to Draft Article 20, *supra* note 55, pp. 118-119, paragraph 2. The ILC said that "[i]n ecosystems, everything depends on everything else and nothing is really wasted".

[91] *Ibid.*, p. 119, paragraph 3.

ment, including harm to human health or safety, to the use of the waters for any beneficial purpose or to the living resources of the watercourse".[92]

In a statement of understanding pertaining to Articles 21 to 23, it is stated that "these articles impose a due diligence standard on watercourse States".[93] This statement of understanding clearly reinforces the conclusion reached in Section 5.2.1 above that the obligation not to cause significant harm is of the nature of an obligation of due diligence.

An essential element of the obligation to prevent, reduce, and control pollution that may cause significant harm is the concept of "pollution". A definition of pollution in the context of international watercourses is not provided in any relevant treaties relating to international watercourses. Some definitions were included in resolutions of the International Law Association and the Institute of International Law.[94] In the 1997 UN Watercourse Convention, however, a definition has been incorporated. Article 21(1) defines "pollution of an international watercourse" as "any detrimental alteration in the composition or quality of the waters of an international watercourse which results directly or indirectly from human conduct". It should be noted that the definition refers to "any detrimental alteration" and it does therefore not prejudge the question of the threshold at which pollution becomes impermissible.[95] In other words, the obligation to prevent, reduce, and control pollution that may cause significant harm does not contain a threshold of pollution, but only a

---

[92] See also 1992 UNECE Watercourse Convention, *supra* note 1, Article 2(a).

[93] See UN Doc. A/51/869 (1997), p. 5.

[94] See, e.g., the 1966 ILA Helsinki Rules, *supra* note 5, Article IX; and 1979 IIL Resolution on the Pollution of Rivers and Lakes and International Law, Article 1, <http://www.idi-iil.org/idiE/resolutionsE/1979_ath_02_en.PDF>. Article 2(33) of the EU Water Framework directive defines polluition as "the direct or indirect introduction, as a result of human activity, of substances or heat into the air, water or land which may be harmful to human health or the quality of aquatic ecosystems or terrestrial ecosystems directly depending on aquatic ecosystems, which result in damage to material property, or which impair or interfere with amenities and other legitimate uses of the environment"; see EU Directive 2000/60/EC of the European Parliament and of the Council of 23 October 2000 establishing a framework for Community action in the field of water policy, *OJ* L327, 2000, p. 1-73.

[95] See the ILC's commentary to Draft Article 21, *supra* note 55, p. 121, paragraph 2.

threshold of harm. The ILC has deliberately presented it as a factual definition without any legal connotations.

There is a certain amount of disagreement in doctrine of international environmental law as to the standard of conduct of states in relation to existing and new forms of pollution.[96] It is said that new forms of pollution require more stringent standards, whilst existing forms of pollution are obligations of due diligence. Some support for this distinction can be found in the 1982 ILA Rules on Transfrontier Pollution (Article 3(1)) and the 1966 ILA Helsinki Rules (Article X). State practice in this respect is not uniform and the 1992 UNECE Watercourse Convention or the 1997 UN Watercourse Convention, for example, do not include such a distinction.

5.3 The Relationship between the Principle of Equitable Utilization of International Watercourses and the Obligation not to Cause Significant Harm

There is an inherent possibility of conflict between the principle of equitable utilization and the obligation not to cause significant harm. The role of the principle of equitable utilization is to strike a balance between the degree of detriment to some states users of a watercourse and the benefits to other states, so that it has a mitigating effect on the obligation not to cause significant harm. As former Special Rapporteur Stephen McCaffrey explains:

> "if the 'no-harm' rule persisted, a later-developing upstream state would not be permitted to construct a dam that would cause significant harm to its downstream neighbour. If the equitable utilization doctrine took precedence, harm to the downstream state would be one factor to be taken into account in determining whether the dam would be permissible".[97]

The question of how to reconcile these two principles, or what should happen when reconciliation is impossible – i.e. which of them then prevails – is the most complicated and controversial problem of the law of the non-navigational uses of international watercourses. In practice, four

[96] See A. Nollkaemper, *supra* note 13, pp. 57-58.

[97] S. McCaffrey, *supra* note 8, p. 399.

situations (to which reference will be made in the following discussion) may arise:

1. the harm-causing state has been diligent, and the use is equitable and reasonable;
2. the harm-causing state has been diligent, but the use is not equitable and reasonable;
3. the harm-causing state has not been diligent, but the use is equitable and reasonable;
4. the harm-causing state has not been diligent, and the use is not equitable and reasonable.

The 1991 ILC Draft Articles were rather straightforward in their approach: the equitable utilization principle was subordinated to the obligation not to cause significant harm.[98] The equitable nature of a particular use of a watercourse could not legitimise the occurrence of significant harm. However, subsequently, Special Rapporteur Robert Rosenstock proposed inclusion of the following paragraph in order to clarify the relationship between the equitable utilization principle and the obligation not to cause significant harm:

> "watercourse States shall exercise due diligence to utilize an international watercourse in such a way as not to cause significant harm to other watercourse States, absent their agreement, except as may be allowable under an equitable and reasonable use of the watercourse".[99]

The result of this proposal would have been the reversal of the priority and would have subordinated the obligation not to cause significant harm to the principle of equitable utilization.

The ILC, in its 1994 Draft Articles, however, opted for a different solution. Pursuant to Article 7, the obligation not to cause significant harm was to be applicable irrespective of whether the use was equitable and reasonable or not. The ILC has attempted to further clarify the relation-

---

[98] "Report of the ILC to the General Assembly on the work of its Forty-third Session", (1991), *supra* note 78, p. 63.

[99] See R. Rosenstock, "First Report on the Law of Non-Navigational Uses of International Watercourses", UN Doc. A/CN.4/451, *YILC* (1993), Vol. II, (Part One), p. 185.

ship between the principles of equitable utilization and the obligation not to cause significant harm by adding a second paragraph to Article 7. Article 7(2) of the 1994 ILC Draft Articles reads as follows:

> "[w]here, despite the exercise of due diligence, significant harm is caused to another watercourse State, the State whose use causes the harm shall, in the absence of agreement to such use, consult with the State suffering such harm over:
> (a) the extent to which such use is equitable and reasonable taking into account the factors listed in article 6;
> (b) the question of ad hoc adjustments to its utilisation, designed to eliminate or mitigate any such harm caused and, where appropriate, the question of compensation".

In view of the qualifying phrase "despite the exercise of due diligence", the provision would only be activated if the harm-causing state has been diligent. If the harm-causing state has not been diligent, it has committed an internationally wrongful act irrespective of whether the harm-causing use was equitable and reasonable or not (situations 3 and 4).

However, the new paragraph embodies a certain degree of ambiguity itself. It imposes an obligation on a diligent harm-causing state to enter into consultations with the affected state on the extent to which a particular harm-causing use is equitable and reasonable. The provision is nonetheless silent on the legal consequences of a positive or negative finding resulting from these consultations. The ILC has observed that:

> "[i]n certain circumstances 'equitable and reasonable utilization' of an international watercourse may still involve significant harm to another State. Generally, in such instances, the principle of equitable and reasonable utilization remains the guiding criterion in balancing the interests at stake".[100]

Hence, even if a state has been diligent, the lawfulness of a harm-causing use is apparently thus still to be determined by the principle of equitable utilization (situations 1 and 2).

Article 7(2) does explicitly recognise the possibility that a harm-causing use may nevertheless be reasonable and equitable. However, in its

---

[100] Commentary to Draft Article 7, *supra* note 55, p. 103, paragraph 2.

Commentary to the 1994 ILC Draft Articles, the ILC suggested an important limitation to what may be regarded as an "equitable and reasonable use". It opined that "[a] use which causes significant harm to human health and safety is understood to be inherently inequitable and unreasonable".[101] This view found support in Draft Article 10 which, having established the general principle of no *prima facie* priority between different types of uses of a watercourse, nonetheless, singles out human needs as calling for special regard.

Furthermore, the relationship between subparagraph (a) and subparagraph (b) of Article 7(2) was unclear. There was no indication, in particular, whether the provisions of subparagraph (b) are activated if a use is found to be equitable and reasonable, or only if it is found not to be so. The former Special Rapporteur, Stephen McCaffrey, seems to be of the opinion that it would be activated in both cases (situations 1 and 2).[102] However, it could also be argued that Article 7(2) is only activated if the harm-causing state has been diligent and has acted in conformity with the principle of equitable utilization (situation 1). In situations 2, 3, and 4, the harm-causing state would have breached an international obligation and could be held liable for an internationally wrongful act.

Article 7(2.b) first requires a diligent harm-causing state to enter into consultations with affected states on (a) the question of *ad hoc* adjustments to a use, designated to eliminate or mitigate the harm caused. If a harm-causing use by a diligent state is not equitable and reasonable (situation 2), the affected state may require the harm-causing state to adjust the use because of breach of the principle of equitable utilization. The obligation to consult with affected states on the adjustment of the use would have added value only if a harm-causing use by a diligent state has proven to be equitable and reasonable.

Article 7(2.b) also requires harm-causing states to consult with affected states, "where appropriate", on the question of compensation. In this respect, it is relevant to note that the origin of the two subparagraphs of Article 7(2) is different: subparagraph (a) has its origin in the 1994 ILC Draft Articles, whilst subparagraph (b) has its origin in the ILC Draft

[101] *Ibid.*, p. 104, paragraph 14.

[102] S. McCaffrey, *supra* note 8, (1995), p. 399.

Articles on State Liability,[103] pursuant to which states are obliged to negotiate on compensation for the effects of harmful activities that do not follow from an internationally wrongful act.[104] This supports the view that Article 7(2.b) only provided a rule for situation 1.

The proposal of the ILC to add a new paragraph to Article 7 is reflected in the final text of the 1997 UN Watercourse Convention, but in a different form. Article 7(2) of the Convention reads as follows:

> "[w]here significant harm nevertheless is caused to another watercourse State, the States whose use causes such harm shall, in the absence of an agreement to such use, take all appropriate measures, having due regard for the provisions of articles 5 and 6, in consultation with the affected State, to eliminate or mitigate such harm and, where appropriate, to discuss the question of compensation".

In a self-evident statement of understanding pertaining to Article 7(2), it is said that "[i]n the event such steps as are required by Article 7(2) do not eliminate the harm, such steps as are required by Article 7(2) shall then be taken to mitigate the harm".[105]

The changes made by the drafters of the Convention are significant. First, it appears that the provision has changed from a mere procedural obligation into an obligation with both substantive and procedural elements.[106] In contrast to the 1994 ILC Draft Articles, the Convention requires the harm-causing state to take, in consultation with the affected states, all appropriate measures to eliminate, or at least to mitigate, the harm. Secondly, the reference to the concept of "due diligence" has been deleted, and this is a logical consequence of the deletion of a similar reference in Article 7(1) of the Convention. It is noteworthy that this reference has not been replaced by the phrase "despite the adoption of appropriate measures". However, a similar effect has been brought about by the inclusion of the word "nevertheless" in Article 7(2), which suggests

---

[103] Cf., J. Barboza, "Sixth Report on International Liability for Injurious Consequences Arising out of Acts not Prohibited by International Law; General List of Draft Articles" (Article 2(h)), Doc. A/CN.4/428, *YILC* (1990) Vol. II (Part One), p. 90.

[104] See J. Barboza, *supra* note 103; R. Lefeber, *supra* note 72, p. 233.

[105] See UN Doc. A/51/869 (1997), p. 5.

[106] Cf., also S. McCaffrey and M. Sinjela, *supra* note 2, at 101-102.

that the second paragraph is only activated if the harm-causing state has not adopted "all appropriate measures" and, hence, has not exercised "due diligence". Third, it is noteworthy that the provision no longer provides (explicitly) for an assessment of the equitableness and reasonableness of the use by the states concerned. It has been replaced by a mere reference to Articles 5 and 6. Accordingly, the use is either unlawful in which case there is a violation of Article 5 (situation 2) or the use is lawful in which case the conduct of the harm-causing state is in conformity with the Convention (situation 1). Hence, neither the principle of equitable utilization nor the obligation not to cause significant harm prevails: they both have to be complied with. The deletion of subparagraph (a) thus puts beyond doubt that Article 7(2) only applies to lawful uses (situation 1) and has its origin in the ILC Draft on State Liability. However, the addition of substantive elements to the provision indicates that lawful conduct may nevertheless entail new obligations if significant harm is caused to other states. This is an innovation and a progressive development of international law.

It is not surprising, then, that Tanzi and Arcari describe the relationship between these two concepts as a Gordian knot.[107] On the basis of their illuminating study of the problem, they suggest, and it is submitted, rightly, Articles 5-7 of the 1997 Watercourse Convention set an abstract principle, the practical application of which is left to States.[108]

5.4 Procedural Obligations Relating to the Use of International Watercourses[109]

Procedural obligations do not focus directly on the prevention of transboundary harm or on the equitableness or reasonableness of a certain use, but on the formal aspects of co-operation between states in relation to the use of international watercourses. They apply when planning, operating, or terminating a certain use of an international watercourse.

---

[107] A. Tanzi and M. Arcari, *supra* note 2, p. 175.

[108] *Ibid.*, pp. 175-179.

[109] On procedural obligations in international environmental law, see P. Okowa, *State Responsibility for Transboundary Air Pollution in International Law*, (2000), pp. 131-171.

According to one theory, procedural obligations are derived from the general obligation to co-operate in good faith.[110] For example, Article 8 of the UN Watercourse Convention provides that "[w]atercourse States shall cooperate on the basis of sovereign equality, territorial integrity, mutual benefit and good faith in order to attain optimal utilization and adequate protection of an international watercourse". According to another theory, procedural obligations are inherent in the obligation not to cause significant harm.[111] Whatever their theoretical basis, these obligations have been spelled out in most documents of hard and soft law, including the 1997 UN Watercourse Convention (see further Articles 9 and 11 to 19). Accordingly, they bind states in many cases independently of the general obligation to co-operate or the obligation not to cause significant harm.

The prevention of transboundary harm and the verification of the equitableness and reasonableness of a certain use is particularly important when planning a certain use of a watercourse. At this stage, a watercourse state should make an assessment of the possible transboundary effects of a contemplated use. It will, however, not always be possible to assess in advance whether a contemplated use will infringe the rights of other states, in particular whether it will produce an inadmissible amount of harm on the other side of the border or will prove not to be equitable or reasonable. The states involved may well disagree on the effects of a contemplated use and/or the rights involved. In these cases, unless it is abundantly clear that rights of other watercourse states will be infringed, the requirement of the consent of potentially affected states does not do justice to the exclusive character of a state's sovereignty within the limits of its national jurisdiction. In the *Lac Lanoux* case, the Tribunal held that it falls within the competence of a planning state to take a decision in doubtful cases, but also that the planning state is accountable for such a decision:

---

[110] See, e.g., the 1972 UN Declaration on the Human Environment (Principle 24); 1992 UNCED Declaration on Environment and Development (Principle 27 and others); 1992 UNECE Watercourse Convention (Articles 2(6) and 9), *supra* note 1; 1994 ILC Draft Articles (Article 8), *supra* note 7; and 1997 UN Watercourse Convention (Article 8), *supra* note 1. The obligation to co-operate was also a guiding principle in the *Lac Lanoux* arbitration, 24 *ILR* 101 and XII *UNRIAA* 281 (in French).

[111] See R. Lefeber, *supra* note 72, p. 34 et seq.

> "[i]t is for each State to evaluate in a reasonable manner and in good faith the situations and the rules which will involve it in controversies; its evaluation may be in contradistinction with that of another State; in that case, should a dispute arise the Parties normally seek to resolve it by negotiation or, alternatively, by submitting to the authority of a third party; but one of them is never obliged to suspend the exercise of its jurisdiction because of the dispute except when it assumes an obligation to do so; by exercising its jurisdiction it takes the risk of seeing its international responsibility called into question, if it is established that it did not act within the limits of its rights".[112]

In the same case, the Tribunal stated that international law imposes restrictions on the freedom of a planning state to permit the carrying on of activities within the limits of its national jurisdiction, even if it does not consider the rights of other states to be at stake. The arbitrators stipulated that not only should the rights of other states be respected, but that also their interests should be taken into account.[113] The planning state is under an obligation to balance in good faith all interests involved. The Tribunal stated that:

> "according to the rules of good faith, the upstream State is under the obligation to take into consideration the various interests involved, to seek to give them every satisfaction compatible with the pursuit of its own interests, and to show that in this regard it is genuinely concerned to reconcile the interests of the other riparian State with its own".[114]

In this context, the Tribunal stressed the interaction between substantive and procedural obligations.[115] From the judgment it emerges that proper balancing of interests requires the observance of specific procedural obligations. However, the emphasis put on the observance of procedural obligations does not alter the fact that the balancing test is conducted by the

---

[112] *Supra* note 109, 24 *ILR* 101, at 132 (paragraph 16), and XII *UNRIAA* 281, at 310.

[113] 24 *ILR* 101, at 139 (paragraph 22), 140 (paragraph 23), and XII *UNRIAA* 281 (French), at 315 and 316; see also *Fisheries Jurisdiction* case (United Kingdom v. Iceland), Merits, Judgment, *ICJ Rep* (1974), p. 3 at 34 (paragraph 79), where the Court refers to the "obligation to pay due regard to the interests of other States" with respect to the conservation and use of natural resources.

[114] 24 *ILR* 101, at 139 (paragraph 22), and XII *UNRIAA* 281 (French), at 315.

[115] 24 *ILR* 101, at 141 (paragraph 24), and XII *UNRIAA* 281 (French), at 317.

planning state. Otherwise, third states would be in a position to paralyse the exercise of jurisdiction by the planning state. As appears from the above quotation, it may be revealed by an *ex post facto* evaluation of the conduct of the planning state whether that state has balanced interests in good faith. Obviously, the latter requirement has only been met if potentially affected states have been given the opportunity to make their views known. The observance of procedural obligations thus becomes a crucial factor in assessing whether the planning state has balanced interests in good faith.

Procedural obligations include the prior notification of a contemplated use, the exchange of information, and the entering into consultations and negotiations. In order sincerely to live up to its obligation to take into account the interests of third states, the planning state should normally – taking into account its own security interests – give prior notification of the contemplated use to potentially affected states and provide these states with all relevant data concerning the contemplated use in order to enable these states to make an assessment of the impact which the activity may have in their respective territories.[116] In addition, the planning state should comply with requests of potentially affected states to enter into consultations in order to enable these states to make a more detailed assessment of the impact which a planned measure may have in their respective territories.[117] Thus, potentially affected states will be in a posi-

[116] For evidence of this obligation, see, e.g., in treaty instruments, the 1997 UN Watercourse Convention (Article 12); the 1992 UNECE Watercourse Convention on the Protection and Use of Watercourses and International Lakes (Article 6); the 1991 UNECE Convention on Environmental Impact Assessment in a Transboundary Context (Article 3); in soft law instruments, the 1992 UNCED Declaration on Environment and Development (Principle 19); the 1974 Charter of Economic Rights and Duties of States (Article 3); 1974 OECD Principles Concerning Transfrontier Pollution (paragraphs 6, 8); in non-governmental instruments, the 1982 ILA Montreal Rules of International Law Applicable to Transfrontier Pollution (Article 5); the 1986 WCED Elements for a Draft Convention on Environmental Protection and Sustainable Development (Articles 15, 16); and, in case law, the *Lac Lanoux* case, 24 *ILR* 101, at 138 (paragraph 21), and XII *UNRIAA* 281 (French), at 314.

[117] For evidence of this obligation, see, e.g., in treaty instruments, the 1997 UN Watercourse Convention (Article 17); the 1992 UNECE Watercourse Convention on the Protection and Use of Transboundary Watercourses and International Lakes (Article 10); in soft law instruments, the 1992 UNCED Declaration on Environment and Development (Prin-

tion to contribute constructively to the assessment of the impact of the planned measure by informing the planning state of the effects which the activity may have in their respective territories.

However, if in spite of consultations, the states involved continue to disagree over points of fact or law, they cannot be required to enter into negotiations to settle the dispute, because there is no *general* obligation of states to negotiate in a dispute over rights, let alone in a dispute over interests.[118] However, several treaties concerned with the protection of the environment oblige parties to enter into negotiations in case of a dispute over rights and to conduct these negotiations in good faith in an attempt to settle the dispute.[119] Ideally, they should make use of other peaceful means to settle the dispute if negotiations do not result in a satisfactory solution for both parties. Pursuit of this procedure would result in a final solution, if it were not for the fact that states are generally not required to

ciple 19); the 1974 OECD Principles Concerning Transfrontier Pollution (paragraphs 7, 8); in non-governmental instruments, the 1986 WCED Elements for a Draft Convention on Environmental Protection and Sustainable Development (Article 17); the 1982 ILA Montreal Rules of International Law Applicable to Transfrontier Pollution (Article 5); and in case law, the *Lac Lanoux* case, 24 *ILR* 101, at 133 (paragraph 17), and XII *UNRIAA* 281 (French), at 310. For national state practice, see, e.g., the construction of the Poplar River Thermal Power Station in Canada near the international border of the United States, Digest of United States Practice in International Law 1978, at 1116 et seq. (request), and *Digest of United States Practice in International Law* 1979, at 1103 et seq.; see also J.G. Merrills, *International Dispute Settlement* (3rd edn., 1998), p. 7 considers that the process for developing procedures for consultations has been too slow.

[118] See, e.g., J.G. Merrills, *ibid.*, p. 26: "there is no general duty to settle disputes by negotiation".

[119] See, e.g., the 1997 UN Watercourse Convention "with a view to arriving at an equitable resolution of the situation" (Article 17(1)); the 1992 OSPAR Convention for the Protection of the Marine Environment of the North-East Atlantic "with a view to negotiating a cooperation agreement" (Article 21(1)); the 1982 UN Convention on the Law of the Sea "with a view to taking the measures necessary" (Article 118); see also the 1986 WCED Elements for a Draft Convention on Environmental Protection and Sustainable Development (Article 12). See also the *Railway Traffic between Lithuania and Poland*, Advisory Opinion, PCIJ Series A/B, No. 42 (1931), p. 108 at 116 ("with a view to concluding agreements"); *North Sea Continental Shelf*, Judgment, *ICJ Rep* (1969), p. 3 at 46-47 (paragraph 85) "with a view to arriving at an agreement" on the delimitation of the continental shelf; *Fisheries Jurisdiction* (United Kingdom v. Iceland), Merits, Judgment, *ICJ Rep* (1974), p. 3 at 32 (paragraphs 74-75) and 34 (paragraph 79), "for the equitable solution" of their respective fishery rights.

reach an equitable compromise solution or to submit disputes to binding third party settlement if they fail to settle the dispute among themselves.[120] Thus, conflicting rights will not be accommodated if the planning state and/or potentially affected states refuse to enter into meaningful negotiations and/or to use other peaceful means of dispute settlement.

Notwithstanding the obligation of the planning state to comply with these procedural obligations to notify, consult, and negotiate, they do not deprive the planning state of its right to take the final decision on a contemplated activity. To comply with its obligation to balance interests in good faith, the planning state should duly take into account the information provided by potentially affected states as well as the results of consultations and negotiations. In an *ex post facto* analysis, this will be a factor in assessing whether subsequent acts of the planning state were justified. In this respect, it would also be of importance that private persons who reside outside the planning state, and are potentially affected by a contemplated use, have a right of equal access to administrative and judicial institutions of the planning state to request judicial review of decisions to carry on or to permit the carrying on of a contemplated use. These procedures should not be discriminatory as regards either legal standing or the availability of legal remedies.[121]

[120] See the *Lac Lanoux* case, 24 *ILR* 101, at 128 (paragraph 11) and 130 (paragraph 13), and XII *UNRIAA* 281 (French), at 306 and 308; see also commentary to Article 8 of the 1982 ILA Montreal Rules of International Law Applicable to Transfrontier Pollution (1982 Montreal Report), *Report of the Sixtieth Conference*, Montreal, 1983, p. 176; C.B. Bourne, "Procedure in the Development of International Drainage Basin: The Duty to Consult and Negotiate", 10 *CYIL* (1972), p. 225. See also *Railway Traffic between Lithuania and Poland*, Advisory Opinion, PCIJ Series A/B, No. 42 (1931), p. 108, at 116 ("an obligation to negotiate does not imply an obligation to reach an agreement"); the *International Status of South-West Africa*, Advisory Opinion, *ICJ Rep* (1950), p. 128 at 140 ("an obligation merely to negotiate does not of itself assure the conclusion of Trusteeship Agreements"); *North Sea Continental Shelf*, Judgment, *ICJ Rep* (1969), p. 3 at 47-48 (paragraph 87) ("an obligation to negotiate did not imply an obligation to reach agreement"). But see the 1986 WCED Elements for a Draft Convention on Environmental Protection and Sustainable Development which prescribes submission to third-parties if negotiations do not result in an agreement (Article 12).

[121] For evidence that the obligation to make available review proceedings on a non-discriminatory basis has entered the body of positive international water law, see, e.g., the 1997 UN Watercourse Convention (Article 32); and 1974 Nordic Environmental Protection Convention. For non-binding instruments, see, e.g., the 1992 UNCED Declaration on

Thus, at the end of the process, the planning state is entitled to decide unilaterally whether a planned measure will be carried out or not. However, the planning state is required to take into account the interests of potentially affected states. This means that these interests will have to be considered as if they were its own interests and that, if the planning state decides to continue with the contemplated use, it will seek to accommodate the interests of potentially affected states by the adoption of such risk-minimising measures as are technically possible and economically feasible. Yet, if such measures are not possible or not feasible, the planning state is entitled to continue with the contemplated use, provided that such decision is based on a careful balancing of interests and that the interests of potentially affected states are taken into account as much as possible. After all, international law protects rights, not interests.

The 1997 UN Watercourse Convention contains a detailed and complicated system of procedural obligations in relation to a contemplated use of an international watercourse (Articles 11 to 19). Pursuant to Article 11, states are required to exchange information and consult each other and, if necessary, negotiate on "the possible effects of planned measures" on the condition of an international watercourse. According to the ILC's commentary, this procedural obligation relates to all types of effects of planned measures on the state of an international watercourse, whether adverse or beneficial, in order to avoid problems arising from unilateral assessments.[122] It does, however, not oblige states to send an official notification to other watercourse states of each and every planned measure, and permits the planning state to assess unilaterally whether a planned measure may have adverse effects or not. The planning state must comply with a number of strict procedural obligations laid down in Articles 12 to 18 of the 1997 UN Watercourse Convention only if the planning state concludes that the planned measure may have "a signifi-

---

Environment and Development (Principle 10); the 1977 OECD Recommendation for the Implementation of a Regime of Equal Right of Access and Non-Discrimination in relation to Transfrontier Pollution; the 1976 OECD Recommendation on Equal Right of Access in Relation to Transfrontier Pollution; for non-governmental instruments, see the 1986 WCED Elements for a Draft Convention on Environmental Protection and Sustainable Development (Articles 6, 20).

[122] See the ILC's Commentary to Draft Article 11, *supra* note 55, p. 111, paragraph 3.

cant adverse effect". These obligations include an obligation to send a timely notification of planned measures which may have a significant adverse effect; rules on the reply to such notification; an obligation to enter into consultations and negotiations if, according to the potentially affected states, the planned measures are inconsistent with the principle of equitable utilization or the obligation not to cause significant harm; and a special procedure in the absence of a notification. If the planned measure is proven to be inconsistent with the principle of equitable utilization or the obligation not to cause significant harm, the planning state cannot proceed with the contemplated use without the consent of the potentially affected states. However, if the states concerned are not in agreement over the consistency of the planned measures with these general principles, the planning state may unilaterally decide on the contemplated use taking into account the results of the exchanges of information, consultations, and negotiations. Such a unilateral decision by the planning state may, of course, be subject to an *ex post facto* analysis. Although the general procedure embodied in Article 11 is arguably part of international customary law and the special procedure embodied in Articles 12 to 18 appears to be a progressive development of international law, both procedures do follow the general system of procedural obligations outlined above.

Compliance with the procedures in relation to a contemplated use enables the planning state to assess what protection and safety measures should be taken to avoid the occurrence of adverse effects in the normal course of operation of a certain use of an international watercourse and to minimise the risk of accidental occurrence of such effects. On the international level, a state should, once a certain use is in operation, continue to provide information to and consult with potentially affected states, if appropriate.[123] It should, furthermore, monitor the impact of the use in order to evaluate whether its actual impact remains within the limits set by international law.[124] On the national level, compliance with the principle

---

[123] See, e.g., the 1997 UN Watercourse Convention, *supra* note 1, Article 9.

[124] See, e.g., the 1992 UNECE Watercourse Convention on the Protection and Use of Transboundary Watercourses and International Lakes (Article 9); for a non-governmental instrument, see the 1986 WCED Elements for a Draft Convention on Environmental Protection and Sustainable Development (Article 4(b)).

of equitable utilization and the obligation not to cause significant harm will require the enactment of regulations on the use of the watercourse, including rules on the issuing of permits, the supervision of compliance with such regulations, and the investigation of violations of them. Examples of such regulations are the establishment of emission standards and rules for the treatment of waste, the prescription of specific technical equipment, the use of incentives and disincentives to encourage or, respectively, discourage the production of certain goods and services, and/or the use of certain manufacturing techniques. To minimise risks, states should adopt safety measures, such as the use of the best available technology, the employment and training of skilled personnel, the drafting and testing of emergency plans, and the installation of early warning systems.

Despite the adoption of measures to prevent their occurrence, adverse effects may occur during the life cycle of a certain use of an international watercourse and cause or threaten to cause significant harm or to encroach upon the equitableness or reasonableness of a certain use. In this respect, a distinction must be made between (1) effects which result from the normal operation of a use and (2) accidental effects.

Once in operation, it may appear that a certain use causes more adverse effects than anticipated. However, the occurrence of adverse effects does not automatically give the affected state the right to claim an injunction. For example, the use in question may continue to be admissible if it proves to be possible to reduce the amount of adverse effects below the threshold of significant harm within a reasonable period of time.[125] This approach was also that followed by the arbitrators in the *Trail Smelter* case. In its final award, the Tribunal permitted the continued operation of a trail smelter, but imposed a regime to ensure that in all probability no

---

[125] For evidence that an obligation of this kind has entered the body of positive international law, see, e.g., the 1997 UN Watercourse Convention (Article 21(2)) and especially the commentary to the 1994 ILC Draft Articles, *supra* note 55, p. 122, paragraph 4; the 1992 UNECE Watercourse Convention on the Protection and Use of Transboundary Watercourses and International Lakes (Article 2); for non-governmental instruments, see the 1982 ILA Montreal Rules of International Law Applicable to Transfrontier Pollution (Article 3(3)); the 1966 ILA Helsinki Rules on the Uses of the Waters of International Rivers (Arts. X(1)b j. XI(2)), *supra* note 5.

significant harm would be caused by its future operation.[126] Interestingly, the Tribunal permitted the operation of the smelter, even though significant harm would be caused south of the border notwithstanding the maintenance of the regime.[127] However, the operation of the smelter under these circumstances was subject to the payment of compensation and the procedure for the amendment of the regime could be set in motion at the request of either party,[128] with the aim of removing the cause of the occurrence of significant harm in the State of Washington.

Following the actual occurrence of accidental adverse effects or when faced with a real threat of such effects, a state should take abatement measures to minimize the consequences of such effects.[129] To this effect, the state should take clean-up and containment measures to prevent or minimise potential harm and clean-up measures to eliminate or mitigate actual harm, and should execute contingency plans, if appropriate. Affected states as well as states that are likely to be affected should receive early notification of any actual or threatened adverse effects, and should be provided with data on the nature of the effects, be given advice on how to combat them, and be offered material assistance in mitigating the effects within their territories.[130]

---

[126] II *UNRIAA* 1905, at 1966 et seq.

[127] *Ibid.*, p. 1978, 1980.

[128] *Ibid.*, p. 1973, 1978.

[129] See also the 1986 WCED Elements for a Draft Convention on Environmental Protection and Sustainable Development (Article 10); 1982 ILA Montreal Rules of International Law Applicable to Transfrontier Pollution (Article 3).

[130] For evidence that obligations of this kind have entered the body of positive international water law, see, e.g., the 1992 UNECE Watercourse Convention on the Protection and Use of Transboundary Watercourses and International Lakes (Articles 14, 16); the 1976 Bonn Convention for the Protection of the Rhine against Chemical Pollution (Article 11); for non-binding instruments, see the 1992 UNCED Declaration on Environment and Development (Principle 18); the 1988 OECD Decision on the Exchange of Information Concerning Accidents Capable of Causing Transfrontier Damage; the 1974 OECD Principles Concerning Transfrontier Pollution (paragraphs 9, 10); for a non-governmental instrument, the 1986 WCED Elements for a Draft Convention on Environmental Protection and Sustainable Development (Article 19). See also *Corfu Channel* case, Judgment of April 9th, *ICJ Rep* (1949), p. 4 at 22, where the Court refers to the obligation to notify states of imminent dangers, in this case the existence of a minefield (this obligation is, *inter alia*, based on "every State's obligation not to allow knowingly its territory to be used for acts contrary to the rights of other states"; *Military and Paramilitary Activities in*

If it is decided to terminate a certain use of an international watercourse, the state should take measures to ensure that the dismantling of the facilities used to carry on the use will not become a source of future adverse effects. This may, for example, require the installation of special devices before dams or power plants are abandoned. If, in spite of such measures, a risk of future effects continues to exist, the site should be monitored and, if necessary, additional measures should be taken.

6. Liability for Damage to International Watercourses[131]

Two conventions are relevant to the question of liability for damage to international watercourses in the Nordic context in particular: the 1974 Convention on the Protection of the Environment between Denmark, Finland, Norway and Sweden (the "Nordic Convention") and the 2003 Protocol on Civil Liability and Compensation for Damage Caused by the Transboundary Effects of Industrial Accidents on Transboundary Water to the 1992 Convention on the Protection and Use of Transboundary Watercourses and International Lakes and to the 1992 Convention on the Transboundary Effects of Industrial Accidents (the "2003 Protocol").[132]

The fundamental rule of 1974 Convention is that "in considering the permissibility of environmentally harmful activities, the nuisance which such activities entail or might entail in another Contracting State shall be equated with a nuisance in the States where activities are carried out" (Article 2). Another basic rule of the Convention is that it is applicable to any person affected or who may be affected by a nuisance caused by environmentally harmful activities in another contracting State. These per-

and against Nicaragua (Nicaragua v. United States of America), Merits, Judgment, *ICJ Rep* (1986), p. 14 at 112 (paragraph 215), pp. 147-148 (paragraph 262).

[131] Signed on 19 February 1974, entered into force on 5 October 1976; see also A. Boyle, "Making the Polluter Pay? Alternatives to State Responsibility in the Allocation of Transboundary Environmental Costs," in *International Responsibility for Environmental Harm*, F. Francioni and T. Scovazzi (eds.), (1993), pp. 363-379.

[132] Signed during 2nd Joint Special Session of the Governing Bodies of the UNECE Conventions on the Protection and Use of Transboundary Watercourses and International Lakes and on Transboundary Effects of Industrial Accidents (Kiev, 21 May 2003), not in force. Text at <http://www.unece.org/env/civil-liability/documents/protocol_e.pdf>.

sons shall have the right to institute proceedings before the appropriate court or administrative authority of that State concerning the permissibility of the activities, including proceedings on measures necessary to prevent damage, and to lodge an appeal against the decision of the court or the administrative authority to the same extent and in the same way as a legal entity of the State in which activity is under way. These rules also apply to compensation (Article 3). Thus citizens of the Parties to the Convention enjoy equal status as regards the right to institute proceedings concerning the permissibility of environmentally harmful activities in any of those countries.

Article 1 of the Convention defines environmentally harmful activities as a discharge from soil or from buildings or installations of solid or liquid waste, gas or any other substance into watercourses, lakes, sea and the and the use of land, the seabed, buildings or installations in any other way that entails or may entail environmental nuisance by water pollution, noise, vibration, changes of temperature, ionising radiation, light, etc. Each country appoints a special supervisory authority whose task is to safeguard general environmental interests insofar as it regards nuisance arising out of environmentally harmful activities in another Party. These authorities have the right to institute proceedings or be heard by the competent court or the same authority in another Party, regarding the permissibility of the environmentally harmful activities if an authority or other representative of general environmental interests in that State can institute proceedings or be heard in the matters of this kind, as well as the right to appeal against the decision of the court of the administrative authority (Article 4). These supervisory authorities are also empowered to inspect damage. Article 10 states as follows:

> "[i]f necessary for determining the damage caused in another State by environmentally harmful activities, the supervisory authority of that other State shall upon request of the examining authority of the State in which the activities are being carried out make arrangements for on-site inspection. The examining authority or an expert appointed by it may be present at such an inspection. Where necessary, more detailed instructions such as referred to in preceding paragraph shall be drawn up in consultation between the countries concerned".

The Nordic Convention is an unusual treaty that gives an equal access to justice for individuals before the courts of parties to the Convention. This solution presupposes a certain similarity in the legal systems and substantive laws of the parties (as is the case with the Nordic States).

The 2003 Protocol sets out in considerable detail all aspects of the damage it covers. The objective of this protocol "is to provide for a comprehensive regime for civil liability and for adequate and prompt compensation for damage caused by the transboundary effects of industrial accidents on transboundary waters" (Article 1). Article 2 defines damage under this Protocol. It includes loss of life or personal injury; loss of, or damage to, property other than property held by the person liable in accordance with the Protocol; loss of income directly deriving from an impairment of a legally protected interest in any use of the transboundary waters for economic purposes, incurred as a result of impairment of the transboundary waters, taking into account savings and costs; the cost of measures of reinstatement of the impaired transboundary waters, limited to the costs of measures actually taken or to be taken; the cost of response measures, including any loss or damage caused by such measures, to the extent that the damage was caused by the transboundary effects of an industrial accident on transboundary waters (Article 2). Article 3 specifies that this Protocol only applies to damage caused by the transboundary effects of an industrial accident on transboundary waters and only to damage suffered in a Party other than the industrial accident has occurred.

The Protocol establishes a system of strict liability (Article 4) and fault-based liability (Article 5). The main principle in Article 4 is that the operator will be liable for damage caused by an industrial accident. Liability is limited in cases where the operator proves that despite that all safety measures were applied, the damage that occurred was the result of an act of armed conflict hostilities, civil war insurrection; the result of a natural phenomenon of exceptional, inevitable, unforeseeable and irresistible character; wholly the result of compliance with compulsory measure of a public authority of the Party where the industrial accident has occurred; or wholly the result of the wrongful intentional conduct of a third party. If a person who incurred damage or a person for whom he or she is responsible under domestic law has by his or her fault caused damage or contributed to it, the compensation may be reduced or disallowed having regard to all the circumstances. In cases of liability of more than one operator, the claimant shall have the right to seek full compensation for the damage from any or all of the operators liable. However, the operator who proves that only part of the damage was caused by an industrial accident shall be liable for that part of the damage only. Fault-based liability exists without prejudice to Article 4 and in accordance with the relevant rules of applicable domestic law including laws on the liability of servants and agents, any person shall be liable for damage caused or contributed to it his of hers wrongful intentional, reckless or negligent acts or omissions. Article 7 specifies who is entitled to a right of recourse in accordance with the rules of procedure of the competent court or arbitral tribunal established under Article 14 of the Protocol against any other person also liable under this instrument. However, nothing in this Protocol shall prejudice any right of recourse to which the person liable might be entitled either as expressly provided for a contractual arrangements or pursuant to the law of the competent court. Article 8 regulates implementation of the Protocol and also introduces the right to access to information and justice accordingly, with due regard to the legitimate interest of person holding the information, in order to promote objectives of the Protocol.[133]

The limits of financial liability under Article 4 are specified in part one of Annex II. However, financial liability under Article 5 is unlimited. The limitation period is fifteen years (Article 10) and the operator has to be insured (Article 11).

However Article 12 provides that "the Protocol shall not affect the rights and obligations of the Parties under the rules of general international law with respect to the international responsibility of States". This provision seems to indicate that there is a parallel applicability of civil liability under the Protocol and of general international law governing State responsibility, as set out in the International Law Commission in 2001 Articles on State Responsibility.[134]

---

[133] On public participation in international law in general, see J. Ebbesson, "The Notion of Public Participation in International Environmental Law", 8 *YIEL* (1997), pp. 51-98; see also: M. Fitzmaurice, "Some Reflections on Public Participation in Environmental Matters as a Human Right in International Law", 2 *Non-State Actors and International Law* (2002), pp. 1-22.

[134] International Law Commission, "Report on the Work of its Fifty-third Session", UNGA, Official Records Fifty-fifth Session, Supplement No.10 (A/56/10), <http://www.un.org/law/ilc/reports/2001/english/cover.htm>.

The Protocol contains extensive rules regarding procedures. It deals the following aspects: competent courts as compensation (Article 13); arbitration (Article 14); lis-pendens/related actions (Article 15); applicable law (Article 16); relationship between the protocol and the applicable domestic law (Article 17); mutual recognition and enforcement of judgements and arbitral awards (Article 18); relationship between the Protocol and bilateral, multilateral or regional liability agreements (Article 19); relationship between the Protocol and the rules of the European Community on jurisdiction, recognition and enforcement of judgements (Article 20). The provisions of this Protocol thus seem to provide for a comprehensive civil liability regime, and in that regard, the Convention fulfills its objective as stated in Article 1.

Civil liability regimes such as those contained in this Protocol move from the principles of state responsibility and liability towards a system that requires polluters to take responsibility for polluting.[135] These regimes are designed to facilitate the resolution of cases involving harm, given the well-known difficulties involved in such cases.[136] The above

---

[135] B. Baker Roben, "Civil Liability as Control Mechanism for Environmental Protection at International Level", in F.L. Morrison and R. Wolfrum (eds.), *International, Regional and National Environmental Law* (2000), p. 821; see also, R.R. Churchill, "Facilitating (Transnational) Civil Liability Litigation for Environmental Damage by Means of Treaties: Progress, Problems, and Prospects", 12 *YIEL* (2001), pp. 3-41; G. Fernando et al., "The Basel Liability Protocol on Liability and Compensation for Damage Resulting from Transboundary Movement of Hazardous Wastes and Their Disposal", *ibid.*, pp. 69-105; A. Daniel, "Civil Liability Regimes as a Complement to Multilateral Environmental Agreements: Sound International Policy or False Comfort?", 12 *RECIEL*, Issue 3, (2003), p. 225; and on dams, M. Faure and W. Hui, "The International Regimes for the Compensation of Oil -Pollution Damage: Are They Effective?", *ibid.*, p. 242.

[136] R.R. Churchill, *supra* note 135, pp. 5-6. The role of the so-called "polluter pays principle" as such, in this context, is however, not quite clearly defined in civil liability regimes. On one view is submitted that they "flesh out" the polluter pays principle, while on another, "[c]ivil liability conventions, for a variety of reasons, do not favour a polluter pays model of loss distribution but instead either leave much of the loss to lie where it falls, or allocate it equitably across the industry as a whole or among participating states as a whole". See A. Boyle, *supra* note 131. See also, generally, EU Directive 2000/60/EC of the European Parliament and of the Council of 23 October 2000 establishing a framework for Community action in the field of water policy, *supra* note 94, especially Articles 9, as well as paragraphs 11 and 38 of the preamble, for the use of the polluter pays principle in water management policy.

Protocol is by no means an exception and joins the list of other civil liability regimes for example in the areas of nuclear energy; shipping and hazardous wastes.[137] The basic principles of this Protocol are very similar to other instruments setting out civil liability regimes.

7. Settlement of Disputes

In general, watercourse states, in international agreements, follow the principles and methods of peaceful settlement of disputes set out in the UN Charter. First of all, they are bound by Article 2(3) which states that "[a]ll Member States shall settle their international disputes by peaceful means in such a manner as not to endanger international peace and security, and justice". Article 33 of the UN Charter enumerates peaceful means of settlement of disputes, viz. negotiation, enquiry, mediation, conciliation, arbitration, and judicial settlement.[138] The 1966 ILA Helsinki Rules provide for a dispute-settlement procedure that follows Article 33 of the UN Charter.

The 1997 UN Watercourse Convention also contains provisions on settlement of international disputes (Article 33). It is one of the articles that has undergone major redrafting since its inclusion in the 1994 ILC Draft Articles. The provisions of this article are residual in nature and only apply if the watercourse states concerned do not have an applicable agreement for dispute settlement (paragraph 1). The ILC Draft Articles provided for a gradual mechanism of dispute resolution, involving consultation and negotiations followed by an obligatory fact-finding commission, or optional mediation or conciliation if agreed by both parties to the dispute. If parties failed to settle the dispute by means of a fact-finding

[137] See, e.g., 1999 Basel Convention on the Transboundary Movement of Hazardous Waste Protocol on Liability and Compensation for damage Resulting from Transboundary Movement of Hazardous Wastes and Their Disposal, <http:// www.unep.ch./basel/COP5/ liabilityJ172000.html>; 1996 Convention on Liability and Compensation for Damage in Connection with the Carriage of Hazardous and Noxious Substances by Sea, signed on 3 May 1996, not yet in force, 35 *ILM* 1415 (1996).

[138] See S. McCaffrey, "Sixth Report on the Law of the Non-Navigational uses of International Watercourses", Doc. A/CN.4/427, *YILC* (1990), Vol. II, (Part Two), p. 67.

commission, they could agree to submit the dispute to arbitration of judicial settlement.

Article 33 of the Convention abandons in part the gradual approach to recourse to settlement of disputes. Article 33(2) lists all the means, including arbitration and judicial settlement. The first step is negotiation, which may be requested by one of the parties to the dispute. If they do not succeed, parties may jointly seek good offices or request mediation or conciliation by a third party or make may use, if appropriate, of any joint watercourse institutions that may have been established by them or agree to submit the dispute to arbitration or the ICJ. If parties to the dispute fail after six months to achieve settlement by any of the means listed above (including arbitration and the ICJ), they may unilaterally have recourse to an independent fact-finding commission, unless they agree otherwise (Article 33(3)). Thus, according to the procedure adopted, methods of peaceful dispute settlement whose decisions are of a legally binding nature do not constitute the usual last resort open to the parties to the dispute. Article 33(6) describes the duties of the parties to the dispute in relation to the work of the fact-finding commission and its tasks. Article 33(10) provides for the possibility of compulsory jurisdiction before the ICJ or before the arbitral tribunal in respect to any dispute. The optional procedure of such an tribunal has been annexed to the Convention. The adoption by both parties to the Convention of compulsory jurisdiction of the ICJ and of an arbitral tribunal cancels the obligation to have resource to the fact-finding commission.

These (typical) provisions underline the fact that compulsory dispute settlement is not the norm in the international legal order. However, it has been noted that " he availability of a broad and growing range of mechanisms for the dispute settlement, including the compulsory jurisdiction of certain regional and sectoral courts and other international bodies, suggests an important and growing role for independent international adjudication".[139] With regard to the Nordic states, the procedures that exist for the settlement of disputes as provided for in bilateral agreements will be considered further in Chapter 5.

---

[139] P. Sands, *Principles of International Environmental Law* (2003), p. 228.

8. International River Commissions: the Institutional Aspect

International Rivers Commissions constitute the institutional aspect of international watercourses. It has been said that this is the most neglected aspect of the law of international watercourses.[140] Several reasons for this state of affairs may be advanced: the variety of international rivers commissions makes it difficult to draw any general conclusions; their practice is little known and not readily available; and, finally, their development was not regarded as being as interesting and important as that of other international organisations.[141]

There is indeed an infinite variety of the forms of international river commissions. This aspect is widely emphasised in the literature on the subject.[142] They may assume the forms of one organ-single purpose bodies, such as the Central Rhine Commission, or of hierarchically structured entities, such as the Niger Basin Authority.[143] This variety is also evident in the powers of international river commissions represent different patterns. Some function only as advisory organs with limited powers, while others are vested with broad decision-making and executive powers.

The international river commissions in northern Europe illustrate this variety of forms, powers and functions: they may perform advisory functions only, but may also carry out a wide range of important tasks, such as planning, licensing, pollution prevention, and fishing regulations. Some of them are also involved in dispute settlement.[144]

The legal personality of international river commissions, on both the international and the national level, is as diversified as their powers and functions.[145] They usually have international and national personality, in-

[140] See L. Caflisch, "The Law of International Watercourses in its Institutional Aspects", in W. Haller, A. Koltz and G. Muller (eds.), *Im Dienst an der Gemeinschaft, Festschrift für D. Schindler zum 65 Geburtstag* (1989); L. Caflisch, *supra* note 35, pp. 22-221.

[141] See L. Caflisch, *ibid.*, p. 22.

[142] See P.K. Menon, "Institutional Mechanism for the Development Of International Water Resources", 8 *RBDI* (1972), p. 81.

[143] See L. Caflisch, *supra* note 35, at 23.

[144] *Ibid.*, p. 25.

[145] See, e.g., H. Schermers and N. Blokker, *International Institutional Law* (3rd edn. 1995), Chapter 11, p. 980: "Since the 1970s, there has been little discussion in doctrine

cluding diplomatic privileges and immunities, and can conclude international treaties and private law contracts. Some of them, however, do not enjoy legal personality expressly granted by their constitutive instruments, such as the Central Rhine Commission, "yet the issue is not without interest in connection with the regulatory activities of those bodies".[146] Other international river commissions are the subject of special arrangements that do not fall in any category. The nature and extent of the personality in question depends on the constituent instrument of the institution and its functions, which will be discussed in detail in Chapter 5.

9. Concluding Remarks

In conclusion, it is clear that the international regulation of the use of international watercourses has developed significantly in the course of the twentieth century. Its basis has moved from the doctrine of absolute territorial sovereignty, through the community of interests principle and equitable utilization, to sustainable development.[147] It is based on co-operation between riparian states, including the duty to enter into consultations and negotiations and exchange of information, as well as the establishment of institutions to manage and facilitate this co-operation.[148] On the whole, however, it appears that the principle of equitable utilization, the basis of the modern law, is not adequate for the purpose of dealing with all the issues that currently require attention in this area of the law, such as environmental protection, sustainable utilization and conservation of natural resources. A broader environmental perspective is required, as was recognized in the ICJ's judgment in the *Gabcíkovo-Nagymaros* case, where the Court stated that international environmental law is not static but

concerning the question of international personality of international organizations. It is generally recognized that organizations have that capacity, unless there is clear evidence to the contrary".

[146] See L. Caflisch, *supra* note 35, p. 25.

[147] See Chapter 6 below.

[148] See Chapters 4 and 5 below on the practice of the Nordic States in this regard. The general trend is evident in the European Union's Water Framework Directive, *supra* note 94.

dynamic and developing, and therefore subject to constant review in the light of new developments. In any event, the practice of the Nordic States, discussed in the following chapters, is to be considered against this background.

Chapter 3
INTERNATIONAL WATERCOURSES AND THE RIGHTS OF INDIGENOUS PEOPLES: THE SAAMI OF LAPLAND AND FINNMARK

1. Introduction

In this chapter the legal position of indigenous populations with interests in the use of watercourses will be considered. The Saami of Lapland and Finnmark are a good subject for a case study of this issue, given their dependence on watercourses in the region and the fact that their interests have been the subject of consideration in the establishment of legal regimes governing the use of watercourses in Lapland and Finnmark. The approach taken here will include consideration of the rules of international and national law concerning the identification of the subjects of the rights accorded to indigenous peoples and minorities, as well as pertinent questions of international environmental law.

The Saami are an indigenous people who live in Lapland in the very northern part of Finland, Norway, Sweden, and north-western Russia. There are approximately 80,000 to 90,000 Saami people, most of whom still live in the traditional territories that they have occupied from time immemorial.[1] No clear evidence exists of where Saami came from, nor,

[1] See L. Hannikainen, "The State of Minorities, Indigenous Peoples and Immigrants and Refugees in Four Nordic States", 65 *NJIL* (1996), pp. 1-71, at p. 6. See also S. Jentoft, H. Minde, R. Nilsen (eds.), *Indigenous Peoples,* (2003), in particular the papers by J. Age Riseth, "Sami Reindeer Management in Norway: Modernization Challenges and Conflicting Strategies", pp. 229-248; J. Nyyssonen, "The Environmental Sustainability of the Property Rights Regimes in Inari: The Performance of the Forest Government and Reindeer Herding Co-operatives", pp. 249-274; and S. Tuulentie, "For and Against the Rights of Sami Peoples: The Argumentation of the Finnish Majority in the Debate on the Sami Rights", pp. 275-296. There is some debate as to the exact number of Saami people. According to Beach, the number is 60,000 out of which approximately 40,000 live in Norway, 15,000 in Sweden, 6,000 in Finland, and 2,000 in Russia; see H. Beach, "The Saami of Lapland", in Minority Rights Group (ed.), *Polar Peoples: Self-Determination and Development* (1994), pp. 149-150.

more pertinently, at what point in time various groups of the North merged into the group now known as the Saami. Recent evidence shows that the Saami already inhabited the area of Härjedalen in Sweden as far back as AD 1000. However, it is believed that the Saami came to areas now known as Finland and eastern Karelia during or after the last ice age, following herds of reindeer. Skis dating back some 4000 years have been found by the Arctic Sea, indicating that some type of Saami culture already existed at that time. About 1,500 rock drawings have also been found in the areas where they lived, some of them 1,500 years old.[2]

It has been said that the Saami identity is best considered as being based on their nomadic-hunter-gatherer way of life rather than on anything genetic; people who adopted the Saami way of life became Saami.[3] There are different types of Saami: Forest Saami, *Fjeld* Saami, Sea Saami, and Kola Peninsula Saami. The Forest Saami live in coniferous forests, mainly in Finland and Sweden, where they engage in fishing and hunting. Families live in large villages (*siida*) usually along riverbanks. The size of a *siida* can vary from a few families to as many as 20 or 30, which may include some hundred individuals. The individual *siida* has a collective right to hunt and fish within the area. A special group of the Forest Saami lives north of Lake Inari; their language is different from that of the rest of the Forest Saami. The *Fjeld* Saami are also known as the Reindeer Saami, because the reindeer is the most important part of their economy. They live on the *fjelds* between Norway and Sweden and on the highlands north of the *fjelds*.[4] This way of life is different from and is less common than the style of living of the half-nomadic Forest Saami. Other activities of the *Fjeld* Saami are fishing and willow grouse (ptarmigan) trapping. A special group within this category is the River Saami that live around the river Deatnu/Tana and its tributaries. Traditionally, they made their living from salmon fishing, but at present they farm domestic animals and are involved in agriculture. They live in more permanent settlements than the *Fjeld* Saami. The Sea Saami live in northern

---

[2] See section by Kari Yli-Kuha, "The Sami", at <http://www.lysator.liu.se/nordic/scn/faq23.html#2.3.1>.

[3] Ibid.

[4] A *Fjeld* is a type of a mountain found in Scandinavia countries with a round top that is mostly bare.

Norway. The Kola Peninsula Saami, numbering just under 2,000 people, are the original inhabitants of the area. They make their living by fishing and reindeering.

The Saami are the main users of these vast watercourses in Lapland (the northern areas of Finland and Sweden), which has more than 188,000 lakes, and in Finnmark (the northern area of Norway). Fishing and farming are the most important means of livelihood for the Saami.[5] The land area is covered by forests,70% of which is populated by large numbers of animals. The Saami have a special and spiritual relationship with the natural environment in which they live. In particular reindeer play a fundamental role in the culture of the Saami. Their relationship with the environment has resulted in the promulgation of domestic legislation with respect to their rights to land, hunting, and fishing in this region, as will be seen below in Sections 3 and 4 of this chapter.

The Saami are politically conscious. They have numerous organisations at both national and international level. At the national level, there are for example the Confederation of Norwegian Reindeer Herders; the Saami Confederation; the Swedish Saami National Union and the Confederation of Swedish Saami. At the international level, the Saami of Finland, Sweden, and Norway are members of the World Council of Indigenous People. Another international organisation is the Saami Council which has been established to promote the rights of the Saami, made up of the Saami of Finland, Norway, Sweden, and Russia. In 1973, the Nordic Saami Institute was founded in Norway. This Institute promotes Saami culture, traditions, language, and rights.[6]

In the Nuuk Declaration of 16 September 1993,[7] the ministers of the Arctic countries recognised the special role that indigenous people, such

---

[5] See <http://odin.dep.no/odin/engelsk/norway/history/032005-99043/index-do000-b-n-a.html>.

[6] H. Beach *supra* note 1, at p. 187. Regarding Russia, Saami culture was endangered during the communist regime in the Soviet Union. Private ownership of reindeer was abolished and the Saami were forced to administer their herds collectively. After the collapse of the communist regime, the Saami organised themselves into the Kola Saami Association with its seat in Murmansk. The ownership of herds has yet to be determined and grazing rights clarified. Nonetheless, the Saami of Russia participate in the Saami Council and are involved in the furthering of their cultural and political causes.

[7] See <http://arcticcircle.uconn.edu/NatResources/Policy/nuuk.html>.

as the Saami, play in the protection of the Arctic environment. Similar references were included in the Declaration on the Establishment of the Arctic Council where participating countries acknowledge the importance of traditional practices and pledged their support for the sustainable development of indigenous people in the region.[8] Mention must also be made of the Inari Declaration adopted on the occasion of the Third Ministerial Meeting of the Arctic Council.[9] This Declaration stressed the importance of the development of an action plan for sustainable development. It also mentioned the importance of the role of women in developing viable Arctic communities and the encouragement of the integration

[8] See the website of the Arctic Council: <http://www.arctic-council.org/index.html>. The Arctic Council was established on 19 September 1996 in Ottawa, Canada. See Declaration on the Establishment of the Arctic Council, available at: <http://www.arctic-council.org/establ.asp>. The Representatives of the Arctic states, i.e. the governments of Canada, Denmark, Finland, Iceland, Norway, the Russian Federation, Sweden, and the United States of America, established the Arctic Council in order to "further provide means for promoting cooperative activities to address Arctic issues requiring circumpolar cooperation, and to ensure full consultation with the involvement of indigenous people and their communities and other inhabitants of the Arctic in such activities". Furthermore, "the Arctic Council is established as a high level forum to: a) provide a means for promoting cooperation, coordination and interaction among the Arctic States, with the involvement of the Arctic indigenous communities and other Arctic inhabitants on common arctic issues, in particular issues of sustainable development and environmental protection in the Antarctic; b) oversee and coordinate the programme established under the AEPS on the Arctic Monitoring and Assessment Programme (AMAP); Conservation of Arctic Flora and Fauna (CAFF); Protection of the Arctic Marine Environment (PAME); and Emergency, Preparedness and Response (EPPR); c) adopt terms of reference for and oversee and coordinate a sustainable development program; disseminate information, encourage education and promote interest in Arctic related issues. 2. Members of the Arctic Council are: Canada, Denmark, Finland, Iceland, Norway, the Russian Federation, Sweden and the United States of America, (the Arctic States); The Innuit Circumpolar Conference, the Saami Council and the Association of Indigenous Minorities in the far North, Siberia, the East of the Russian Federation are the Permanent Participants in the Arctic Council. Permanent participation is equally open to other Arctic organisations of indigenous peoples with majority Arctic indigenous constituency, representing a. single indigenous people resident in more than one Arctic State; or b. more than one Arctic indigenous people resident in a single Arctic State. The determination that such an organization has this criterion is to be made by decision of the Council. The number of Permanent Participants should at any time be less than the number of members".

[9] See Inari Declaration, Arctic Council 3rd Meeting, Inari, 9-10 October (2002), at <http://www.arctic council.org/files/inari2000/inari-declaration.pdf>.

of gender equality and women and youth perspectives in all efforts to enhance human living conditions in the Antarctic. The Declaration also emphasised the value of the continued co-operation in health issues, including among others the relationship between pollution and health, the sharing of information on promoting healthier lifestyles, and the role of education and training in improving the health and well being of children and young people.

In addition, the Declaration dealt specifically with problems of pollution, with a view to taking action to reduce pollution affecting the Arctic and the adoption of appropriate steps to ensure that Arctic concerns were adequately addressed at the regional and global levels. The Declaration adopted the position that the overall protection of the Arctic against pollution required a more integrated and co-ordinated approach in order to address the challenges of the Arctic coastal and marine environment and in order to develop a strategic plan for the protection of the Arctic marine environment. The Declaration also stressed the importance of the conservation of biodiversity and of the sustainable use of natural resources. To this end close co-operation with non-arctic States was also deemed necessary. Monitoring was deemed an essential part of responsible management of fauna and flora of the Arctic.

The European Union has adopted two Northern Dimension Action Plans.[10] The first Action plan was the product of an initiative of the Helsinki European Council in December 1999 that invited the Commission to prepare, in co-operation with the Council and in consultation with the partner countries, an Action Plan for the Northern Dimension. The Feira European Council in June 2000 adopted the Action Plan in the external and cross-border policies of the European Union. The First Northern Dimension Action Plan sets out perspectives and objectives for actions during 2000-2003 on a number of issues, including the preservation of the traditional ways of life of the indigenous populations of the Arctic in the Nordic countries and North Western Russia.[11] The second Northern

---

[10] First Northern Dimension Action Plan 2000-2003: <http://europa.eu.int/comm/external_relations/north_dim/ndap/06_00_en.pdf>; Second Northern Dimension Action Plan 2004-2006: <http://europa.eu.int/comm/external_relations/north_dim/ndap/ap2.pdf>

[11] First Northern Dimension Action Plan 2000-2003, *supra* note 10, paragraph 73: "...All actions supported by the Community should promote equal opportunities and the

Dimension Action Plan sets out a framework of priorities, objectives and actions to be pursued in the implementation of the Northern Dimension in the external and cross-border policies of the European Union over the period 2004-2006. The document focuses on five priority sectors: economy and infrastructure, social issues (including education, training and public health), environment, nuclear safety and natural resources, justice and home affairs and cross-border co-operation. Within each of these sectors, it sets out strategic priorities and specific objectives, and indicates the priority actions to be pursued in achieving these objectives. The Action Plan also stresses the necessity to pay special attention to areas of the Northern Dimension region with particular development needs, such as the Arctic and sub-Arctic areas and the Kaliningrad region. The need to take into consideration the rights of indigenous peoples as well as the need to involve them in all pertinent decision-making is underlined throughout the Plan.[12] Particular emphasis is placed on the principle of subsidiarity, ensuring the full involvement of all stakeholders in the implementation of the Action Plan, and including partner countries, regional bodies, local and regional authorities and civil society generally.

In Finland, Norway, and Sweden, Saami Parliaments have been established in order to promote and support Saami cultural and political rights and development. The Finnish Saami Parliament is composed of 20

special needs of indigenous peoples in the Arctic regions"; paragraph 80: "...Research should further concentrate on the preservation of bio-diversity, the effects of climate change and the socio-economic and cultural interests of indigenous peoples...". Others areas of concern include addressing the environmental problems in the region, e.g., the treatment of waste water in St. Petersburg, Kaliningrad and the Baltic States, as well as atmospheric pollution and other problems, which are a threat to the surrounding arctic environment; improving the level of nuclear safety and nuclear waste management in the area where thousands of spent nuclear fuel elements have been stored and dumped into the sea (e.g., in the Kola Peninsula area), and where there are several nuclear power plants in operation; facilitating co-operation in the energy sector and developing efficient transport and border-crossing infrastructure.

[12] Second Northern Dimension Action Plan 2004-2006, *supra* note 10. The text is replete with references to indigenous people, see, e.g., section 3.6.2 "The Arctic: ...Encouraging the economic development of the Arctic region is of crucial importance; such development however must take place in full respect of the fragile environmental situation of the region, and must involve local populations and indigenous people in the decision-making process at all levels".

representatives, who have been elected by the Saami, but have been approved by the Government. Elections are held every fourth year. The Norwegian Saami Parliament (*Sameting*) consists of 39 representatives elected for four years. The same is the case with the Swedish Saami Parliament. In fact, Saami Parliaments in general are departments of governments "subject to governmental directives and beside some administrative duties, in possession of only advisory status".[13] Knowledge of the Saami language is the main criterion for eligibility for electoral lists. Representatives of Saami Parliaments attend the Nordic Council meetings as observers.

Great influence on the future of indigenous people in general and on their relationship with the environment in particular will be exerted by the Declaration on the Rights of Indigenous People which is in the process of being finalised by the UN Working Group on Indigenous Population.[14] For example, draft Article 25 states that "[i]ndigenous peoples have the right to maintain and strengthen their distinctive spiritual and material relationship with the lands, territories, waters and coastal seas and other resources which they have traditionally owned or otherwise occupied or used, and to uphold their responsibilities to future generations". The "intricate and salutary" relationship between indigenous people and the earth, which is basic to their existence and culture, has often been noted.[15] This phenomenon was recognised by the Sub-committee on the Prevention of Discrimination and Protection of Minorities, which concluded that "[a]ll indigenous communities have, and uphold, a complete code of rules of various kinds which are applicable to the tenure and conservation of lands as an important factor in the production process, the foundation of family life and the territorial basis for the existence of their people as such. The whole range of emotional, cultural, spiritual and religious considerations is present where the relationship with the land is concerned [...] the land forms part of their existence".[16]

---

[13] See H. Beach, *supra* note 1, p. 200.

[14] UN Doc. E/CN.4/Sub.2/1994/2/Add.1 (1994).

[15] See W.A. Shutkin, "International Human Rights Law and the Earth: The Protection of Indigenous People and The Environment", 31 *VJIL* (1991), p. 484.

[16] W. Shutkin, *ibid*, p. 484; See also the UN Subcommittee on Prevention of Discrimination and Protection of Minorities, Study of the Problems of Discrimination against Indigenous Populations, UN Doc. E/CN.4/sub.2/1986/7 and Adds.1-4 (1986), p. 28.

2. The Protection of Indigenous Peoples under International Law

Identifying the Saami under international law is more difficult than identifying them in terms of the national laws of the Nordic States. This problem of definition arises from the lack of clarity concerning the position of "indigenous groups" and "minorities" in international law, and from the lack of clarity concerning the definition of the term "peoples".

The history of indigenous people has been very troubled. They have been the victims of genocide and colonization. Their treatment reflected a patronising attitude in relation to their cultures and style of life that often resulted in attempts to eradicate or modernise them.[17] The recognition in international law of the particular interests of indigenous people in relation to natural resources and the environment did not begin until the second half of the twentieth century.[18] Some attempts were made during the period of the League of Nations to regulate the position of indigenous people within the framework of the protection of minorities under colonial rule. Nonetheless, the colonial powers were reluctant to accord any substantial rights to indigenous people. It was only in 1973, when a "Decade of Action to Combat Racism and Racial Discrimination" was declared, that indigenous people were identified as a separate group by the United Nations.[19]

The rights of indigenous people originate in title dating back to a time before the process of colonization, such as the Lapp Codicil of 1751,[20] or

[17] See P. Thornberry, *International Law and the Rights of Minorities* (1991), p. 133. On the history of indigenous people, see G.C. Marks, "Indigenous People in International Law: The Significance of Francisco Vittoria and Banolome di Casa", 13 *AYIL* (1992), pp. 1-51; J.S. Davidson, "The Rights of Indigenous People in Early International Law", 5 *CLR* (1994), pp. 39-423. On indigenous people in general, see R. Moody, *The Indigenous Voice, Visions and Realities* (1988), and F. Wilmer, *The Indigenous Voice in World Politics*, (1993).

[18] It must be stressed that NGOs have played and continue to play an important role in enhancing the position of indigenous people in relation to the environment. In particular, the IUCN is very active and has established the Inter-Commission Task Force on Indigenous People, which prepared a guidebook entitled *Indigenous Peoples and Sustainability: Cases and Actions* (1997).

[19] See J. Sutherland (with the assistance of D. Craig and D. Posey), "Emerging New Legal Standards for Comprehensive Rights", 27 *EPL* (1997), p. 15.

[20] See <http://www.cwis.org/fwdp/Eurasia/sami88.txt>.

on treaties between an indigenous group and its colonizer. Traditionally, these instruments were treated as the only source of rights for indigenous people. At present however, they are only considered to be detailed documentation of the rights of indigenous people before their colonization. From the point of view of the right of self-determination, territorial rights and separate cultural identity are more important than historical title. However, historical or pre-existing rights cannot be extensively restored due to the existence of new populations and the formation of new states. Historical title does not solve the dilemma concerning how to avoid discrimination between indigenous people and the non-indigenous population.[21]

The term "indigenous groups" relates to a number of different types of groups of people, including nomadic tribes, who have inhabited ancient lands from time immemorial and may constitute a minority or a majority in the state in which they live.[22] It is undisputed that the Saami are such an indigenous group. According to Brölmann and Zieck, four criteria to define indigenous groups may be distinguished: (a) pre-existence or historical continuity; (b) distinct cultural forms; (c) non-dominance; and (d) self-identification. These criteria are applicable to the Saami. This definition does not include, however, other criteria germane to a proper understanding of the true identity of an indigenous group, such as language, occupation of ancestral lands, and – probably the most crucial element of all – their relationship with the land that constitutes the heart of indigenous claims.[23] The relationship with land seems to distinguish

---

[21] See D. Sanders, "Self-Determination and Indigenous Peoples", in C. Tomuschat (ed.), *Modern Law of Self-Determination* (M. Nijhoff Publishers; Boston, 1993), p. 55, at pp. 71-72.

[22] See C. Brölmann and M. Zieck, "Indigenous Peoples", in C. Brölmann, R. Lefeber and M. Zieck (eds.), *Peoples and Minorities in International Law* (1993), p. 187; see also C.J. Iorns, "Indigenous Peoples and Self Determination: Challenging State Sovereignty", 24 *CWRJIL* (1992), p. 200.

[23] See C. Brölmann and M. Zieck, *supra* note 22, pp. 191-197; See also M. Cobo, *Study of the Problem of Discrimination Against Indigenous Populations,* UN Doc. E/CN 4/Sub 2/1986/7 and Add. 1 to 4 (1986); Also see: UN Doc. E/CN.4/Sub.2476 and Add. 1-6; UN Doc. E/CN.4/Sub.2/1982/2 and Add. 1-7; UN Doc. E/CN.4/Sub.2/1983/21 and Add. 1-8, paragraphs 196 and 215

indigenous groups from other groups, such as minorities.[24] It has been said that historical continuity may arise from the occupation of ancestral lands, from common ancestry with the original occupants of the land, or from a distinctive culture, language, or residence in certain regions of the country. For example, the historic rights of the Saami were recognised in the Lapp Codicil,[25] appended to the border treaty of 1751 at the time when Norway and Sweden extended their borders northwards.

The attribution of rights to groups or members of such groups under international law corresponds to the legal qualification of a group of human beings as "minorities" or as "peoples". It is generally accepted that only peoples possess the right of self-determination, and that minorities do not.[26] Hence, a narrow interpretation of the term "peoples", i.e. one that excludes minorities, restricts the scope of the right of self-determination.[27] Thus, if indigenous groups belong both to the category of "minorities" and at the same time to the category of "peoples", a paradoxical (but not contradictory) situation would arise in which they would both have and, at the same time, not have the right of self-determination. For that reason, indigenous groups have rejected the distinction between "minorities" and "peoples", and opted instead for the concepts of self-identification and their historical relationship with the territory as constituting factors that entitle them to self-determination. Moreover, indigenous groups have become minorities due to the process of colonisation or state expansion and to treat them as mere minorities is to deny their colonial origins.[28]

---

[24] See R. Kapashesit and M. Klippenstein, "Indigenous Group Rights and Environmental Protection", 36 *MLJ* (1991), pp. 934-936. Their relationship with land constitutes a distinguishing feature of indigenous groups. Indigenous environmental ethics do not distinguish between nature and humans. Humans and animals have the qualities of persons, as signified by the Cree word *primatisiiwin*. Humans and nature are not competing, but complementing elements in relation to the earth. Indigenous groups integrate secular and spiritual life. Life is connected with the earth, and the earth is sacred.

[25] See <http://www.cwis.org/fwdp/Eurasia/sami88.txt>.

[26] See R. Müllerson, *International Law, Rights and Politics* (1994), p. 73, for the view that "it would be more accurate to say that they can exercise the right to self-determination together with the rest of the population of a given state, as a part of this population".

[27] See S.J. Anaya, Indigenous Peoples in International Law (1996), p. 77.

[28] See E. Spiry, "From 'Self-Determination' to a Right to 'Self-Development' for Indigenous Groups", 38 *GYIL* (1995), p. 139.

In general terms, the category of "minorities" comprises ethnic, religious, and linguistic groups which differ from the rest of the population of a state. There are other pertinent characteristics which single out a minority. Minorities are numerically inferior to the rest of the population and "show if not implicitly, a sense of solidarity, directed towards preserving their culture, traditions, religion or language".[29] It would therefore seem that the Saami constitute a minority in each of the Nordic States. It has been said that "[n]early all indigenous peoples form minorities and are entitled to minority protection".[30] However, this does not necessarily exclude the fact that indigenous groups also belong to the category of "peoples".[31]

"Peoples" represent communities which consist of social structures rather than autonomous individuals.[32] To determine whether a group of human beings constitutes a people, a distinction is made between objective and subjective criteria. Objective criteria include distinctive anthropological characteristics, such as language, culture, and religion. It is not clear which of these characteristics are sufficient or necessary for a group of human beings to constitute a people. In view of the anthropological heterogeneity of peoples, the identification of objective criteria would itself seem to be context-dependent.[33] Subjective criteria involve some degree of cohesion and a sense of difference experienced by the group of human beings concerned. It would seem therefore that indigenous groups fall within both the categories of "peoples" and "minorities", because some distinctive characteristics, such as separate cultural forms and non-dominance, are the same for minorities and peoples.[34]

However, having regard to the legal implications, there is considerable reluctance to recognise indigenous groups as "peoples" in international instruments. This issue surfaced, for example, at the United Nations

---

[29] F. Capotorti, "Study on the Rights of Persons belonging to Ethnic, Religious and Linguistic Minorities", Report to the UN Sub-Commission on the Prevention of Discrimination and Protection of Minorities, UN Doc. E/CN.4/Sub.2/384/Rev. 1, (1979), p. 96.

[30] See L. Hannikainen, *supra* note 1, p. 3.

[31] Cited from C. Brölmann and M. Zieck, *supra* note 22, p. 194.

[32] See S. J. Anaya, *supra* note 27, p. 77.

[33] See also J. Crawford, "The Rights of Peoples: Some Conclusions", in J. Crawford (ed.), *The Rights of Peoples* (1988), pp. 160-175, at 168-169.

[34] See C. Brölmann and M. Zieck, *supra* note 22, p. 191.

World Conference on Human Rights in Vienna in 1993. The 1993 Vienna Declaration and Programme of Action uses the term "indigenous people" which has a different connotation and, hence, different legal implications than the term "indigenous peoples" (Article 20).[35] The ILO Convention Concerning Indigenous and Tribal Peoples in Independent Countries (Convention 169)[36] provides further illustration of this issue. Article 1(3) of this Convention provides that "[t]he use of the term 'peoples' in this convention shall not be construed as having implications as regards the rights which may be attached to the term under international law". The following comment was made in the records of the proceedings of the Committee: "[i]t is understood by the Committee that use of term 'peoples' has no implication as regards the right of self-determination as understood in international law".[37]

A fundamental question in relation to the protection of groups is what type of rights are accorded to a particular group and its members: individual rights, group rights, or collective rights. In some cases, the differences between the types of rights are blurred; for example, the right to equality is an individual right and a group right at the same time. Sanders argues that every group right constitutes an individual right, but that not all individual rights are group rights.[38] According to Sanders there is a theoretical distinction between group and collective rights. Group rights are individual rights aimed at benefiting the individual members of a particular group, while collective rights are intended to be for the benefit of the group as a whole. In short, collective rights are distinct from group rights in so far as they override the individual right and serve the goals and preservation of collectivity – their aim is collective. Nonetheless, the lack of clarity as to the distinctions between rights is a stumbling block in any attempt to formulate firm divisions. For example, group rights and

---

35 See <http://www.unhchr.ch/huridocda/huridoca.nsf/(Symbol)/A.CONF.157.23.En?OpenDocument>.

36 See 1989 Convention (No. 169) Concerning Indigenous and Tribal Peoples in Independent Countries, at <www.unhchr.ch/html/menu3/b/62htm> adopted on 29 July 1989 and entered into force on 5 September 1991.

37 See International Labour Organization, "Report of the Committee on Convention 107", International Labour Conference, Provisional Record 25, Seventy-sixth Session at p. 25, paragraph 31.

38 See D. Sanders, "Collective Rights", 13 *HRQ* (1991), p. 369.

collective rights in fact both have a collective dimension, i.e. they both exist for the benefit of a certain organised group or a collective entity, such as minorities, groups or states.[39]

In this context, there is the general issue of a human right to water. Water management was the subject of Chapter 18 of the Agenda 21,[40] which sets out a wide-ranging set of principles relevant to water management.[41] Is there a human right to water? And if so what are the features of such a right?[42] McCaffrey assesses this problem from two aspects: the right to water as a human right; and the right of one state to receive water from a co-riparian state. As to the former, it may be said that the right to food should be interpreted as the right to receive life-sustaining nourishment, including the right to potable drinking water, sufficient to sustain life; "[a] state's due diligence obligation to safeguard these rights to sustenance should therefore be interpreted to require the state to accord priority to ensuring that such vital human needs are met". Regarding the latter, he writes that "[o]n the international level, it seems equally clear that one state cannot deny a co-riparian state water necessary for the survival of the latter's population on the ground that the water is needed for the economic development of the former. The conditions on which equitable allocation would be affected would vary from case to case, but

[39] See J. Crawford, "The Rights of 'Peoples' or Governments?" in J. Crawford (ed.), *supra* note 33, p. 58.

[40] See Agenda 21, "Report of the United Nations Conference on Environment and Development", UN Doc. A/Conf.51/26, Annex II (1992). It was stated that "[w]ater is needed in all aspects of life. The general objective is to make certain that adequate supplies of water of good quality are maintained for the entire population of this planet, while preserving the hydrological, biological and chemical functions of ecosystems, adapting human activities within the capacity limits of nature and combating vectors of water-related diseases [...]. The multisectoral nature of water resources development in the context of socio-economic development must be recognised, as the multiinterest utilization of water resources for water supply and sanitation, agriculture, industry, urban development, hydropower generation, inland fisheries, transportation, recreation, low and flat lands management and other activities".

[41] See H.I.F. Saeijs and M.J. van Berkel, "The Global Water Crisis: The Major Issue of the Twenty-First Century, A Growing and Explosive Problem", in E.H.P. Brans, E.J. de Haan, J. Rinzema and A. Nollkaemper (eds.), *The Scarcity of Water. Emerging Legal and Policy Responses* (1997), p. 15.

[42] See S. McCaffrey, "A Human Right to Water: Domestic and International Implications", 5 *GIELR* (1992), pp. 1-20.

certainly human lives or even health should take precedence over economic development".[43] This should apply equally to people and to "peoples".

The question of a human right to water was addressed by ECOSOC in General Comment No. 15, in relation to Articles 11 and 12 of the UN Covenant on Economic Social and Cultural Rights where it was stated with clarity that: "The human right to water is indispensable for leading a human life of dignity. It is a prerequisite for the realization of other human rights", and a number of factors, crucial in the enjoyment of that right, were identified, namely availability, quality, physical and economic accessibility and non discrimination.[44] The same position was adopted at the Fourth meeting of the Working Group on water management established under the auspices of the 1992 UNECE Helsinki Convention. The Working Group in a working paper entitled "Integrated Water Resources Management (IWRM) Including Transboundary River Basin Issues" stated in its opening phrase: "Access to safe water is a fundamental need and a human right, vital for dignity and health of all people".[45]

Other multilateral instruments specifically address the rights of indigenous people, including the 1957 ILO Convention Concerning the Protection and Integration of Indigenous and Other Tribal Populations or Semi-Tribal Populations in Independent Countries (Convention 107),[46] and its substitute, i.e. the 1989 ILO Convention Concerning Indigenous and Tribal Peoples in Independent Countries (Convention 169),[47] and the draft Declaration on the Rights of Indigenous Peoples.[48] Norway is the only Nordic State that has signed and ratified Convention 169. It did not however become a party to Convention 107.

---

[43] *Ibid,* p. 10.

[44] General Comment No. 15, "The right to water (Articles 11 and 12 of the International Covenant on Economic, Social and Cultural Rights", UN Doc. E/C.12/2002/11 (Twenty-ninth session, 2002) at <http://www1.umn.edu/humanrts/gencomm/escgencom15.htm>.

[45] See <http://www.unece.org/env/water/meetings/wgwm/4meeting/wp3e.pdf>.

[46] See 328 *UNTS* 247.

[47] See 28 *ILM* 1382. Adopted on 27 June 1989, entered into force on 5 September 1991. *Supra* note 36.

[48] *Supra* note 14, adopted by the Sub-Commission on Prevention of Discrimination and Protection of Minorities (at present Sub-Commission on the Protection and Promotion of Human Rights).

Convention 107 bestows on governments primary responsibility for developing co-ordinated and systematic action for the protection of the populations concerned and their progressive integration into the life of their respective countries. Some bilateral treaties between Nordic states had the same paternalistic attitude towards the Saami. For example, according to one such treaty,

> "[t]he Contracting States have agreed to the following arrangement concerning the Lapps [...] dwelling in the Valley of the Pasvik (Patsjoki), who formerly engaged in salmon fishing in the Norwegian Fjords of Bökfjord and Jarfjord. The Norwegian Government, being desirous of compensating the Lapps for the loss of aforesaid fisheries, though not admitting any obligation to do so or recognizing that the Lapps have any fishing rights in those waters, undertakes to hand over, for their benefit, the sum of 12,000 gold Norwegian crowns (Kr. 12.000). This sum shall be paid to the Government of Finland in exchange for a formal declaration on the part of the above mentioned Lapps renouncing on behalf of themselves and their successors, all claims to the said fisheries or any further compensation in this respect. The Government of Finland, being concerned for the welfare of the Lapps in question, undertakes, for its part, to advise them to accept arrangement referred to above, and should they fail to do so, the Government of Finland undertakes [...] not to support any claim which Lapps may subsequently advance in regard to this matter".[49]

ILO Convention 169 is different. Broadly speaking, this convention abandoned the patronising and paternalistic[50] attitude towards indigenous people that characterised Convention 107. One of the most important changes in Convention 169 is the substitution of the term "indigenous population" by "indigenous peoples". It has already been explained that this new formulation is only a formal one and does not constitute any ground for according the right of self-determination to indigenous people. In general terms, Convention 169 recognises "the aspirations of indig-

---

[49] Article II of the Final Protocol to the 1924 Convention between the Republic of Finland and the Kingdom of Norway Concerning the Frontier between the Province of Finnmark and the Territory of Petsamo, signed on 28 April 1924, entered into force on 26 September 1924, XXX *LNTS* 49.

[50] See C. Brölmann and M. Zieck, *supra* note 22, p. 203; see also E. Spiry, *supra* note 28, p. 130.

enous peoples to exercise control over their institutions, ways of life and economic development and to maintain and develop their identities, language and religions, within the framework of the States in which they live".[51] The Convention constitutes a significant development towards the recognition of indigenous people as a distinctive group with distinctive rights.[52] Notably, the Convention confers on indigenous peoples the participatory right to share in decision-making with the government of the state in which they live on matters of their concern (Article 7(1)).

Among the most important rights accorded to indigenous peoples by Convention 169 are rights related to land. The Convention requires parties to "respect the special importance for the cultures and spiritual values of peoples concerned of their relationship with the lands or territories [...] and in particular the collective aspects of this relationship" (Article 13(1)). The general right to land comprises the right to ownership and possession as well as management rights.[53] The term "land" includes the concept of territories which covers the "total environment of the areas which the peoples concerned occupy or otherwise use" (Article 13(2)). According to the Convention, "the rights of ownership and possession over the lands which they traditionally occupy shall be recognised. In addition, measures shall be taken in appropriate cases to safeguard the right of the peoples concerned to use lands not exclusively occupied by them, but to which they traditionally had access for their subsistence and traditional activities" (Article 14(1)). The Convention upholds the right of indigenous peoples to natural resources and the right to participate in the use, management, and conservation of such resources (Article 15). These "territorial" rights to land and natural resources are of a collective character.[54] The above-mentioned right is quite broad, because it provides for the right of consultation in cases in which the state retains the ownership of mineral or sub-surface resources (Article 15(2)).

Convention 169 also accords other rights to indigenous peoples, such as the right to cultural integrity. Article 5 provides that "[t]he social, cul-

[51] See Convention No. 169, *supra* note 36, fifth paragraph of the Preamble.

[52] See G.T. Morris, "In Support of the Right of Self-Determination for Indigenous People under International Law", 29 *GYIL* (1986), p. 311.

[53] See S. J. Anaya, *supra* note 27, p. 106.

[54] *Ibid.*

tural, religious and spiritual values and practices of these peoples shall be recognised". The Convention also introduces the right of indigenous peoples to non-discrimination in social welfare and education. Accordingly, "[s]ocial security schemes shall be extended progressively to cover the peoples concerned, and applied without discrimination against them";[55] and "[m]easures shall be taken to ensure that members of the peoples concerned have the opportunity to acquire education at all levels on at least an equal footing with the rest other nationals community".[56] However, Article 34 could weaken the rights conferred by the Convention as a whole, in providing that the measures taken by Parties shall be determined in a flexible manner, having regard to the conditions characteristic of each country.

There are also several soft-law instruments concerning indigenous peoples.[57] The most important is the Draft Declaration on the Rights of Indigenous Peoples of 1994. It took the UN Working Group on Indigenous Population (hereinafter the Working Group) nine years to finalise the text of the Draft Declaration. It was subsequently adopted by the UN Sub-Commission on Prevention of Discrimination and Protection of Minorities.[58] The Declaration covers all aspects of the position of indigenous

[55] See Part V, Social Security and Health, Article 25.

[56] See Part VI, Education, Article 26.

[57] See, e.g., the *Draft Declaration on Principles for the Defence of Indigenous Nations and Peoples of the Western Hemisphere*, developed and circulated by indigenous participants at the Non-Governmental Organization Conference on Discrimination Against Indigenous Population, Geneva (1977), reprinted in UN Doc. E/CN.4/Sub.2/476/Add.5, Annex 4 (1981); *Declaration on Principles of Indigenous Rights*, adopted by the Fourth General Assembly of the World Council of Indigenous Peoples, Panama (1984), reprinted in UN Doc. E/CN.4/1985/22, Annex 2 (1985); *Declaration on Principles on the Rights of Indigenous Peoples*, adopted by representatives of indigenous peoples and organizations meeting in Geneva (1985), in preparation for the fourth session of the United Nations Working Group on Indigenous Populations as reaffirmed and amended by representatives of indigenous peoples and organizations meeting in Geneva (1987), in preparation for the working group's fifth session, reprinted in UN Doc. E/CN.4/Sub.2/1987.22, Annex 5 (1987).

[58] See Resolution 1994/45 (26 August 1994) at <http://www.unhchr.ch/huridocda/huridoca.nsf/(Symbol)/E.CN.4.SUB.2.RES.1994.45.En?OpenDocument>. On the draft Declaration, see C. Brölmann and M. Zieck, "Some Remarks on the Draft Declaration on the Rights of Indigenous Peoples", 8 *LJIL* (1995), pp. 103-113. See also C. Brölmann and M. Zieck, *supra* note 22.

peoples, such as cultural, religious, and economic identity; land and natural resources; indigenous institutions; language; and education. It contains some fundamental provisions which regulate the general position of indigenous people. The cornerstone of the Draft Declaration is Article 42 which states that "[t]he rights recognised therein constitute the minimum standards for the survival, dignity and well-being of the indigenous peoples of the world". The Declaration identifies the rights of indigenous people as individual and collective rights. For example, it provides that "[i]ndigenous peoples have the collective right to live in freedom, peace and security as distinct peoples..." (Article 6), and that "indigenous peoples have the collective and individual right not be subjected to ethnocide and cultural genocide including the prevention and redress for (a) Any action which has the aim or effect of depriving them of their integrity as distinct peoples, or their cultural values or ethnic identities; (b) Any action which has the aim or effect of dispossessing them of their lands, territories or resources; (c) Any form of population transfer which has the aim of violating or undermining any of their rights; (d) Any form of assimilation or integration by other cultures or ways of life imposed on them be legislative, administrative or other measures; (e) Any form of propaganda directed against them" (Article 7).

3. International Legal Instruments and the Rights of the Saami with respect to the Environment

The Saami and other indigenous peoples are also the subject of international agreements which are not directly related to human rights. For example, the rights of indigenous peoples in relation to the environment have been recognised in the revised Operational Guidelines for the Implementation of the World Heritage Convention.[59] These Operational Guidelines also apply to cultural landscapes and contain specific techniques of sustainable land use, which are based on a spiritual relationship to nature.

[59] See UNESCO, Intergovernmental Committee for the Protection of the World Cultural and Natural Heritage, *Operational Guidelines for the Implementation of the World Heritage Convention*, WHC/2Revised, February 1995, p. 11.

The continued existence of traditional forms of land-use supports and enhances biological diversity in many regions of the world.[60]

The importance of the culture of indigenous people was also emphasised during the 1992 United Nations Conference on Environment and Development (UNCED).[61] The Rio Declaration adopted at UNCED states that "[i]ndigenous people and their communities, and other local communities, have a vital role in environmental management and development because of their knowledge and traditional practices. States should recognise and duly support their identity, culture and interests and enable their effective participation in the achievement of sustainable development" (Principle 22).

Special provision was made for the Saami when Finland and Sweden acceded to the European Union. Protocol 3 of the Act of Accession in the 1994 Treaty of Accession deals with the Saami.[62] The Protocol recognises the obligations and commitments which both these countries have with regard to the Saami under international and national law. Article 1 provides that notwithstanding the provisions of the EC Treaty, exclusive rights to reindeer husbandry within traditional Saami areas may be granted to the Saami people. Finland and Sweden are committed to preserving and developing the means of livelihood, language, culture, and way of life of the Saami. Article 2 provides that the Protocol may be ex-

---

[60] The rights of indigenous people, especially rights related to the environment and culture, are at present taken into consideration by the World Bank in its lending and development policy. The World Bank has developed guidelines on environmental impact assessment, cultural integrity, and indigenous self-development. See *Tribal Peoples in Bank-Funded Projects,* World Bank Operational Manual, statement 2.34 (1982); World Bank, *Indigenous Peoples*, World Bank Operational Directive 4.20 (1991), <http://wbln0018.worldbank.org/Institutional/Manuals/OpManual.nsf/toc2/0F7D6F3F04DD70398525672C007D08ED?OpenDocument>; <http://lnweb18.worldbank.org/ESSD/sdvext.nsf/63ByDocName/IndigenousPeoples>; See <http://lnweb18.worldbank.org/ESSD/sdvext.nsf63ByDocName/Policies>. See also R.L. Barsh, "Indigenous Peoples in the 1990s: From Object to Subject of International Law", 7 *HHRJ* (1994), pp. 33-86 at 68.

[61] United Nations Conference on Environment and Development (Rio), Declaration, UN Doc. A/CONF.151/26/Rev.1, Report of the UNCED, Vol. 1.

[62] *OJ* C 241, 29 August; <http://europa.eu.int/eur-lex/en/treaties/dat/AU_FI_SV_accession.html#0352020030>

tended to take into account any further development linked to their traditional means of livelihood.[63]

The Convention on Biological Diversity, which was signed at Rio in 1992, also acknowledges the special position of indigenous people. According to the preamble, "[t]he Contracting Parties [...] recognising the close and traditional dependence of many indigenous and local communities embodying traditional lifestyles on biological resources, and the desirability of sharing equitably benefits arising from the use of traditional knowledge, innovations and practices relevant to the conservation of biological diversity and the sustainable use of its components [...] have agreed as follows". Article 8 (j) of this Convention also provides that

> "[e]ach Contracting Party shall, as a far as possible and as appropriate: ...[s]ubject to its national legislation, respect, preserve and maintain knowledge, innovations and practices of indigenous and local communities embodying traditional lifestyles relevant for the conservation and sustainable use of biological diversity and promote their wider application with the approval and involvement of the holders of such knowledge, innovations and practices and encourage the equitable sharing of the benefits arising from the utilisation of such knowledge, innovations and practices".

The principal means of livelihood of the Saami people, i.e. reindeer herding, hunting and fishing, are based on large extent on traditional knowledge and practices. The Swedish Parliament has initiated co-operation among the Nordic Saami communities in order to analyse the

---

[63] See also paragraph 13 of the European Union's Water Framework Directive (Directive 2000/60/EC, *OJ* L 327, 2000, p. 1-73); "There are diverse conditions and needs in the Community which require different specific solutions. This diversity should be taken into account in the planning and execution of measures to ensure protection and sustainable use of water in the framework of the river basin. Decisions should be taken as close as possible to the locations where water is affected or used. Priority should be given to action within the responsibility of Member States through the drawing up of programmes of measures adjusted to regional and local conditions". Article 14 provides that "the success of this Directive relies on close cooperation and coherent action at Community, Member State and local level as well as on information, consultation and involvement of the public, including users". See further also paragraphs 18 and 46 on subsidiarity. The substance of the provisions on public information and participation are set out in Article 14. The directive does not, however, make further reference to indigenous peoples in general or to the Saami in particular.

implications of the Biodiversity Convention provisions on respecting, preserving and promoting the wider application of traditional knowledge and practices and to consider how equitable sharing of the benefits arising from the utilisation of such knowledge can be achieved.[64] In Finland, this Article 8(j) is implemented through the careful use of biological resources in the Northern part of the country. This is relevant in particular to reindeer husbandry, fishing, hunting, gathering and other traditional Saami forms of land use, in relation to forestry, mining, trekking, tourism and the regulation of land sue in larger protected areas within the Saami region.[65] In Norway, the Saami Parliament adopted a resolution stating that the Norwegian implementation of Article (8)(j) must not conflict with traditional Saami interests. It considered that the problem might arise in connection to a management regime determined by the central authorities and including elements such as the establishment of national parks, wetlands and coniferous forest reserves in the Saami settlement area.[66]

The position of the Saami people regarding reindeer herding features prominently in the implementation of the 1992 Convention on Biological Diversity, as is evident from the first national reports from Finland,[67] Sweden[68] and Norway[69] on the implementation of the Convention. Reindeer husbandry is one area that has been the focus of attention in the context of the debate over Saami land rights. Reindeer husbandry may cause some habitat alteration in the specially protected areas under the IUCN

[64] See First National Report of Sweden, p. 35 at <http://www.biodiv.org/doc/world/se/se-nr-01-en.pdf>. See also Arctic Council Project on Co-Management of Marine Resources in Arctic Areas With Respect to Indigenous Peoples and Traditinal Ecological Knowledge at <http://www.arctic-council.org/sdwg_projects.asp>.

[65] See National Action Plan for Biodiversity in Finland for 1997-2005 at <http://www.biodiv.org./doc/world/fi/fi-nr-01-en.pdf>, paragraphs 6.3 and 6.10.

[66] See Norway's National Report on Implementation of the Convention on Biological Diversity <http://www.biodiv.org/doc/world/no/no-nr-01-en.pdf>, p. 53.

[67] See National Action Plan for Biodiversity in Finland, 1997-2005, <http://www.biodiv.org/doc/world/fi/fi-nr-01-en.pdf>.

[68] See Sweden's National Report under the Convention on Biological Diversity, <http://www.biodiv.org/doc/world/se/se-nr-01-en.pdf>.

[69] See Norway's National Report on Implementation of the Convention on Biological Diversity, <http://www.biodiv.org/doc/world.no/no-nr01-en.pdf>.

and world heritage sites under the 1972 World Heritage Convention[70] and may impact on parts of the landscape, through, for example, the building of cabins and fences. However, reindeer herding is a livelihood in some of these areas, such as in the Lapponian Area (Norrbotten county) in Sweden.[71] Reindeer husbandry can also constitute an environmental threat due to over-grazing, trampling by reindeer and the use of motor vehicles in wilderness areas. The Arctic Council has initiated a special project on "Sustainable Reindeer Husbandry", under its "Sustainable Development Working Group".[72] The main goal of this project is to assess circumpolar reindeer herding and husbandry in relation to economic/ social sustainability in the Arctic. The project will involve a thematic survey and assessment of reindeer husbandry in the region (Norway, Sweden, Finland, Russia, Alaska), with reference to social and economic conditions, national management and legal status in reindeer husbandry. The Report on Sustainable Reindeer Husbandry was presented at the Ministerial Meeting in Arctic Council in Inari, held on 10 October 2002. The workshop identified a number of challenges, including the following: the lack of infrastructure, which hampers economic development; in certain areas industrial development, disturbance by traffic and pollution have resulted in a loss of traditional pasture land; there is a need for legal protection of reindeer herding rights and pasture land; an increase in the number of predators and changes in wild reindeer migration have negative impacts on reindeer husbandry; and in some areas the number of animals needs to be adjusted to the carrying capacity of the pasture land. The project will help to improve existing databases and scientific knowledge in circumpolar husbandry, to identify problems and shortcomings in reindeer husbandry, with account taken of cultural variety and adaptation to the natural resources base.[73]

---

[70] Adopted on 16 November 1972, entered into force on 17 December 1975, 11 *ILM* 1358.

[71] See 1971 Reindeer Husbandry Act, <http://www.unep-wcemc.org/sites/wh/lappon.htm>.

[72] Report of the Council's Sustainable Development Working Group (2002) available from <http://www.arctic-council.org/files/inari2002sao/sdwg_report.pdf>

[73] See <http://www.reindeer-husbandry.uit.no>.

4. The Protection of the Rights of the Saami under the Laws of Finland, Norway and Sweden

In the past, legislation in Norway and Sweden did not take much account of the interests of the Saami. Indeed, the Saami in both Norway and Sweden (under the 1928 laws) were actually relocated to the Southern regions in order to break the special relationship with their lands. In the 1970s, the Nordic States began to assist the Saami to achieve better conditions economically and in terms of health, with a higher degree of autonomy. For example, the Saami in Sweden had their own Saami sheriff to carry out policing, and the *samebys* became exclusively responsible for reindeer policy. The difficulty which characterised this period was that the Nordic States were unable "to integrate their strict economic herding policies with their native minority policies".[74]

At present, there is a considerable amount of legislation protecting the Saami, which, coupled with the growing awareness of the Saami as a group, is believed to have contributed to their survival as a distinct ethnic and cultural group in Nordic countries. Much of the current national legislation in the Nordic States relating to the Saami relates to reindeer herding, with herding rights being reserved for the Saami in most cases. Saami herding rights were the subject-matter of the *Kitok* case before the United Nations Human Rights Committee. The Applicant in this case had lost his right to return to his *sameby* with full rights as a member, having been away for three years. He based his claim on Article 27 of the International Covenant of Civil and Political Rights. According to Swedish law, the above-mentioned right was accorded only to full-time reindeer herders. After the lapse of three or more years, return was only possible with special permission. Kitok had obtained such permission, but it acknowledged his rights only partially. The Human Rights Committee agreed with the reasoning of the Swedish Government and supported the limitation of full rights to those of the Saami who base their livelihood exclusively on reindeer herding.[75] Unlike the situation in Sweden, in Fin-

---

[74] See H. Beach, *supra* note 1, p. 179.

[75] See Communication No. 197/1985, Report of the Human Rights Committee, UN Doc. A/43/40, pp. 221-230.

land the non-Saami population can own and herd reindeer provided that they live in the reindeer-herding area.[76]

The importance of the enjoyment of culture by the Saami was confirmed by the Human Rights Committee in the *Ilmari Länsman* case.[77] The applicants, forty-eight Saami reindeer breeders, challenged a decision of the Central Forestry Board to permit quarrying. The committee observed that a State might wish to encourage development of economic activity, but without ignoring its obligations under Article 27 of the International Covenant on Civil and Political Rights (ICCPR). The Human Rights Committee expressly rejected the European doctrine of the margin of appreciation and held that measures that infringe the right to culture are not compatible with the Covenant, although measures that simply restricted the way of life of a person belonging to a minority may not necessarily violate the Covenant. The Committee also referred to its General Comment on Article 27, according to which measures must be taken to ensure the effective participation of members of minority communities in decisions that have an impact on them. The Committee came to the conclusion that the amount of quarrying that was carried out did not constitute a denial of the applicants' right to culture. The Human Rights Committee also determined that due attention had been paid to the need to minimise the effect of quarrying on reindeer herding and on the environment. The State party was under an obligation to bear this in mind when either extending existing contracts or granting the new ones.

The position regarding Saami rights to land, water and reindeer is generally much less favourable. The argument put forward by the Saami is based on the premise that hunting and fishing rights are due to Saami villages as a part and parcel of reindeer herding rights, which they do enjoy; but as the Norwegian Saami Rights Commission stated, "[t]he land title question will be the real test for minority rights in Norway".[78]

In Sweden, for example, the Reindeer Herding Ordinance of 1993[79] deprived the Saami of their exclusive fishing and hunting rights in their

[76] See H. Beach, *supra* note 1, pp. 179-180.

[77] See Communication No. 511/1992, Ilmari Lansman et al. v. Finland, Human Rights Committee, Final Decisions, 74, CCPR/C57/1 (1996).

[78] See L. Sillanpää, Political and Administrative Responses to Saami Self-Determination (1994), p. 162.

[79] See SFS 1993:383, paragraph 3.

lands. Prior to the enactment of this law, the Saami retained the exclusive right to dispose of these rights, by selling hunting and fishing licences to outsiders. The law was promulgated in "the name of equal rights",[80] and is in contrast with a decision of 1981, in the Taxed Mountain case,[81] in which the Swedish Supreme Court stated that Saami reindeer-herding rights constitute a special form of property right based upon immemorial ancestral use.[82] The precise character of this special property right is not clear. It has been said that "[t]he encroachment of the Swedish State on Saami hunting and fishing rights must be seen in this perspective. It forms part of a pattern which includes rivers and lakes being used for hydropower purposes with consequent flooding of Saami settlements and pasture; reindeer pasture in the forests being destroyed by extra large-scale forestry, roads and other communication links being built across pasture; and other aspects of what is otherwise held up to be a positive social trend, but which for Saami and the Saami culture has meant and still means encroachment on, and destruction of, their natural basis of life and work".[83] The scope of the new law extends to fisheries, which fall within the field of the powers of the Finnish-Swedish Commission.[84] It is questionable whether the decisions of the Swedish authorities are compatible with the management of water resources in the region under the jurisdiction of the Commission.[85]

---

[80] See L. Hannikainen, *supra* note 1, p. 34.

[81] See NJA 1981, p. 1

[82] One speaks of an immemorial right "when one has had some real estate or right in undisputed possession and drawn benefit and utilised it that no one remembers or can in truth know his forefathers or he from whom the rights were acquired first came to get them"; cited from H. Beach, *supra* note 1, p. 191. The citation is originally from the 15th chapter of the old Swedish Code of land Laws (Jordabalken) from 1734, at present retained in paragraph 6 of the new Jordabalken.

[83] See Bohlin, J., "Human Rights and Access to Natural Resources", 64 *NJIL* (1995), pp. 495-499

[84] See Chapter 5 below.

[85] There is also further evidence of the infringement of the right of the Saami to land and natural resources. Such violation has occurred, for example, in the case of the construction of a hydroelectric-power dam in Alta in northern Norway in the early 1980s. The Norwegian Water and Energy Administration (NVE) issued comprehensive plans in 1970 to develop Alta-Kautokeino water system on the Finnmark plate. These plans included a dam that would inundate the community at Masi. These plans were subsequently modified. However, a major hydroelectric project remained pending, including a 100-meter

In Norway, the legal position as regards Saami land rights is slightly different. This is due to the fact that Norway has ratified ILO Convention 169. One of the Convention's requirements is the recognition of "[t]he rights of ownership and possession of the peoples concerned over the lands which they traditionally occupy" (Article 14). Norway has interpreted the right of usage accorded to the Saami under the law of Norway as being in sufficient compliance with the requirements of the Convention, even if full ownership is not provided for. In Norway, the Saami enjoy strong usage rights over their territories, such as exclusive rights of reindeer herding, fishing, and hunting in the northernmost part of the country. The establishment of the Saami Parliament in Norway resulted in 1988 in an addendum to the Norwegian Constitution. This addendum stipulated that Norway was under an obligation to ensure proper conditions for the Saami in order to enable them to develop their culture, their language, and their social life.[86] In Finland, the Saami have also a right of usage, but not the full right of ownership over their land. They can hunt and fish freely in the lands occupied by them. The possibility of according the Saami full rights of ownership is under consideration by the Saami Parliament in Finland, in co-operation with the Ministry of Justice of Finland.[87]

---

high dam across the river canyon. It also involved the building of a road across the reindeer grazing land and calving areas. The reindeer owners were affected by this development and the Norwegian Society for the Conservation of Nature took the State to the Court to stop these developments in 1979. Demonstrations by the Saami and environmentalists took place at the building site and Saami activists started a hunger strike in front of the Storting. A group of Saami women staged a sit-in strike at the office of the Prime Minster. Nevertheless, the dam was completed but the issue of the Saami people received public attention and paved the way for a better political climate for the Saamis in the 1980s. See <http://www.odin.dep.no/odin/engelsk/norway/history/032005-990463/index-dok000-b-n-a.html>.

[86] See H. Minde, "A Century of Norwegian Research into Sámi Rights", in A. Victorin (ed.), 31 *Scandinavian Studies in Law* (1995), pp. 109-140. Further legislation (a "Finnmark Act") is currently under consideration in Norway, relating to legal relations and management of land and natural resources in the county of Finnmark. On this see State Secretary A.J.H. Eira, "Facts and Myths regarding the Finnmark Act", <http://odin.dep.no/krd/engelsk/aktuelt/taler/articles/016091-990091/index-dok000-b-f-a.html>; compare the views of the Saami Council, who point out, *inter alia*, that no rights of ownership are conferred as required by international law including Convention 169, and that the Act merely furthers the aim of the Norwegian Government of "Norwegianization" of the Saami, at : see, e.g. <http://www.saamicouncil.net/?deptid=2193>.

[87] See, e.g., S. Tuulentie, "For and Against the Rights of the Sami People: The Argumentation of the Finnish Majority in the Debate on the Sami Rights", in *Indigenous Peoples: Resource Management and Global Rights*, S. Jentoft, H. Minde and Ragnar Nilsen (eds). 2003, Chapter 14.

The interests of the Saami are taken into consideration in relevant international river commissions. The Finnish-Swedish Frontier River Commission ("FSFRC")[88] includes three representatives appointed by Finland and Sweden. One of the Finnish members is appointed on the recommendation of the Lapland County Administration, and one of the Swedish members on the basis of a recommendation of the Norrboten County Administration. Their task is to ensure that the interests of the Saami people are taken into consideration and that their rights are not harmed or impaired.[89] The presence of representatives of the Saami people on the Commission aims to ensure that management of the resources is not detrimental to the interests of Saami people. For its part, the Finnish-Norwegian Commission[90] consists of six members, with each of the parties to the Agreement appointing three members, as is the case with the Finnish-Swedish Commission. The members of the Finnish-Norwegian Commission are appointed on the basis of proposals made, on the part of Norway, by the Regional Commissioner of Finnmark and, on the part of Finland, by the Lansstyrelsen, i.e. the local government in Finnish Lapland. One of the members appointed by each state must have knowledge of watercourses issues and another must be familiar with the conditions in the areas, so as to represent Saami interests.

The interests of the Saami people have also been secured in other bilateral agreements between Finland and Norway, such as the 1977 agreement on fishing in the area of the river Neiden.[91] The purpose of this Agreement is to encourage fishing (especially salmon) in this area. In

---

[88] Signed on 24 April 1964 and entered into force on 6 May 1965, 537 *UNTS* 231; discussed in depth in Section 4 of Chapter 5.

[89] The possibility of increased Saami representation in the work of the FSFRC appeared has been discussed in parliament, with a negative outcome-the proposed expansion was considered too expensive and unnecessary. It was assumed that all the members of the Commission were sufficiently versed in the problems of the region. See the response to the Parliamentary question asked by the Minister of Agriculture on 18 June 1987, Esko-Juhani Tennila, 1987, KK No. 86 (Finnish Parliamentary Reports).

[90] 1980 Agreement concerning a Norwegian-Finnish Commission for Transboundary Watercourses signed on 5 March 1980, entered into force 1 May 1981, *Suomen säädöskokoelman* 1981, No. 32. (Translation of text on file with authors).

[91] Agreement between Finland and Norway concerning Fishing in the Fishing Area of the Naatamo (Neiden) River, signed 14 December 1977, entered into force on 1 June 1978, 1215 *UNTS* 121.

order to supervise fishing, the Agreement establishes a system for common Finnish-Norwegian surveillance patrols. Responsibility for the drafting of general conditions concerning surveillance and the setting up of patrols has been left, on the Norwegian side, to the Chief Administrative Officer of Finnmark, and on the Finnish side, to the Lansstyrelsen. These authorities are required to represent Saami interests. An amendment to the 1977 Agreement provides that the implementation of quotas of fish allowed to be caught in the river Neiden will be carried out by these authorities in Finnmark and Finnish Lapland.[92] Fishing in Lapland is subject to strict licensing, and in Finland and Norway licenses for hunting and fishing are granted by the Saami villages, while in Sweden licensing rights have been taken away from these villages and conferred on the Government in 1993. The recognition of the importance of maintaining the Saami's livelihood is also reflected in other agreements, for example the Frontier Agreement between Finland and Russia of 1960;[93] one of the tasks of the Joint Commission that was set up under this Agreement is to supervise the transfer of reindeers across the frontier.

5. Concluding Remarks

The position of the Saami is a very good illustration of the position of States with respect to groups; Norway and Finland generally appear to accord them more rights, in contrast to the position in Sweden. As we have seen, Swedish authorities have taken away from the Saami the right to issue licenses for hunting and fishing in their territories, while Norway is bound by the "pro-'peoples'" ILO Convention 169, and Finland is yet to become a party to that Convention. Sweden is not a party and is unlikely to become one in the near future. It may be noted however, that none of the Nordic States has granted a full right of ownership of land to

[92] Agreement between Finland and Norway concerning Fishing in the Fishing Area of the Naatamo (Neiden) River, 3 May 1984, that entered into force on 1 June 1984, 1372 *UNTS* 213.

[93] Agreement Concerning the Regime of the Finnish-Soviet State Frontier and the Procedure for the Settlement of Frontier Incidents, signed on 23 June 1960, entered into force on 5 October 1960, 379 *UNTS* 277.

the Saami, notwithstanding international obligations which require this. But the rights accorded to the Saami in respect of reindeer herding and fishing, and also their representation in the institutions charged with managing the use of watercourses, would seem to provide a model for the inclusion of the interests, if not the rights, of peoples in the use of watercourse resources. Of course, the question that arises is that of the maintenance of the precarious balance between the Saami and the non-Saami population in the northern parts of these states. Many are already of the view that the Saami already have more rights than they deserve, to the detriment of other citizens in these countries, even in a region with ample watercourse resources. On balance, however, it could be said that, in view of the extent to which Saami rights are protected, and more specifically the extent to which their interests are taken into account in watercourse management policy, the practice of the Nordic countries favours the rights of indigenous peoples.[94]

[94] See K. Kinnunen, "Experiences of Finnish-Norwegian co-operation in common water" at <http://www.environment.fi/default.asp?contentid=37001&lan=en> (the internet site of the Finnish Lapland Regional Environment Centre, where it lists as some of the lessons learned in the course of the work of the Commission, the following; "It is very important to include the interests of the local population in the transboundary water agreements. This is a particularly significant concern in the present case, because the area covered by the agreement is the home area of the only indigenous people in the EU, the Saami and that", and "When implementing the proposals of the Commission, ownership of the local population and the decision-making ministries is essential".

Chapter 4
NORTHERN EUROPEAN CO-OPERATION REGARDING WATERCOURSES

1. Introduction

The international river regimes in the countries under consideration fall into two very different categories. On the one hand, there are the simple intergovernmental agreements, based upon the enforcement by each state of agreed common rules. The agreements made by Norway with Finland, Russia and Sweden fall into this category. On the other hand, the agreements made by Finland with Russia and Sweden are bold examples of supranationalism in the regulation of frontier waters.

The more conservative agreements are treated first in this Chapter. Among them, the 1929 Convention between Norway and Sweden on Certain Questions Relating to the Law on Watercourses[1] is considered in particular detail, as an example of a regime based not on the creation of a supranational authority but rather on the traditional principles of *bon voisinage*.

2. Norway and Sweden

The 1929 Swedish-Norwegian Watercourse Law Convention[2] (which suffers from very poor French and English translations in the *League of Nations Treaty Series*) establishes a regime based upon co-operation and consultation, without any permanent or supranational organisational framework. It is, in essence, a regime based on a conception of *voisinage* (or, perhaps more accurately, of *bon voisinage*[3]) and in particular upon

---

[1] See 1929 Agreement on Certain Questions Relating to the Law on Watercourses, signed on 11 May 1929 and entered into force on 1 August 1931, CXX *LNTS* 277.

[2] The Preamble to the Convention specifies this short title, reversing the order of the names of the States Parties given in the full title.

[3] See P. Iftene, *Voisinage et bon voisinage en droit international,* (1980).

the principles of consultation, co-operation, and national treatment which constitute the most common applications of *voisinage*. That was the conceptual framework within which multilateral initiatives of the period, such as the 1921 Convention and Statute on the Regime of Navigable Waterways of International Concern[4] and the 1923 Convention relating to the Development of Hydraulic Power affecting more than one State,[5] were conceived and drafted.

The Swedish-Norwegian regime applies to all works (called "undertakings" or "travaux" in the English and French versions) on watercourses in one State which cause appreciable changes in the depth, volume, direction, etc., of water, or detrimentally affect fishing, in the other State (Articles 1.1 and 1.3), or have an adverse impact on navigation on frontier waters (Article 1.2).[6] It does not apply to major works involving the transfer of water from one drainage basin to another: such works are to be the subject of special negotiations outside the scope of the Convention (Article 2).

The basic scheme is as follows. It is intended that the States Parties legislate so as to require authorisation before works to which the Convention applies are undertaken.[7] Proposed works must be notified to the State in which they are to be carried out (Article 14). It is envisaged that the competent authorities will notify the corresponding authority in the other State of the application, and that the terms of the application will be published to interested parties (Articles 14.3 and 15). The handling of the application is a matter for the law of the State concerned (Articles 3, 8 and 15). However, when deciding on the application, the authorities must take into account the effects that the works would have in each of the States, although the benefit is normally to be considered as confined (it seems) to

[4] Signed on 20 April 1920 and entered into force on 31 October 1922, VII *LNTS* 37. See also League of Nations, *First General Conference on Communications and Transit (Barcelona Conference)* (1921), Verbatim Records and Texts relating to the Convention on the regime of navigable waterways of international concern.

[5] Signed on 9 December 1923 and entered into force on 30 June 1925, XXXVI *LNTS* 77. See also League of Nations, *Second General Conference on Communications and Transit, Records and Texts* (1921), League of Nations Document C.30.M.16.1924.VIII, Annex I, at 6 et seq.

[6] The meaning is more evident in the French translation.

[7] This appears to be one of the purposes, or at least one of the effects, of Article 3.

the place or person who carries out the works. Authorities in each State may ask those in the other for information necessary to determine what the likely effects of the works will be (Article 16). This is, then, a system based upon prior notification and consultation. However, the consultations do not occur through high level diplomatic channels, but rather at the level of the authorities charged under the law of each State with the implementation of controls over the works in question and in accordance with their normal procedures for consulting with interested parties in their own States (Articles 14.1 and 16). This "localization" of regulatory procedures, with the interests of national of the other State concerned directly and alongside the interests of the nationals of the regulating State, is characteristic of the regime of *voisinage.*

No authorisation may be given for works which may involve considerable inconvenience to navigation or fishing, or considerable disturbance to the conditions of the water-supply, unless the other State has given its approval (Article 15).[8] The other State must decide on approval according to its national rules governing similar works; and its approval may be conditional, but the conditions must be confined to the planning of the work and the minimising of public damage or nuisances (Article 13). In particular, the Convention excludes the possibility of ordering cross-frontier transfers of power in order to compensate for nuisance or damage or to safeguard interests in the other State (Article 9). A State may regard detriment to its inhabitants as a matter of public damage or nuisance, but there is probably a right for individual inhabitants of each State to make objections based upon the risk of private damage before the authorities of the other State.[9]

There is a provision made for the examination at the request of either State Party of "questions which concern both countries" (Article 18.1) by an *ad hoc* Commission of two, four or six members, half of whom are to be nominated by each State (Article 17). This would enable controversial proposals to be examined by a bilateral body, entitled to call upon expert assistance where necessary (Article 18.1). A commission delivers to both

[8] The threshold for the requirement of approval is, curiously, phrased slightly differently from the threshold for the application of the Convention set out in Article 1.

[9] The Convention is not clear on this point, but it seems to follow from the general principle of equality of treatment of the nationals of each State: see, e.g., Article 24.1.

States its opinion as to whether and how the works should be carried out, and on matters such as the amount of any financial securities which should be charged against the completion of the works (Article 19).

The outcome of this consultative process is set out, in confusing terms, in Articles 20 and 21. Article 20 provides that

> "[t]he question whether the consent of the other country is required for an undertaking and if so whether such consent should be given and on what conditions, shall be decided by the King".

This seems to deal with two situations. First, the King of the State where the works are to be carried out decides if the consent of the other State is needed. If not, the matter may, *ex hypothesi*, be decided by the King's own State alone. Secondly, the phrase "and if so whether [...] conditions" seems to deal with a quite different situation. It appears to mean that if the consent of the other State is required it is for the King of the other State to decide whether and on what conditions to give it. It cannot mean what a strict interpretation of its grammar requires – that the King of the State where the works are to be carried out decides both whether the consent of the other State is needed and whether the other State gives that consent. The confusion of the roles of the King is continued in the second sentence of Article 20, which specifies that

> "[i]f such consent is required and if it has been subjected to special conditions, the question whether the undertaking is permissible and on what conditions shall also be decided by the King in the country in which the work is to be carried out".

Here the King of the State where the works are to be carried out is authorised to take the decision on authorisation, having received the consent of the other State.[10] If the other State has attached conditions to its consent (Article 13), the "territorial" King may decide that the works should not go ahead at all, or that they should go ahead subject to those conditions, perhaps with further conditions imposed by the "territorial" King.

[10] A point made clearer by the first sentence of Article 21.1.

All such conditions are set out in the authorization issued by the competent authorities in the State where the works are to be carried out (Article 21); even so, the works may not proceed until the applicant has obtained a certificate from the competent authorities in the other State, certifying that the Convention procedures for approval of the works have been completed (Article 22). The approvals, therefore, do not have an inherent supranational authority; to borrow the language of the European Community, they lack direct effect and direct applicability. Similarly the supervision and maintenance of any works are to be monitored by the authorities of the State in which they are located (Article 24). There is no system of cross-frontier policing of the kind that exists, for example, under certain bilateral agreements concerning cross-frontier seabed resources, such as the 1976 Frigg Field Agreement made by Norway and the United Kingdom.[11]

Throughout the Norway-Sweden regime the principle of national treatment is observed, with nationals of each State having the same rights and obligations in relation to, for instance, the "opening, maintenance or use for transport or floating" of the watercourses (Article 26).[12] The practical application of the principle is facilitated in an unusual provision under which anyone authorised under the Convention to carry out works may require the authorities in the other State to appoint an agent to represent him in proceedings in that other State, for example by receiving notice of proceedings instituted against him (Article 29). Provision is made in the Convention for the recognition and enforcement in each State of final non-penal judgments, awards, or other decisions on matters covered by the Convention emanating from the other State (Article 30).

The scheme of the Norway-Sweden agreement is modest and cautious. It is based upon national control and national treatment, i.e. the control of river works and uses is left in the hands of the national – that is, the territorial State – State, but that State is obliged in various ways not to discriminate between its own nationals and those of the other State. In this

---

[11] 1977 *UKTS* 113; K.R. Simmonds (ed.), New *Directions in the Law of the Sea*, Vol. V, (1995), p. 380.

[12] Subject to an exception permitting nationals of the other state to be required to give security for obligations which they incur by carrying out floating on the waterways. On national treatment, see also Articles 27, 31 and 32.

respect it is a child of its time. Arrangements for boundary rivers were conservative both in their procedural and their substantive provisions.

As far as procedures are concerned, the pattern before 1945 was to leave controls in the hands of the riparian States.[13] There were exceptions. For instance, there might be a degree of joint action in the case of works of common importance – as, for instance, in the provision for a joint technical commission and joint dredging of the frontier waterways in the Agreement regarding the Improvement of Navigation on Frontier Rivers, made in 1934 by the USSR and Manchukuo,[14] and in the provision for a special joint commission to rectify the course of frontier rivers after changes by natural causes.[15] Some such commissions could have considerable powers. The mixed commission established under the 1927 Turkey-USSR Convention regarding the Use of Frontier Waters, for instance, was given powers to determine the quantities of water each State might take from the river, and to decide on sites where hydroelectric stations and mills might be erected.[16] But all of these provisions were focused upon co-operation between the States as such: they were not focused upon procedures applicable between the nationals of the States. To that extent, they were even more conservative than the Norway-Sweden scheme. True, there were commissions for the great navigable rivers of Europe, such as the Rhine, the Elbe, the Oder and the Danube, which had powers touching directly upon the activities of citizens of riparian States. But those commissions[17] were established primarily in order to safeguard

[13] See, e.g., 1926 Persia-Russia Convention regarding the Mutual Use of Frontier Rivers and Waters, signed on 20 February 1926, entered into force on the same day, translation in L. Shapiro, *Soviet Treaty Series. Volume I, 1917-1928* (1950), p. 314, which is concerned with the division of waters between the two states and contains barely any stipulations on the uses of those waters or on co-operation in the resolution of disputes.

[14] Signed on 4 September 1934, entered into force on the same day, translation in L. Shapiro, *Soviet Treaty Series, Volume II, 1929-1935* (1955), at 110. The Stimson Doctrine of Non-Recognition had a lesser effect than is sometimes assumed.

[15] 1932 Poland-USSR Convention regarding Juridical Relations on the Frontier, Article IX, signed on 10 April 1932, entered into force on 4 October 1934, CXLI *LNTS* 349, translation in L. Shapiro, *Soviet Treaty Series, Volume II, 1929-1935* (1955), at 48.

[16] Signed on 8 January 1927], entered into force on the same day, translation in L. Shapiro, *Soviet Treaty Series, Volume I, 1917-1928* (1950), at 324. See Articles IV, VIII and X.

[17] As to which, see, e.g., C.J. Colombos, *International Law of the Sea* (6th edn., 1967), Chapter VI, and references therein.

strategic interests in particular waterways of vital concern, which are in any event by no means always boundary waters. They have their roots more in the balance of power than in the concept of *voisinage*, with which this text is concerned.

As far as substantive rules are concerned, some agreements of the pre-1945 period concerning frontier waters spelled out more of the implications of *voisinage* than did the Norway-Sweden Agreement. For example, the 1932 Poland-USSR Convention regarding Juridical Relations on the Frontier deals explicitly with duties not to pollute boundary waters or to interfere with fisheries in those waters (Articles VI-XVIII),[18] and, as will be seen in the context of Finnish-Soviet relations, there were many bilateral agreements concerned with particular uses of frontier waters, notably fishing and timber floating. The absence of such detailed provisions from the 1929 Swedish-Norwegian Agreement is perhaps explicable partly on the basis of the relatively small economic importance of the waters in question, and partly on the basis of the confidence felt by each State in the good neighbourliness of the other (and it should be recalled that from 1814, when it ended a union of more than 400 years with Denmark, until 1904, Norway was united with Sweden).[19]

The approach of the Norway-Sweden regime was reflected in other arrangements entered into by Norway. The agreements that it made with Finland and Russia, and the multilateral agreement concerning Lake Inari, display an equally modest and conservative approach. They will be described briefly, before turning to the more adventurous regimes established by the Finland-Russia and Finland-Sweden agreements.

3. Finland and Norway

Finnish-Norwegian co-operation over frontier rivers has been largely

---

[18] For reference, see note 15.

[19] Though there are other Swedish-Norwegian treaties concerned with uses of boundary waters, such as the Exchange of Notes of 22 July 1969 concerning the Free Passage of Salmon to and from Lake Vänern, signed on 22 July 1969 and entered into force on 22 July 1969, 968 *UNTS* 253 and the Agreement of 5 December 1991 concerning the Fishing for Salmon and Trout in Svinesund, Iddefjorden and Enningsdalelva (text on file with authors).

concerned with fisheries.[20] Agreements in 1953,[21] 1959,[22] 1960,[23] 1972,[24] and 1989,[25] for example, established common regulations for fishing in the area of the Tana River. The scheme is simple. Each State issues fishing licenses, valid in both the Finnish and the Norwegian portions of the river. Joint Finnish-Norwegian fishery patrols, with one bailiff from each State, patrol the area, and basic rules for the conduct of fishing are laid down.[26] Further regulations may be adopted by the local authorities in the two States. Similar agreements have been made concerning fishing in the area of the Näätämö (Neiden) river.[27]

[20] There have been agreements concerned with other matters, such as the flow of water. See, e.g., 1951 Agreement concerning the Transmission from the Neiden Watercourse, of Water from Garsjoen, Kjerringvatn and Forestevannene, to the Gandvik Watercourse, signed on 25 April 1951 and entered into force on the same date, *Suomen Asetuskokoelman* 1951, No. 8-9.

[21] 1953 Agreement between Norway and Finland Regarding Fishing Regulations For the Fishing Area of the Tana River, signed on 20 May 1953 and entered into force on 20 May 1953, 173 *UNTS* 163.

[22] 1959 Exchange of Notes Constituting an Additional Agreement to the 1953 Agreement between Norway and Finland Regarding Fishing For the Fishing Area of the Tana River, signed on 2 June 1959 and entered into force on 1 June 1959, 338 *UNTS* 373.

[23] 1960 Agreement between the Kingdom of Norway and Finland Regarding New Fishing Regulations for the Fishing Area of the Tana River, signed on 15 November 1960 and entered into force on 1 January 1961, 383 *UNTS* 178.

[24] 1972 Agreement concerning Common Regulations for Fishing in the Fishing Area of the Tana River signed on 12 May 1972 and entered into force on 1 January 1973, 1289 *UNTS* 105.

[25] 1989 Agreement concerning Common Regulations for Fishing in the Fishing Area of the Tana River signed on 1 March 1989 and entered into force on 1 January 1990, 1588 *UNTS* 195.

[26] Including a curious provision for alternating between the sides of the river on which licensees of each State must fish: see Article 6.

[27] 1964 Agreement Between the Republic of Finland and the Kingdom of Norway Regarding Fishing in the Fishing Area of the Naatamo (Neiden Watercourse, signed on 9 June 1964 and entered into force on 9 June 1964, 503 *UNTS* 205; 1977 Agreement concerning Fishing in the Fishing Area of the Näätämö Area (Neiden) River, signed on 14 December 1977 and entered into force on 1 June 1978, 1215 *UNTS* 121, as amended in minor respects by the Agreement of 3 May 1984 that entered into force on 1 June 1984, 1372 *UNTS* 213.

A more general arrangement was made in the 1980 Agreement concerning a Norwegian-Finnish Commission for Boundary Watercourses.[28] The Commission established by that Agreement is, however, endowed only with the most modest powers. The six member Commission (three members from each State) is the vehicle for co-operation and co-ordination between the two States on questions concerning boundary watercourses, but it possess no more than advisory powers. It has the right to receive notifications from the Contracting States of works that may affect boundary waters, and it may make proposals concerning the management of the waters, but it has no power to adopt binding measures (Articles 1 and 9). The closest that the Commission gets to a supranational authority is the right that its members have to cross the frontier when their work requires it: but even then they must notify their crossing in advance (Article 8). Finally it is interesting to note the inclusion of a relatively progressive provision in Article 5 which stipulates that the Commission "shall also obtain the points of views of representatives of local inhabitants".

4. Norway and Russia

The frontier between Norway and Russia was demarcated by a Mixed Soviet-Norwegian Commission for the Demarcation of the State Frontier, under the terms of an agreement of 18 December 1947. That agreement was followed by the 1949 Agreement concerning the Regime of the Norwegian-Soviet Frontier and Procedure for the Settlement of Frontier Disputes and Incidents.[29] The 1949 Agreement includes provisions regarding navigation, timber floating, and fishing in the frontier waters, which are the Pasvikelv (Pasvik, Patso-joki) river and the Jacobselv (Voriema) river, and the lakes formed by them (Part II, Articles 7-15). The regime that it establishes was, however, extremely simple. In essence, it does no

[28] 1980 Agreement concerning a Norwegian-Finnish Commission for Transboundary Watercourses signed on 5 March 1980, entered into force 1 May 1981, *Suomen säädöskokoelman* 1981, No. 32. (Translation of text on file with authors)

[29] Signed on 29 December 1949 and entered into force on 30 October 1950, 83 *UNTS* 342.

more than delegate to officials the power of the States to agree upon the handling of minor frontier incidents and disputes.

The 1949 Agreement establishes freedom of navigation of the frontier waters in daytime for nationals of the two States, although boats are obliged to anchor or tie up in their own State at night (Articles 8 and 9). Similarly, nationals enjoy the right to float timber and, with certain restrictions, to fish in frontier waters (Articles 10-13). The Contracting States are obliged to take steps to prevent frontier disputes, and to investigate and settle any disputes that may arise (Articles 19). Frontier Commissioners appointed by each State are given the immediate responsibility for the handling of disputes and incidents, except those of particular gravity, which are to be referred for settlement "through the diplomatic channel" (Part V, Articles 20-37). Decisions of the Commissioners are final, but subject to confirmation by the Contracting States if they involve the award of compensation of more than US $500 (Article 26). It appears from the absence of provisions on majority voting that the Commissioners are expected to take all decisions by consensus.

There is little in the way of further international regulation of the frontier rivers between Russia and Norway. In 1957 an Agreement was made on the utilisation of water power on the Pasvik (Paatso) river.[30] That Agreement sets out the terms on which the two Contracting States may use the waters of the Pasvik river for the generation of water power, and provides for the use of each other's territory in connection with the permitted works. The Agreement contains interesting provisions defining the nature and limits of liability for damage arising from the works (Articles 9-12); but it creates no institutional mechanism to oversee its implementation. Similarly, the Agreement of 1971 concerning the regulation of fishing and the preservation of fish stocks in the Grense-Jacobs

[30] 1957 Agreement between the Norway and the Union of Soviet Socialist Republics Concerning the Utilisation of Water Power on the Pasvik (Paatso) River, signed on 18 December 1957 and entered into force on 27 June 1958, 312 *UNTS* 274. Minor modifications were effected by the 1976 Agreement concerning the Outlet of Water at the Norwegian Part of the Pasvik River (Paatsojoki) above the Boris Gleb Power Plant, signed on 20 May 1976 and entered into force on the same date (text on file with authors).

(Voriema) and Pasvik rivers is a simple statement of agreed fishery rules.[31] No supervision mechanism is established.

5. Finland, Norway and Russia

Before turning to the more innovative frontier waters regimes established by Finland, on the one hand, and Russia and Sweden, on the other, mention must be made to the set of multilateral agreements, made by Finland, Norway and Russia (USSR), concerning Lake Inari. Agreements for the regulation of Lake Inari in connection with the use of the Niskakoski Dam were signed by Finland and Russia on 24 April 1947, and amended in 1954 and 1956.[32] These instruments set out rules for the operation of the hydroelectric plant on the lake, and include provisions designed to accommodate other uses of the waters, such as fishing and timber floating. No supranational machinery is established. These bilateral agreements were superseded by the Agreement made by Finland, Norway and Russia on 29 April 1959.[33]

---

[31] 1971 Agreement concerning the Regulation of Fishing and the Preservation of Fish Stocks in the Grense-Jacobs River (Voriema) and the Pasvik River (Patsojoki), signed on 7 December 1971 and entered into force on the same date (text on file with authors).

[32] 1947 Agreement between Finland and the USSR concerning the Regulation of Lake Inari by means of the Niskakoski Control Dam, signed on 24 April 1947, *Suomen Asetuskokoelman* 1947, No. 10; 1954 Protocol for the Implementation of the Agreement of 24 April 1947 between Finland and the USSR concerning the Regulation of Lake Inari by means of the Niskakoski Control Dam, signed on 29 April 1954, 243 *UNTS* 147; 1956 Protocol between Finland and the USSR concerning Amendments to the Regulations of 24 April 1947 for the Regulation of Lake Inari in connexion with the Use of the Niskakoski Dam and to the Protocol of 29 April 1954 concerning Amendments to paragraph 2 of the Said Regulations, signed on 24 February 1956 and entered into force on the same date, 243 *UNTS* 147. See also Treaty between USSR and Finland on the Transfer to Territory of the Soviet Union of Part of the State Territory of Finland in the Region of the Jäniskoski Hydroelectric Power Station and the Niskakoski Control Dam, signed on 3 February 1947, entered into force 18 April 1947, 216 *UNTS* 231.

[33] 1959 Agreement (with Annexes) between Finland, Norway, and the USSR concerning the Regulation of Lake Inari by means of the Kaitakoski Hydroelectric Power Station and Dam, signed on 29 April 1959 and entered into force on the same date, 346 *UNTS* 167.

The trilateral Agreement of 1959, and the associated Regulations of the same date, adopt a rather different approach, giving the USSR the right within prescribed limits to regulate the lake by means of the Kaitakoski Hydroelectric Power Station and Dam (Articles 1 and 2, and the annexed Regulations). The Government of Finland undertakes not to carry out or authorise measures likely to affect the regime of the lake or of the river Paatsjoki (Pasvik) (Article 4). Each of the three States appoints a representative to oversee the implementation of the Agreement (Article 5). Disputes are to be referred to a Mixed Commission to which each State appointed two members, but if the Commission fails to resolve them (presumably by consensus, since no provisions for majority decision-making are included), the matter has to be referred to the Governments of the three States (Article 7). The regime is, therefore, a relatively rudimentary one in institutional terms. The institutions – the three representatives and the Mixed Commission – can handle uncontroversial matters; but anything controversial is diverted to the traditional diplomatic channels.

6. Finland and Russia

The Finish-Russian frontier waters regime is of a different character to those so far examined. While by no means as innovative as the Finish-Swedish regime (see this Chapter, Section 7), it does take the critical step of ascribing responsibility for the routine implementation of parts of the regime to genuinely international bodies, with powers to take binding decisions.

There is a close historical relationship between Finland and Russia.[34] Part of Sweden until 1809, when it became an autonomous grand duchy

[34] For an interesting reflection of this point, see Article XI of the 1923 Convention regarding the Navigation of Finnish Merchant and Cargo Vessels on the Neva between Lake Ladoga a and the Gulf of Finland, signed on 5 June 1923 and entered into force on 20 August 1923, XVIII *LNTS* 217, translation L. Shapiro, *Soviet Treaty Series, Volume I, 1917-1928* (1950), at 217, which states: "[t]he decisions of this Convention, which are a consequence of the special geographical position of Finland and of its immediate neighbourhood to Russia, cannot by virtue of the most favoured nation principle be extended to the vessels of all third states, with the exception of the Soviet Republics, which are united to R.S.F.S.R. *(sic)*".

of the Russian Empire, Finland declared its independence in 1917 but was invaded by the Soviet Union in 1939 and forced to cede to the USSR around 10% of its territory, including its access to Lake Ladoga and to the Arctic Ocean in the River Pasvik area. In that way, key segments of what were in 1917 boundary waters between the two States were taken over by the Soviet Union after 1939. While the treaty relations between the two States are in many respects model applications of the principle of *bon voisinage*,[35] the historical context of Finno-Russian relations should be borne in mind.

The treaty record is a rich one. In 1920, a Treaty of Peace (the Treaty of Dorpat) was concluded by Finland and the USSR.[36] It provides, *inter alia*, for the demilitarisation of Lake Ladoga, at that time a boundary lake (Article XVI), for national treatment in the context of the navigation of frontier waters (Article XXXII.6), and for the maintenance, in the absence of agreement to the contrary, of the water level in Lake Ladoga (Article XVIII). But more significant than these provisions is the development that the Treaty of Dorpat anticipated. It provides for further negotiations with a view to the conclusion of an agreement on rights related to timber floating (based on an MFN rather than the more national standard) (Article XXI), and for the establishment of a Finnish-Russian commission to deal with the implementation of the Treaty of Dorpat (Article XXXVII). Shortly after the making of the Treaty of Dorpat, Finland, and the RSFSR made an agreement on the regulation of fishing activities in the Gulf of Finland.[37] That agreement has no supranational elements: it simply lays down obligations to be observed by fishermen of either State in the area, leaving enforcement in the hands of the national authorities. October 1922, however, saw a flurry of further diplomatic activity in the Mixed Finnish-Russian Central Commission (a body established under Article XXXVII of the Treaty of Dorpat to negotiate agreements between the two countries) in Helsinki and the conclusion of a number of altogether more adventurous treaties.

---

[35] See P. Iftene, *supra* note 3.

[36] Signed on 14 October 1920 and entered into force on 31 December 1920, III *LNTS* 6, translation in L. Shapiro, *Soviet Treaty Series, Volume I, 1917-1928* (1950), at 69.

[37] 1922 Convention regarding Fishing Regulations in the Gulf of Finland, signed on 20 September 1922 and entered into force on same day, XIX *LNTS* 143; translation in L. Shapiro, *Soviet Treaty Series, Volume I, 1917-1928* (1950), at 191.

Finland and the USSR signed a series of treaties concerning fishing. On 21 October 1922, Finland and the USSR signed a convention dealing with fishing and sealing in the territorial waters of the Arctic Ocean.[38] That Convention embodies the principle of national treatment in many detailed provisions relating to access to the fisheries covered by the Convention. The following week, Conventions were signed dealing with fishing and sealing in Lake Ladoga,[39] and the maintenance of river channels and regulation of fishing on watercourses forming part of the frontier between Finland and Russia.[40] The former Convention, largely concerned with the detailed application of the principle of national treatment in access to fisheries, acknowledges in Article VIII that the fisheries of Lake Ladoga can be fully protected only by the adoption of joint and simultaneous measures taken by Finland and Russia. The States go no further than an undertaking to negotiate over proposals for fishing or sealing regulations; but the provision marks a step in the direction of joint regulation of one use of those boundary waters. The second of the Conventions, on the maintenance of river channels, took a different approach. It sets out detailed prescriptions and prohibitions on hydraulic works and fishing activities in order to safeguard navigation and fisheries in boundary waters. In more detail, this convention regulates protection of migratory fish and contains progressive provisions for the time of its drafting, such as the prohibition of poison, drugs or explosives (Article 5, paragraph 5), regulation of fishing gear and closed seasons (Article 5, paragraphs 2 and 4) and prohibition of establishment of factories or other structures that re-

---

38 1922 Convention regarding Fishing and Sealing in the Territorial Waters of the Arctic Ocean, signed on 21 October 1922 and entered into force on 2 July 1924, XXIX *LNTS* 197; translation in L. Shapiro, *Soviet Treaty Series, Volume I, 1917-1928*, (1950), at 192.

39 1922 Convention regarding Fishing and Sealing in Lake Ladoga, signed on 28 October 1922 and entered into force on 2 July 1924, XXIX *LNTS* 211, translation in L. Shapiro, *Soviet Treaty Series. Volume I, 1917-1928* (1950), at 196; Protocol regarding Article IV of the Convention of 28 October 1922 regarding Fishing and Sealing in Lake Ladoga, signed on 12 July 1924 and entered into force on same day (translation in L. Shapiro, *Soviet Treaty Series, Volume I, 1917-1928* (1950), at 272).

40 1922 Convention concerning the Maintenance of Rivers, Channels and the Regulation of Fishing on Watercourses forming part of the Frontier between Finland and Russia, signed on 28 October 1922 and entered into force on the same day, XIX *LNTS* 183, translation in L. Shapiro, *Soviet Treaty Series, Volume I, 1917-1928* (1950), at 197.

tard the flow of the stream as to cause damage to the fish of the territory of the other State.

A fourth Convention signed on the same day dealt with the floating of timber in watercourses flowing from Finland to Russia and vice versa.[41] It is based upon the principle of national treatment[42] coupled, as in the other conventions of the time, with the recognition that the territorial state possessed exclusive jurisdiction to enforce regulations on its side of the frontier. But this Convention pushes joint action a stage further. In cases where works on the waterways were necessary, the Convention requires that regulations be drawn up and sanctioned conjointly by the competent authorities of the two States (Articles 3.1, 3.2 and 3.3). The regulations may require steps, such as the compulsory acquisition of property in order to enable the necessary works to take place (Article 3.4). Floating is to be regulated largely by associations of timer floaters (which play an important role in the frontier waters regimes), of which both Finnish and Russian floaters are members (Articles 3.5, 3.6 and 3.7). Claims for damage caused by timber floating which are not settled amicably with the owner of the damaged property are to be referred for binding decision to a Valuation Commission. Each State appoints one valuer, and these two jointly elected two chairmen, one for the valuation of damage in Finnish territory, one for the valuation of damage in Russian territory (Article 3.17). While its role is limited, and essentially judicial rather than executive, administrative or legislative, the ascription to this international body of the power to take binding decisions is a significant advance. Broader issues concerning the interpretation or application of the Convention are to be referred for (apparently non-binding) discussion by a special commission to which the two Governments appoint equal numbers of representatives (Article 9).

Further treaties were made on specific matters such as the navigation of Finnish ships on Lake Ladoga,[43] but the USSR made no general fron-

[41] 1922 Convention regarding the Floating of Timber in Watercourses flowing from Finland to Russia or vice versa, signed on 28 October 1922 and entered into force on the same day, XIX *LNTS* 153, translation in L. Shapiro, *Soviet Treaty Series, Volume I, 1917-1928* (1950), at 193; as amended by the Agreement of 15 October 1933 that entered into force on 7 February 1934, CXLIX *LNTS* 243.

[42] See, e.g., Articles 1, 3.10, 5 and 6.

[43] 1923 Convention regarding the Navigation of Finnish Merchant and Cargo Vessels on the Neva between Lake Ladoga and the Gulf of Finland signed on 5 June 1923 and

tier waters treaties with its Scandinavian neighbours before World War Two. The USSR was making general agreements on frontier waters in this period with neighbours elsewhere. The agreements with Persia,[44] Poland,[45] Turkey,[46] and Manchukuo[47] have been referred to above. The explanation for the different practice between the USSR and Finland may lie in the fact that relations between those two States were sufficiently close for frontier matters to be treated without great fuss and on a case-by-case basis, whereas the regulation of frontier questions with the Soviet Union's other neighbours had a more greater political significance. Nonetheless, there was a general conciliation convention concluded by Finland and the USSR, after the fashion of the time.[48] The four person (two Finnish, two Soviet) Commission has competence in "all disputes of whatever nature [...] which cannot be settled within a reasonable time through the diplomatic channel" (Article I), and may submit non-binding proposals to the two States.

After World War Two a number of the earlier treaties, such as those concerning the floating of timber and the maintenance of river channels and the regulating of fishing, were expressly revived by the Treaty of Peace with Finland.[49] As has been noted, the USSR also concluded agree-

---

entered into force on 20 August 1923, XVIII *LNTS* 217, L. Shapiro, *Soviet Treaty Series, Volume I, 1917-1928* (1950), at 217; 1928 Protocol modifying Article VII of the Convention of 5 June 1923 regarding the Navigation of Finnish Merchant and Cargo Vessels on the Neva between Lake Ladoga and the Gulf of Finland, signed on 17 March 1928 and entered into force on 31 July 1928, LXXX *LNTS* 151, translation in L. Shapiro, *Soviet Treaty Series, Volume I, 1917-1928* (1950), at 364.

[44] Signed on 20 February 1926; translation in L. Shapiro, *Soviet Treaty Series, Volume I, 1917-1928* (1950), at 314.

[45] Signed on 10 April 1932; translation in L. Shapiro, *Soviet Treaty Series, Volume II, 1929-1935* (1955), at 48; see also the Convention regarding the Rafting of Timber on Frontier Rivers, Warsaw, signed on 19 June 1993, *ibid.*, at 67.

[46] Signed on 8 January 1927, translation in L. Shapiro, *Soviet Treaty Series, Volume I, 1917-1928* (1950), at 324.

[47] Signed on 4 September 1934, translation in L. Shapiro, *Soviet Treaty Series, Volume II, 1929-1935* (1955), at 110.

[48] 1932 Convention on Conciliation, signed on 22 April 1932 and entered into force on 9 August 1932, CLVII *LNTS* 401, translation in L. Shapiro, *Soviet Treaty Series, Volume II, 1929-1935* (1955), at 51.

[49] See 67 *UNTS* 153 and 157.

ments on Lake Inari with Finland in 1947, and with Finland and Norway in 1959. But much the most important developments occurred in the 1960s, when Finland and the USSR made two agreements that form the basis of a true frontier waters regime.

In 1960, the two States made an Agreement concerning the Regime of the Finnish-Soviet State Frontier and the Procedure for the Settlement of Frontier Incidents.[50] The 1960 Agreement is similar to the 1949 Norway-USSR Border Agreement. Thus, it sets out broad principles concerning freedom of navigation and fishing, and provides for Frontier Commissioners appointed by each State to handle minor frontier disputes and incidents. In 1964, much greater detail was added to this basic framework. The Agreement concerning Frontier Watercourses[51] establishes principles that go far beyond those in the earlier agreements.

Article 2 sets the tone of the 1964 Agreement by prohibiting unilateral measures that might cause damage or harm to the water area, or a danger of flooding, or a significant loss of water, or interfere with a use of a fairway, or "which might in some like manner be prejudicial to the public interest". The frontier waters have ceased to be viewed simply as parts of the territory of the riparian States in which their geographical adjacency requires that there be some common rules. There has been a conceptual shift, with the frontier waters being viewed in this context as a shared resource, whose integrity has to be preserved for the common good.

The Agreement lays down a procedure for the consideration of measures affecting the frontier waters that might be prejudicial to the public interest (Chapter Two, Articles 6-11). A Joint Finnish-Soviet Commission on the Utilization of Frontier Watercourses is established (Article 6). Each State appoints three members and three alternates, and makes experts available to the Commission. The Commission examines and deals with matters concerning the utilisation of the waters, acting either under the direction of the States or on its own initiative. The Contracting States may agree to refer to the Commission proposals for measures that might

---

[50] Signed on 23 June 1960 and entered into force on 5 October 1960, 379 *UNTS* 277.

[51] Signed on 24 April 1964 and entered into force on 6 May 1965, 537 *UNTS* 231. This Agreement superseded the bilateral agreements of 28 October 1922 on the maintenance of channels and regulation of fishing on frontier watercourses, and on the floating of timber, and the Agreement of 15 October 1933 on the floating of timber.

prejudice the public interest in the frontier waters, requesting a decision or opinion from it. The Commission is obliged to consult national authorities whose consent is required by national law for the measures in question; and it may consult technical experts if it wishes. It may stipulate how proposed measures are to be carried out (Article 10); and, while the provisions on decision-making are not altogether clear in their meaning and effect, in at least some circumstances unanimous decisions of the Commission on matters referred to it are "binding upon both Contracting Parties and shall be as valid and enforceable as a decision of the governmental or judicial authorities of the State concerned" (Article 11).[52]

The 1964 Agreement gives the Commission the power to make detailed rules on timber floating (Article 13). Navigation remains regulated by the 1960 Agreement as, apart from the stipulation of some additional principles on fishery conservation, does fishing (Articles 14 and 17).

The 1964 Agreement represents a major development in the history of the regulation of Scandinavian frontier waters. The joint Finnish-Soviet Commission has not removed the need for the conclusion of further bilateral treaties on specific issues.[53] Nor is the composition of the Commission clearly intended to signal a degree of independence from the Contracting Parties, as might have been the case had it been composed of technical experts or judges, for instance. Moreover, the lack of clarity in the provisions setting out the Commission's decision-making powers may evidence a certain reluctance on the part of the Contracting States to surrender powers to it. Nevertheless, the 1964 Agreement took the significant step of giving responsibility for the supervision of the utilisation of frontier waters in the hands of a truly supranational body, whose remit points towards the goal of the administration of those waters as a shared resource in the common public interest. This signal development was carried a stage further in the regime established for the Finnish-Swedish frontier waters.

---

[52] See Articles 10 and 11 for the qualifications.

[53] See, e.g., 1972 Agreement concerning the Production of Electric Power in the part of the Vuoksi River bounded by the Imatra and Svetogorsk Hydroelectric Stations, signed on 12 July 1972 and entered into force on 7 February 1973, 884 *UNTS* 64; and the 1983 Protocol on the Participation of Soviet Organizations in Fish Breeding Activities for the Conservation of the Fish Stocks in Lake Inari, signed on 14 December 1983 and entered into force on the same date, 1351 *UNTS* 141.

7. Finland and Sweden

The Finland-Sweden boundary waters regime began in a limited fashion. The two States made, in 1924, a convention concerning the establishment of a Conciliation Commission,[54] which was to investigate and settle "all disputes of any nature whatever which it has not been possible to settle within a reasonable time through diplomatic channels" (Article 1). Reports of the Commission were, however, not binding (Article 16), and the convention should be seen as an instance of the flurry of bilateral conciliation treaties which were made in the 1920s, rather than as the foundation of a bilateral regime between these Scandinavian neighbours.

Three years later they concluded a convention on the joint exploitation of salmon in the Torne and Muonio Rivers.[55] This was a true application of the principles of *bon voisinage*. With limited local exceptions, the salmon fisheries in boundary rivers were to be exploited jointly, for the profit of the two Contracting States, each of which was entitled to half of the yield of the fisheries (Articles I and III). Detailed provisions are made, in the 1927 Convention and in the Regulations set out in the Declarations annexed to it, concerning the use of certain kinds of fishing equipment, and in particular those that interfere with the floating of timber on the rivers, and also imposing limitations on the right to fish at certain times and in certain places. One notable provision permits courts in one State to try nationals who have committed an offence in the other State, and who no longer resided in that other State.[56] Despite this unusual provision for the allocation of criminal jurisdiction between courts,[57] there is

[54] 1924 Convention concerning the Establishment of a Permanent Commission for Investigation and Conciliation signed on 27 June 1924 and entered into force on 13 September 1924, XXIX *LNTS* 19. In fact, there was a much earlier treaty, the Frontier Regulation Treaty of 20 November 1910, which included provisions on matters such as the right of nationals of each of the riparian States to travel on the river.

[55] 1927 Convention concerning the Joint Exploitation of the Salmon Fisheries in the Tornea (Tornio) and Muonio Rivers, signed on 10 May 1927 and entered into force on 31 December 1927, LXX *LNTS* 201.

[56] Regulations concerning Fishing in the Fishery Zone of the Tornio River, Article 14.1.

[57] And also in civil matters; see the Regulations concerning Fishing in the Fishery Zone of the Tornio River, Article 14.2.

no such explicit system for the sharing of executive powers. The whole scheme is overseen by a Commission to which each State (represented for this purpose by a designated provincial administration) nominates three nationals: one, a fisheries officer; one a forest administration officer; and the third a person acquainted with local conditions (Article XIII). It seems, from the absence of provisions on the procedure of the Commission that it is intended to operate by consensus.

A further treaty on the Torne and Muonio Rivers, this time concerning timber floating, was concluded by Sweden and Finland in 1949.[58] The treaty itself is very simple, permitting nationals of either State to float timber down the river without payment of taxes, and relaxing in the interest of the floating industry other regulations concerning entry and residence in each State. Disputes between the Contracting States concerning the treaty are to be dealt with under the 1924 Convention on conciliation. The 1949 Treaty has annexed to it extensive and precise Regulations. These require those who wished to float timber on anything other than a small scale to join a timber floating association,[59] whose by-laws are to be approved by the local administrations in each State.[60] Detailed rules govern floating operations, and provision is made for mixed teams of inspectors to examine the floatways and make further rules.[61] Disputes arising from floating operations may be submitted to arbitration,[62] and provisions similar to those in the fisheries treaty of 1928 are laid down for the prosecution of criminal offences.[63]

The fisheries and timber floating regimes were subsumed within the 1971 Agreement between Finland and Sweden concerning Frontier Riv-

---

[58] 1949 Agreement concerning Timber Floating in the Torne and Muonio Frontier Rivers, signed on 17 February 1949 and entered into force on 9 July 1949, 197 *UNTS* 123.

[59] Regulations concerning Timber Floating in the Floatway of the Torne and Muonio Frontier Rivers, Article 2.

[60] Regulations concerning Timber Floating in the Floatway of the Torne and Muonio Frontier Rivers, Article 12. Those administrations had the right to appoint non-voting representatives to the association: *ibid.*, Article 13.

[61] Regulations concerning Timber Floating in the Floatway of the Torne and Muonio Frontier Rivers, Article 6.

[62] Regulations concerning Timber Floating in the Floatway of the Torne and Muonio Frontier Rivers, Articles 22-28.

[63] Regulations concerning Timber Floating in the Floatway of the Torne and Muonio Frontier Rivers, Article 36.

ers.[64] Indeed, this Agreement preserves the effect of the 1949 Agreement on timber floating (Article 274), and builds directly on the earlier regulations on fisheries.[65] But the 1971 Agreement has a very different character to its predecessors. True, there are familiar provisions regulating hydraulic works, fishing, and compensation for damage to other river users, and the treaty adopts, in Article 5, the principle of equal sharing of the water volume between the Contracting States. But the similarities to earlier treaties are superficial. This Agreement has a completely different vantage point from its predecessors. They were concerned with adjustments between individuals. The conflicts and abuses that they addressed were envisaged as arising between private parties. The 1971 Agreement stands above private parties and private interests, and is explicitly designed to pursue a measure of social engineering.

The theme is apparent in Chapter 1, Article 4, which states that where an order of priority has to be determined for projects affecting the same waters, "preference shall be given to the project which may be assumed to be of the greatest public and private benefit". The "public interest" approach is more clearly apparent in Chapter 3, Article 3. That permits hydraulic works which permanently diminish the comfort of local residents or which cause significant nature conservancy losses, only if the works are of particular importance from some public standpoint (see also Chapter 4, Article 1). The public interest approach may be seen at work in other contexts. For instance, where significant works are carried out, the developer may be obliged to pay a charge, to be used to minimise damage or inconvenience which cannot properly be compensated, or for other purposes beneficial to the locality affected by the project (Chapter 3, Article 10). Similarly, landowners may be required to tolerate the building on their property of works necessary for sewage purification (Chapter 6, Article 9).

These, and similar, provisions would be unremarkable in the context of any State's domestic planning legislation. They are noteworthy here because, like the provisions of the earlier Finnish-Soviet Agreement, they mark a clear break from the earlier tradition in frontier water regimes. No

---

[64] Stockholm, 16 September 1971, 825 *UNTS* 272.

[65] See Annex B to the 1971 Agreement.

longer are frontier waters treated almost like a geological fault line, where chafing could send serious tremors deep into the territory of the neighbouring State, and where friction had to be eliminated by the delicate adjusting of disputes between individuals. In the 1971 Agreement, the riparian States march boldly in to the frontier zone, regulating it, and imposing and preserving a balancing of interests in the zone for what is perceived to be the greater public good.

More remarkable than these substantive changes are the institutional innovations in the 1971 Agreement. It established the permanent Finnish-Swedish Frontier River Commission (FSFRC) (Chapters 2, 8 and 9, and Annex A), to which each State appoints three persons: one judge, and one technical expert and one person with local knowledge. The FSFRC is empowered to pursue investigations and to call upon the authorities of either State in performing its functions (Chapter 2, Article 3). Its inspectors may enter premises on either side of the river (see Chapter 9, Articles 1-5). Its judicial and legislative powers are equally impressive. It has practically complete control over authorisations for all manner of works on the frontier rivers (see Chapter 8, Article 1 et seq.). Indeed, the courts of the States Parties must refer to the Commission cases affecting the frontier rivers; and it is for the FSFRC to decide whether they fall within its jurisdiction or are to be remitted to the national courts (Chapter 8, Article 3). Each case is to be handled "in the manner appropriate to its nature" (Chapter 8, Article 7). However, the Agreement includes detailed stipulations concerning the publicity to be given to the proceedings of the Commission and the right to address arguments to it, and those should ensure that basic principles of natural justice are observed. Appeals lie from FSFRC to the supreme water right courts of the State where the interests concerned are located. The FSFRC also enjoys extensive administrative powers (Chapter 8, Article 17), including a wide-ranging power to make regulations governing uses of the frontier rivers. These regulations have immediate legal effect and are not subject to any appeal although, in the case of certain fisheries regulations, they are subject to confirmation by the Governments of the two States (Chapter 8, Article 17).

While these powers give the FSFRC very considerable autonomy, the interests of each of the States receive a degree of protection from the requirement that decisions be taken by a majority of at least four, including at least two from each State. In most cases (Chapter 8, Articles 13 and

17), in the absence of such a majority the matter is to be referred to the two governments. This effectively enables any two members from a single State to push the matter back to their governments, and that opportunity might be found attractive by cautious members were the FSFRC to become too radical in its approach. That, coupled with the opportunity for control of its judicial decisions by the supreme water rights courts of the two States, may operate as a significant brake upon any truly innovative use of the FSFRC's very considerable powers.

8. Concluding Remarks

The regimes surveyed here range from straightforward applications of the principles of *bon voisinage*, in the case of the 1929 Norway-Sweden arrangements, to an advanced form of supranationalism, in the case of the 1971 Finland-Sweden regime. The later agreements are the more advanced, in terms of their institutional complexity;[66] but it would be unwise to assume that all regimes must develop in the direction of increased complexity. The nature of the political and economic relationship between the States Parties, the economic and cultural value of the waters in question, and the incidence of major hydraulic works, will vary from one frontier watercourse to another. Some frontier waters simply need less, and less sophisticated, regulation than do others.

It is also unwise to assume that there is necessarily a direct correlation between the sophistication of a treaty regime and the nature of the practice "on the ground". There is no shortage of examples of organisations with extensive and elaborate powers that have never been used, or of organisations where simple provisions have been given subtle and inspired interpretations by officials determined to make the organisation as active and effective as possible. More fieldwork on the actual practice of the Commissions needs to be done before definite hypotheses are framed concerning the strengths and weaknesses of the different approaches to frontier waters regimes that are evident in Scandinavia.

[66] On co-operation regarding the implementation of the 2000 EU Water Framework Directive, 2000/60/EC, *OJ* L327, 2000), see <http://www.environment.fi/print.asp?contentid=58166&clan=EN>.

What is beyond doubt is that, in a relatively small area of the globe, there is a diversity and a richness of practice in the regulation of frontier waters that make it one of the most fascinating testing grounds for international legal institutions in the world today.

Chapter 5
NORTHERN EUROPEAN WATERCOURSE INSTITUTIONS

1. Introduction

In this chapter, institutions established pursuant to agreements some examples of commissions established between states in northern Europe will be examined in detail, in order to appreciate better the actual operation of the rules and principles discussed in previous chapters. Section 2 considers co-operation between Finland and Russia, and Section 3 examines institutional co-operation between Norway and Russia. This provides the opportunity to examine the extent to which meaningful co-operation is possible between states with different national legal systems in addressing problems related to the use of watercourses. Section 4 considers the Norwegian-Finnish Frontier Watercourse Commission, while Section 5 examines one of the most highly developed institution of its kind, namely the Finnish-Swedish Frontier River Commission.

2. Finland and Russia

2.1 The Joint Finnish-Russian Commission on the Utilization of Frontier Watercourses

The Joint Finnish-Soviet Commission on the Utilization of Frontier Watercourses (the "Watercourse Commission") was established by the 1964 Agreement concerning Frontier Watercourses ("Watercourse Agreement" or "WA"), (Article 6).[1] This Agreement regulates in general the use of the common frontier watercourses (see Preamble). This Agreement is closely connected with the Agreement concluded in 1960 between Finland and

[1] Signed 24 April 1964, entry into force on 6 May 1965, 537 *UNTS* 251.

the Soviet Union on their frontier and the settlement of disputes related to that frontier ("Frontier Agreement" or "FA").[2] The Frontier Agreement set up its own Commission ("Frontier Commission"; see Section 2.3).

2.1.1 *Geographical Scope*

The sections of frontier watercourses that are deemed to be frontier waters for the purpose of the Watercourse Agreement are specified in the Frontier Agreement (Article 1 WA).[3] The Frontier Agreement sets out the method of delimitation of the frontier between the Russian Federation and Finland in relation to rivers and lakes (Part I FA). In cases where the frontier intersects standing or running waters, the frontier is an immovable line following a straight course from one frontier mark to the next (Article 2.1 FA). In sectors in which it follows running waters, including lakes, the frontier is a straight, broken or crooked line running from one frontier mark to the next; and in the case of a frontier river or stream, the frontier follows the middle of the river or stream or of its main branch (Article 2.2 FA). Islands in frontier rivers belong to the territory of one Party of the other, according to their position with regard to the frontier line (Articles 2.1, 2.2 and 2.3 FA). Where there are natural variations in the banks of rivers and streams, the frontier line will be drawn in conformity with them (Article 3.1 FA). In the case of rivers intersected by the frontier line, and of any lake or coastal bay along which the frontier line runs, a strip of water 100 meters wide on either side of the frontier river is deemed to be frontier waters (Article 11.1 WA).

2.1.2 *Structure and Composition of the Watercourse Commission*

The Watercourse Commission consists of three members and three alternates (Article 6 WA). Both the members and their alternates are

[2] See Article 6 of the 1960 Agreement concerning the Regime of the Finnish-Soviet State Frontier and the Procedure for the Settlement of Frontier Incidents, signed on 23 June 1960, entry into force on 5 October 1960, 379 *UNTS* 277.

[3] Rivers Pasvik, Tuloma, Kemi, Kovda, Kem, Oulu, Vuoksa, Janisjoki, Tohmajoki, Hintoloujoki, Kilpinjoki, Soskuanjoki, Hounijoki, Tervajoki, Vilajoki, Santajoki, Urpalanjokiand Vaalimanajoki; the Saima Canal; and the Gulf of Finland.

appointed by the Parties. The staff of the Commission includes, as well, a Secretary and, if necessary, experts. At the meetings of the Commission, the Chairmanship is held by a member of the Commission appointed to that position by one of the Parties to the Agreement, alternately (Article 7 WA).

2.1.3 *Functions of the Commission*

(a) General

A general description of the Watercourse Commission's functions can be found in Article 8 WA. The Commission may, on the instructions of the Parties or on its own initiative, deal with all matters relating to the utilization of frontier watercourses, including timber floating, water transport, the conservation of fish stocks, and fisheries; the flow of water; and the quality of water. Furthermore, the Commission has to ensure that the Watercourse Agreement is complied with; to monitor the state of the water in frontier watercourses; and to resolve difference of opinion arising from the interpretation or application of the Watercourse Agreement. As seen below in Subsection 2.1.7, further functions of the Commission flow from an agreement made in 1972 concerning the production of electric power in part of the Vuoksi River.[4]

(b) Water Flow

Contracting Parties must ensure that the frontier watercourses and the structures situated therein are maintained in such a state that no harm or damage is caused as a result from changes in the position, depth, level, or free flow of water (Article 2 WA). In principle, no activities may be carried out that cause harm or damage to the water area, to fisheries, to land, or to structures or property; create a danger of flooding or a significant loss of water; alter the main fairway or interfere with the use of a com-

[4] 1972 Agreement concerning the Production of Electric Power in the Part of the Vuoksi River bounded by the Imatra and Svetogorsk Hydroelectric Stations, which was signed on 12 July 1972 and entered into force on 7 February 1973, 884 *UNTS* 64; see also 1989 Agreement concerning Rules for the Regulation of Lake Saimaa and River Vuoksi, signed on 26 October 1989, entry into force on 9 October 1991, *Suomen säädöskokoelman* 1991, No. 91, 1663 *UNTS* 325.

mon fairway for transport or timber floating; or are otherwise prejudicial to the public interest. The main fairways of the watercourses must be kept open for the free flow of water and for transport, timber floating, and the passage of fish (Article 3 WA). An activity that affects or may affect the water flow may only be carried out if it has been approved in accordance with a special procedure (Section 2.1.5).

(c) Water Quality

Contracting Parties must ensure that frontier watercourses are not polluted by untreated industrial influents and sewage, by waste materials from timber floating or wastes from ships or by other substances that may cause shoaling of the watercourses, harmful changes in composition of water, damage to the fish-stock or substantial scenic deterioration or might endanger public health or have similar harmful effects for the population or the economy. The Contracting Parties shall jointly set water quality standards and co-operate in monitoring the state of the water and adopting measures to increase the self-cleansing capacity of water (Article 4 WA). An activity that affects or may affect the water quality may only be carried out if it has been approved in accordance with a special procedure (see Section 2.1.5).

(d) Timber floating

One of the most important functions of the Watercourse Commission, especially in the past, relates to timber floating. In the event of timber floating in the territory of the other Party, the Commission may, in consultation with competent authorities, authorise timber floating and approve a set of rules governing such floating, in order to define the rights and obligations of the timber floaters and their crews, and may enumerate equipment and installations required for the floating operations. The Parties in any event may conclude special agreements relating to timber floating. Timber floating which is not regulated by the general rules of the Watercourse Agreement, and is not covered by a special agreement, is governed by municipal law of each Party (Article 13 WA).

(e) Transport

Transport in frontier watercourses is also governed by the Frontier Agreement (Article 14 WA). Vessels of the Contracting Parties navigate in the narrow sections of lakes and in the rivers along the frontier line. On lakes and rivers intersected by the frontier line, ships may only navigate up to the frontier line. Ships of either Party navigating in frontier waters may tie up to the other Party's bank, or remain in frontier waters, only in cases of distress (Articles 12.1, 12.2 and 12.3 FA). Ships may only navigate during daylight, and waters are to be kept clean and are not to be artificially polluted or fouled in any way. Likewise, the Parties have to take measures to present wilful damage to the banks or frontier rivers (Article 15 FA). The Parties have a duty to respect each other's rights and to ensure the proper implementation of the Frontier Agreement (Article 16 FA). Failure to comply with the above requirements, causing material loss to one of the Parties, results in liability for compensation which has to be paid by the Party to which the loss is attributable (Article 16 FA). The Parties must ensure that all the waterways are kept in proper condition (Article 19 FA).

(f) Fishing

Under Article 17 WA, of the Contracting Parties may fish in frontier waters up to the frontier line in accordance with the regulations in force in their respective territories. They are prohibited, however, from using explosives, poisonous or narcotic substances, or resorting to other means that result in the large scale destruction or mutilation of fish, and from fishing in frontier waters at night. Technical measures relating to fishing, such as closed seasons, are regulated by special agreement concluded between the relevant authorities of the Parties (Article 21 FA). Pursuant to the Watercourse Agreement, the Contracting Parties shall take joint conservation measures in relation to a number of specified frontier watercourses abounding in salmon and white fish (*siika*) (Article 15 WA) and individually in relation to other frontier watercourses (Article 16 WA).

2.1.4 *Adoption of Decisions and Opinions by the Commission*

A Contracting Party wishing to allow an activity that has or may have the consequences referred to in Articles 2 or 4 WA (see Section 2.1.3 above) must notify the other Party and allow it to make observations (Article 9 WA). The Contracting Parties may refer the matter to the Commission for a decision or an opinion (Article 9 WA). The Commission must take into account the provisions of the law in force in each country (Article 10 WA). From this provision, it follows that the Commission may only take a decision after it has requested the opinion of competent authorities "where, under the law of one of the Contracting States, permission must be obtained from the competent authorities for construction work or other measures in the territory of that State" (Article 10 WA). Apart from where the Commission fails to reach a decision, it must also submit the matter to the two Governments "where a certain measure may have *significant* effects in the territory of one of the Contracting Parties" (emphasis added) (Article 10 WA).

The Commission adopts its decisions either by unanimity or majority voting. Where the Commission reaches a decision on a matter under its consideration unanimously, that decision is binding on the Parties and "shall be valid and enforceable as a decision of the governmental or judicial authorities of the State concerned" (Article 11). When the Commission adopts a decision by a majority vote, it is subject to the system of "contracting-out", i.e. it is binding on the Parties if neither of them expresses an objection within a period of two months (Article 11 WA).[5]

2.1.5 *Compensation Procedure*

On liability for damage, the Watercourse Agreement provides that "[w]here the execution of certain measures by one Contracting Party causes loss or damage in the territory of the other Contracting Party, the Contracting Party permitting such measures in its territory shall be liable to make reparation to the Party suffering the loss or damage" (Article 5 WA).[6] In addition to traditional forms of reparation for internationally wrongful acts, Contracting Parties may agree that reparation is provided in the form of granting privileges to the Party suffering the loss or damage (Article 5 WA).

---

[5] On this mode of expression of consent to be bound, see M. Fitzmaurice, "Expression of Consent to be Bound by a Treaty as Developed in Certain Environmental Treaties", in J. Klabbers and R. Lefeber (eds.), *Essays on the Law of Treaties* (1998), pp. 59-80.

[6] On the interpretation of this provision in relation to the law on state responsibility, see R. Lefeber, *Transboundary Environmental Interference and the Origin of State Liability* (1996), pp. 170-171.

2.1.6 *Dispute Settlement Procedure*

The Watercourse Agreement provides for a three-tiered procedure to settle disputes (Article 19 WA). Firstly, differences of opinion arising from the interpretation or application of the Agreement are to be settled by the Watercourse Commission. Secondly, in the event that they are not settled by the Commission, a Joint Board will be set up consisting of four members, two appointed by each Government. Finally, if this Board fails to reach an agreement, the differences are to be settled through diplomatic channels.

2.1.7 *The Vuoksi Agreement*

Other functions of the Watercourse Commission flow from the 1972 Agreement concerning the Production of Electric Power in the Part of the Vuoksi River bounded by the Imatra and Svetogorsk Hydroelectric Stations ("Vuoksi Agreement").[7] The Vuoksi River is the largest of the frontier watercourses between Russia and Finland. Its catchments area is 69,500 km^2, out of which 77% is within the boundaries of Finland and 23% within Russia. Lake Saimaa is the main lake in the watercourse (4,460 km^2), from where the Vuoksi River runs into Lake Ladoga in Russia (catchment area 258,000 km^2).[8] The Vuoksi Agreement was con-

[7] *Supra* note 4.

[8] Article 1 says as follows: "For the purpose of ensuring efficient use of the hydroelectric stations, the Parties declare that the Svetogorsk hydroelectric station, which regulates the stream flow shall be operated using the water levels approved for it by Russian authorities and the backwater and daily stream flow regulation practice in use since 1948, due regard being had to the water levels agreed in Article 2. The water levels in question and the daily practice shall not be altered in such a way as to cause a loss of stream flow, shall not be altered in such a way as to cause a loss of stream flow or energy at Imatra hydroelectric station greater than stipulated in Article 3". Article 3 says as follows: "Pursuant to Article 1, the daily regulation of stream flow at the Svetogorsk hydroelectric station must be carried out in such a way that the water level in the tail bay of the Imatra hydroelectric station, as measured at the Imatra hydroelectric station, does not exec the average levels, indicated below for various flows of the Vouksi River, as measured at Tainiokoski". On the subject, see M. Ollila and N. Rozkov, "Regulation of the Lake Saimaa and the River Vuoksi Watercourses" in *Cooperation on the Frontier Watercourses during Thirty Years* (published by the Joint Finnish-Russian Commission on the Utilization of Frontier Watercourses, 1995), p. 21.

cluded to ensure the efficient operation of the four hydroelectric power stations in Svetogorsk in Russia and those in Imatra in Finland. The main objective of the Agreement is to regulate the flow of water and energy, especially the water levels. Since the agreed water levels will result in a decline of the flow of water and energy in Finland, Russia provides an annual compensation to Finland by the supply of electric power (Articles 3 and 4). The Water Commission is responsible for the verification of the implementation of the Vuoksi Agreement with respect to matters concerning the use of water resources as well as the settlement of any differences of opinion arising from the interpretation or application of the Agreement (Article 5). The responsibility for the supply of compensatory electric power, however, remains with national public authorities (Article 5).

The regulation of water levels of Lake Saimaa is critical for a number of different uses. These include wood processing plants, timber floating, fishing, and recreation. One of the main reasons for the regulation of water levels of Lake Saimaa is the prevention of flooding. The Watercourse Commission has had to take some preventive measures since it came into existence. Information was exchanged between the Contracting Parties on dangerous water levels (cf., Article 17 FA). Necessary changes to the water flow were arranged at meetings of the Commission or by telephone, in accordance with guidance of the Commission. It has been said that "[t]he co-operation has been flexible and productive".[9] In 1989, an additional agreement was concluded on the discharge of water.[10] Accordingly, the amount of water discharged from Lake Saimaa, and its water level, will follow natural limits, provided that the water level remains within the so-called normal zone, or differs by 50 cm, at most, from the average level (Article 1 of the Rules of Regulation of Lake Saimaa and Vuoksi River).[11] In this last agreement of 1989, the Watercourse Commission is also entrusted with implementation, as well as settling questions of interpretation (Article 2).

---

[9] M. Ollila and N. Rozkov, *ibid.*, p. 24.

[10] *Ibid.*, p. 25.

[11] 1989 Agreement concerning Rules for the Regulation of Lake Saimaa and River Vuoksi, signed on 26 October 1989, entry into force on 9 October 1991, 1663 *UNTS* 325.

Another agreement which, though not directly related, influences to some extent the work of the Commission as it relates to the same geographical area of the Saimaa, provides for the lease by Russia to Finland of part of the Saimaa Canal and the Malyj Vysotsky Island.[12] This Agreement was concluded to enable Finland to use the Canal and the Island for transport and storage purposes (Article 1). An interesting feature of this Agreement is that it introduces freedom of navigation for commercial purposes for third parties going to and from Finland (Article 2). This freedom of navigation does not, however, cover war ships. All goods are exempted from custom duties (Article 9). Each Party nominates its own representative for the purpose of dealing with the matters concerning the management of the Canal and the adoption of decisions relating to the Agreement. All decisions are to be taken by unanimity (Article 14).

2.2 The Agreement concerning Regulation of Lake Inari

2.2.1 *Introduction*

In order to present a full picture of the legal basis of frontier watercourse co-operation between Finland and Russia, mention must also be made of the bilateral arrangements which flow directly from a trilateral agreement between Finland, Norway and Russia on the regulation of the Lake Inari ("Lake Inari Agreement").[13] This Agreement vested in Russia the right to regulate the water levels of Lake Inari by means of the Kaitakoski Hydroelectric Power Station and Dam within the limits of the water levels in the control reservoir of Lake Inari – a minimum of 115.67 metres above sea level and a maximum 118.03 metres above sea level.

---

[12] 1962 Agreement on the Transfer for Rent of the Saimaa Canal and Part of the Island of Maly Vysotsky, signed on 27 September 1962, entry into force on 30 September 1963, 479 *UNTS* 122; 1964 Protocol to the Agreement of 27 September 1962 on the Transfer for Rent of the Saimaa Canal and Part of the Island of Maly Vysotsky, signed on 11 August 1964, entry into force on 13 September 1964, *Suomen Asetuskokoelman* (1964), No. 47.

[13] 1959 Agreement between the Government of Norway and the Government of Finland concerning the Regulation of Lake Inari by Means of the Kaitakoski Hydroelectric Power Station and Dam, which was signed on 9 April 1959, entry into force on the date of signature, 346 *UNTS* 209.

2.2.2 *Participants*

The main participants in the implementation of the Lake Inari Agreement are the Ministry of Electric Power Station Construction of the former USSR [now the Ministry of the Russian Federation], the Royal Norwegian Ministry of Industry and Handicraft and the Ministry of Transport and Public Works of Finland. These Ministries are responsible for the amendment of the Regulation to the Agreement, which constitutes an integral part of the Lake Inari Agreement. The Regulation, indeed, is the operative part of the Agreement, which has to be followed by the Russian Government in relation to its exploitation of Lake Inari. Amendments to the Regulation are to be made by the consent of the three Ministers (Article 2 of the Lake Inari Agreement).

2.2.3 *Compensation Procedure*

The Lake Inari Agreement superseded the 1947 Agreement that ceded the right to regulate the dam at Niskakoski from Finland to the former Soviet Union. The actual right to regulate the lake was granted to the Soviet Nickel Company (Article 1). In return for this exclusive right, the Soviet Union agreed to pay to Finland an amount of 75 million Marks for any harm which might be caused as a result of regulation of the Lake and as a result of the works which Soviet Union was to carry out in connection with the regulation of the Lake (Article 5). The payment was effected prior to the beginning of the works. The Lake Inari Agreement (Article 1 of the Additional Protocol) seems to confirm that this payment under the 1947 Agreement was indeed made and thus "exonerates the Soviet Union from all responsibility for harm caused by the regulation of the Lake".[14] This provision constitutes an interesting example of a case of conditional consent for any harm that would otherwise, under general rules, result in state responsibility for damage.

2.2.4 *Dispute Settlement Procedure*

Any dispute arising between the three Ministries concerning the applica-

[14] See R. Lefeber, *supra* note 6, p. 104.

tion of the Lake Inari Agreement are settled by a Mixed Commission composed of two Members appointed by the Norwegian Ministry and two Members appointed by the Finnish Ministry and two by the Russian Ministry. If agreement is not reached by the Mixed Commission, the dispute is to be settled by the Soviet Government, the Norwegian Government and the Finnish Government through diplomatic channels (Article 7 of the Lake Inari Agreement).

2.2.5 *The Protocol on Fish Breeding and Conservation of Fish Stocks*

The 1983 Protocol on Fish Breeding and Conservation of Fish stocks in Lake Inari is based on the trilateral agreement on Lake Inari.[15] The right of participation in fish breeding activities for the conservation of fish stocks is vested in a formerly Soviet private organization that co-operates with Finnish private organizations. This was effected by the Government of the former Soviet Union expressing its agreement to the wishes of the Government of Finland for such participation (Article 1). Participation in the breeding and conservation of fish stocks is done through the provision of electricity from the Russian Federation to Finland for the establishment of a fish-breeding establishment with fish hatchery constructed in Finland (Article 1). The expenses of the Russian private organization were assumed by the former Soviet Union (Article 2).

2.3 **The Frontier Commission**

2.3.1 *Introduction*

The Frontier Commission is established under the Frontier Agreement (Article 24 FA) and fulfils tasks related to the common frontier, including frontier waters (Part II FA). The Frontier Agreement is relevant to the use of frontier watercourses insofar as it relates to transport and fisheries.

[15] 1983 Protocol between the Government of the Republic of Finland and the Government of the Union of Soviet Socialist Republics on the Participation of Soviet organisations in Fish Breeding Activities for the Conservation of Fish Stocks in Lake Inari, signed on 14 December 1983, entry into force on the date of signature, 1351 *UNTS* 142.

From this it follows that the Frontier Commission has some duties relating to these watercourses. The Frontier Commission consists of Commissioners appointed by Finland and the Russian Federation as well as their deputies and assistants (Article 24 FA). The main task of the Frontier Commission is to prevent and, where applicable, investigate frontier incidents and settle claims arising from them (Articles 29 and 31-33 FA). Such incidents may, amongst others, relate to the illegal crossing of the frontier by river and on ships and boats; discovery of fishing vessels and fishing equipment and timber that happen to be in the territory of the other Party as a result of natural causes; moving, damaging, or destruction of frontier or navigation channel marks; or the movement of reindeer across the frontier.

2.3.2 *The Functioning of the Frontier Commission*

The Commission, consisting of frontier commissioners and their deputies (assistant commissioners), ordinarily performs its functions at formal and informal meetings (Article 35.1 FA). Minor questions may be settled by correspondence or other means of communication between the frontier commissioners unless either commissioner insists that such a question be dealt with at a formal or informal meeting. Assistant commissioners normally perform their functions at informal meetings (Article 35.2 FA). Decisions of assistant commissioners do not have legal effect until confirmed by the frontier commissioners. Matters on which assistant commissioners cannot agree must be referred to the frontier commissioners for settlement. Minutes are drawn up on the occasion of each formal and informal meeting (Article 35.3 FA). A formal or informal meeting takes place at the request of one of the commissioners and if possible at the time mentioned in the request (Article 36 FA). By agreement between the frontier commissioners, formal and informal meetings may also take place between their deputies. Informal meetings between assistants may only take place by order of the frontier commissioners.

2.3.3 *Dispute Settlement Procedure*

The Frontier Commission has a duty to take all measures within its power to settle frontier incidents (Article 32.1 FA). Each commissioner may, at his or her discretion, refer any matter of particular importance for settlement through diplomatic channels after notifying the frontier commissioner of the other Party. Some frontier incidents of particular gravity, such as homicide, are in any event referred back for settlement through the diplomatic channel (Article 32.2 FA). In such cases, however, the frontier commissioners make the necessary inquiries into the incident and record the results at a joint meeting. Any matter may be referred back from the diplomatic channel to the frontier commissioners for settlement (Article 33.3 FA). The decisions taken jointly by the frontier commissioners are final and binding with immediate effect, as soon as the minutes drawn up on the matter investigated are signed (Article 32.4 FA).

Claims for damages are also dealt with by the frontier commissioners. The amount of compensation due to each Party, on the basis of the agreement arrived at concerning damages, is calculated by the frontier commissioners quarterly as of 31 March, 30 June and 31 December. For the determination of amounts to be paid, the frontier commissioners submit appropriate statements to the Ministries of Foreign Affairs of Finland and the Russian Federation. The procedure for the final settlement is effected through diplomatic channels (Article 33 FA).

2.3.4 *Frontier Guards*

The Watercourse Commission has been helped during its thirty-year existence by frontier guards acting on behalf of the Frontier Commission.[16] These frontier guards were particularly effective during the Soviet era in helping to organize meetings of the Watercourse Commission's working groups and to provide assistance to the Watercourse Commission in fulfilment of its many practical tasks. At present the frontier guards still play a considerable role in the organization of meetings at border sections which have no official crossing. The frontier guards, amongst others, supervise the fishing and sampling activities of the Watercourse Commission. The frontier guards, for example, facilitate the access of the Water-

[16] "Frontier Guards Assist the Commission", in *Cooperation on the Frontier Watercourses during Thirty Years, supra* note 8, p. 53

course Commission to Lake Paanajarvi, which is situated entirely within Russia, and also deliver the Watercourse Commission's mail.[17]

2.4 The Reindeer Agreement

As seen in Chapter 3, together with fishing and hunting, the herding of reindeers is one of the activities which traditionally forms part of Saami culture. Water plays an important role in the herding of reindeers. Although the 1965 Agreement concerning Reindeer may not on the face of it appear to be directly linked to the management of frontier watercourses, the interdependence between water and reindeer herding is a factor that is taken into consideration by the Watercourse Commission in its decision-making.[18]

The Reindeer Agreement is related to the Frontier Agreement. The Agreement was concluded to ensure that supervision is exercised over herds of reindeer in their frontier areas with a view to preventing reindeer, in so far possible, from crossing the border (Article 1). The geographical scope of the Reindeer Agreement covers areas adjoining the Finnish-Russian State frontier at the junction of the frontiers of Finland, Russia and Norway. Only domesticated reindeer are covered by the Agreement, not wild reindeer (Article 2).

The frontier commissioners appointed under the Frontier Agreement are designated as competent authorities under the Reindeer Agreement with respect to frontier crossing of reindeer (Article 2). On the basis of the Reindeer Agreement, if herds of reindeer cross the border, the competent authorities of the Contracting Party from whose territory the reindeer came are promptly notified (Article 3). The competent authorities of this Contracting Party have to send a permanent drover team to take the reindeer back, unless the competent authorities of the Contracting Party whose territory the reindeer have entered decide to return the reindeer to the other side of the frontier by use of their own resources (Articles 4 and 5).

---

[17] Frontier Guards Assist the Commission, *ibid.*, p. 55: "[w]e are the only functioning connection between Finland and the Soviet Union and we are still the best. Regardless of time of the day a letter from the Finnish decision-makers is delivered to the border it is forwarded immediately to the Russian decision-makers".

[18] Signed on 4 June 1965, entry into force on 12 March 1966, 560 *UNTS* 180.

The Contracting Party whose territory the reindeer enter is entitled to claim compensation for their unauthorised stay in foreign territory, amounting up to 5% of the value of the reindeer counted (Article 7). The value of the reindeer is determined on the basis of the prices for reindeer prevailing during the second half of November in the country to which the reindeer belong. The competent authorities exchange information concerning these prices in December each year. If, after ten days, the Party to which reindeer belong has failed to comply with a request to send drovers to take the reindeer back, the competent authorities of the Party in whose territory reindeer are present without authorization may send a second notification, upon which that Party will become entitled to claim an additional 10% of the value of the reindeer counted. If this procedure does not produce any effect, the Party to which the reindeer belong forfeits any right to their return (Article 7). This Contracting Party also has to compensate the other Party for the actual costs of searching for reindeer, separating them, and sending them back, as well as for any damage caused by them or the reindeer drovers, on the territory of that other Party (Article 8). The sums due for the unauthorised stay of reindeer on the territory of one Party, calculated under Articles 7 and 8, are paid in the manner prescribed in Article 33 of the Frontier Agreement (see above) and in accordance with the procedure for the settlement of frontier incidents and with the trade and payment agreement between Finland and Russia (Article 9).

2.5 An Overview of Finnish-Russian Institutions

The work of the Watercourse Commission has been very successful so far. Finnish-Russian bilateral watercourse agreements are part of a general network of international legal arrangements which are also connected with, and take into consideration, other legal instruments such as the Frontier Agreement. The variety of legal arrangements reflects a very rich field of co-operation between the two countries, which has a long history, as described earlier in Chapter 4.[19] The achievements of the Commission

[19] Thus, the present Watercourse Agreement, which established the Watercourse Commission, was preceded by agreements from the 1920s and 1930s which mainly covered the operation of channels, log floating and fishing. These earlier treaties, however, lacked

include the environmental regulation of the Saimaa and Vuoksi Rivers (see above) and of the southern Saimaa River, and their protection from wastewater from the pulp and paper industry as well from the Imatra steelworks, and from municipal waste.[20] This waste is treated at biological water purification plants and activated sludge plants, except for the waste waters from Lesogorsk, which is treated at a biological filter plant. Waste water from the Imatra steelworks undergo chemical and mechanical treatment. Waste from the Svetogorsk mills is treated at an activated sludge plant and, in addition, the biologically purified water goes through a flotation filter with a great percentage of purification. At the Kamennogorsk paper mill no purification system is provided for, but the waste from the paper mill containing fibres are treated in a flotator to recover the fibres. In a plastic factory of Lesogorsk no waste water is produced but only cooling water which is led to the Vuoksi River.[21]

Co-operation between Finland and the Russian Federation on the observation of the state of the frontier watercourses started as far back as 1965, i.e. at the time the Watercourse Agreement entered into force. All major frontier rivers were monitored as of 1966. The quality of water in the majority of frontier watercourses has greatly improved, and this is

---

an institutional element. Dr. Manner, who undertook the groundwork in relation to study of the general legal position of watercourses, chaired a committee set up in 1960 by the Finnish Ministry of Trade and Industry in order to study the situation of international watercourses between the then Soviet Union and Finland and to prepare the future watercourse agreement; see S. Jaatinen, "Joint Finnish-Russian Commission on the Utilization of Frontier Watercourses-Cooperation at its Best", *supra* note 8, pp. 11-15.

[20] The town of Imatra (37,000 inhabitants), the Imatra steelworks, the Svtegogorsk (17,000 inhabitants), the Svetogorsk pulp and paper mill (pulp production 233,702 tonnes in 1993 and 144,006 tonnes in 1994), the community of Lesogorsk (3,000 inhabitants), the Kammenogorsk paper mill (paper production 8,000 tonnes in 1994), and the community of Kammenogorsk (6,000 inhabitants) discharge their waste to Vuoksi River, data from R.S. Wirkkala and I. Kettunen, "Water Quality of the River Vuoksi on the Finnish and Russian Sides", in *Cooperation on the Frontier Watercourses During Thirty Years*, *supra* note 8, pp. 61-68.

[21] The Vuoksi River is also polluted by phosphor and nitrogen. The load from the Finnish side accounts for about 9.6% of nitrogen and 9.6% phosphorous. The biggest point source is Svetogorsk paper and pulp mill, accounts for about 2.7% and 9.7% of the pollution load of the Vuoksi River; data from R.S. Wirkkala and I. Kettunen, *ibid.*, pp. 67-68.

mainly as a result of this far-reaching joint monitoring programme established by these two states.

Co-operation between Finland and the Russian Federation also stems from multilateral environmental co-operation, such as the UNECE Convention on the Protection and Use of Transboundary Watercourses and International Lakes.[22] This Convention has been ratified by both Finland and Russia. It has introduced a joint monitoring system (Article 4) that is now followed by both States. This is apparent in the Water Commission's recommendations relating to the Vuoksi and Hiitolanjoki Rivers. The Water Commission recommended to monitor a variable selection of pollutants[23] complemented with total nitrogen, total phosphorous, heavy metals, and certain organic compounds in the Vuoksi and Hiitolanjoki Rivers, thus reconciling the Finnish and Russian concerns.[24] The Water Commission also conducts a broad programme of research in relation of fish, especially salmon, brown trout, perch, etc.[25]

In 1992, a bilateral agreement was concluded between the Russian Federation and Finland on co-operation in relation to the protection of environment.[26] This agreement was concluded in order "to solve ecological problems and exploit rationally natural resources in accordance with the principle of sustainable development" (Preamble). This Agreement was concluded as a follow up to the 1974 Convention on the Protection of the Marine Environment of the Baltic Sea Area which was revised in 1992.[27]

---

[22] 31 *ILM* 1312 (1992), discussed in Chapter 2.

[23] Because these rivers are exposed to loads caused by forest industry, the variables include biological and chemical oxygen demand, suspended solids and sodium. Additionally, the Russians stress monitoring of mineral oils, phenols and anionic tensides.

[24] L. Kauppi, L.S. Tsikurejeva, S. Antikainen and M. Korhonen, "Protection and Monitoring of the Frontier Watercourses", in *Cooperation on the Frontier Watercourses During Thirty Years, supra* note 8, pp. 29-37.

[25] P. Tuunainen, A.M. Kutizov, H. Auvinen and A. Niemelä, "Fish Studies in Joint Finnish- Russian Frontier Water-Courses", in *Cooperation on the Frontier Watercourses During Thirty Years, supra* note 8, pp. 39-51. The research is especially conducted in Lake Pyhäjärvi, River Tuulomajoki, Luttojoki and Nuorttijoki for salmon. Joint fishery regulations are now being drawn up for the Luttojoki and Oulankajoki watercourses.

[26] 1992 Agreement Concerning Co-operation on the Field of Environmental Protection, signed on 29 April 1992, entered into force 14 January 1993, 1721 *UNTS* 362.

[27] Signed on 24 March 1974, entered into force on 3 May 1980, 13 *ILM* 546 (1974). Revised by the 1992 Convention on the Protection of the Marine Environment of the Bal-

The main principle of the co-operation envisaged by this Agreement is included in Article 1 which states that Parties shall develop and strengthen co-operation in the field of environmental protection in accordance with the principle of sustainable development, taking into account interests of both Contracting Parties. The scope of the Agreement is broad and includes in particular protection of the atmosphere, protection of watercourses and the marine environment, protection of biodiversity, management of waste, measures against noise, monitoring of environmental research, technology of environmental protection, ecological upbringing and education, implementation of management and lawmaking in the field of environmental protection, exchange of information, creation of joint technological and economic projects, organization of joint seminars and exhibitions, exchange of experts, and other bilaterally agreed measures. The responsible organs for the implementation of the above measures are in Finland in the Ministry of Environment, and in Russia, the Ministry of Ecological and Natural Resources (Article 6). A special commission was established for the detailed implementation of this Agreement (Article 7). This Special Commission shall confirm the particular tasks and the methods of co-operation, and the organs that are responsible for it. The Commission can, if necessary, establish working groups in order to decide jointly agreed directions and problems. The financing of the co-operation shall be affected on the basis of joint agreed measures between the parties of the Commission (Article 8). The Parties shall broaden the co-operation between the local organs and the companies as well as general organizations in the field of environmental protection of both parties (Article 9).

Another area of watercourse co-operation relates to the so-called "nearby area co-operation". This started in 1992 in the Kymi Water and Environment District – on the Finnish side of the border – and in several authorities, research institutes and industrial units in the St. Petersburg District and the city of St. Petersburg, district of Murmansk – on the Russian side of the border.[28] On the Finnish side, the party responsible for

tic Sea Area, signed on 9 April 1992, entered into force on 17 January 2002, at <http://www.helcom.fi/helcom/convention.html>

[28] The bases of co-operation are: 1992 Agreement on Co-operation between Nearby Areas, signed on 20 January 1992, *Suomen säädöskokoelman* 1992, No. 61-62; 1992

this co-operation is the Environmental Agency of South-East Finland. The scope of co-operation covers the Saimaa Canal and the Vuoksi River as well as the Eastern part of the Gulf of Finland. As pointed out above, these areas are heavily polluted. As part of the co-operation between the nearby districts, the Kymi Water and Environment District has carried out planning of water protection activities, waste water and watercourse studies, comparisons of water analysis methods, and practical training.[29] This co-operation is very broad and and it provides for the establishment of mutual trade relations, the utilization of natural resources, the development of agriculture and food industry, the enhancement of transport and communication, and the safety of nuclear plants, in addition to the establishment of appropriate management mechanisms. The Parties take into consideration the development of cultural and educational links between population, including young people. The list provided in Article 2 of the above mentioned 1992 Agreement is not exclusive and foresees the possibility of broadening of the scope of co-operation if necessary. The Parties also undertook to develop bilateral regional and local co-operation (Article 3).

Agreement Concerning Co-operation in the Field of Environmental Protection, signed on 29 April 1992, entry into force on 14 January 1993, 1721 *UNTS* 362; 1992 Agreement on Water Pollution Action Programme, signed on 26 May 1992, *Suomen säädöskokoelman* 1992, No. 77; 1992 UNECE Convention on the Protection and Use of Transboundary Watercourses and International Lakes, signed on 17 May 1992, entry into force on 6 October 1996, 31 *ILM* 1312 (1992).Agreement on the Protection of the Baltic Sea signed on 24 March 1974, entered into force on 3 May 1980, 13 *ILM* 546 (1974). Revised by the 1992 Convention on the Protection of the Marine Environment of the Baltic Sea Area, signed on 9 April 1992, entered into force on 17 January 2002 See, for further description of the institutional co-operation between the two countries, <http://www.laaninhallitus.fi/lh/lappi/kvasiat/home.nsf/pages/E4E3EFB2151D5C77C2256C55002BDAA9>.

[29] In 1994, co-operation in the field of environment information management was started between St. Petersburg area and the Leningrad district and Finland. The Agreement was signed between Kymi Water and Environment District and the Environmental centre of the national Board of Waters and Environment and Lenkomekologia. In 1995, a programme of the special protection of the Bay of Vyborg has started. See O. Vallo and E. Kleemola, "Nearby Area Cooperation with St. Petersburg and the Leningrad District to Improve Protection of Watercourses", in *Cooperation on the Frontier Watercourses During Thirty Years, supra* note 8, pp. 57-59.

2.6 Conclusions

Finnish-Russian co-operation in the field of watercourses forms a complex and advanced international legal system. It covers, as pointed out above, many areas that are not usually covered by agreements of this type in other regions of the world. The functions of the Water Commission are varied, including pollution control, fisheries, transport energy, and construction activities. It is also important to note the Commission's decision-making procedures. While decisions reached unanimously are directly binding on the Parties to the Watercourses Agreement, in the practice of the Commission, decision are adopted by consensus. Thus, the decisions bind the Parties rather because, after long discussion, agreement is reached and problems solved than because they constitute a peremptory means of international decision-making.

3. Norway and Russia

The Joint Norwegian-Russian Commission on Environmental Co-operation Commission was set up on the basis of an Agreement concluded in 1988 between both states.[30] The duration of the agreement was initially for five years, with automatic renewal unless one of the parties exercises the right to terminate the agreement in the period of six months prior to its expiry (Article 10.1). Article 1 of this Agreement provides that the co-operation between the two parties in relation to the protection of the environment will be conducted on the principles of reciprocity and equality. Among the designated issues of co-operation are the following: atmospheric protection, protection of the marine environment, the protection of ecological systems, rare species of fauna and flora, monitoring the exchange of information on, *inter alia,* scientific research projects and adopted measures (Article 2.2.a-e).

[30] 1988 Agreement between the Kingdom of Norway and the Government of the USSR on Co-operation in the Field of Environmental Protection, signed 15 January 1988, entered into force on same day, text on file with authors.

For the purpose of management and co-ordination relating to the implementation of this agreement, the Parties set up a joint Norwegian-Russian Commission on Co-operation in the Field of Environmental Projection with each Party appointing Commissioners (Article 6.3). This Commission, which meets once a year, assesses proposals relating to co-operation programmes and defines the institutions and organizations responsible for their implementation, and also adopts non-binding recommendations directed at the Parties. The Commission is empowered to establish working groups on special fields and problems of co-operation (Article 6.1-6).

In 1992 the two Parties concluded a second agreement extending and supplementing the agreement of 1989.[31] The fundamental principles remained the same, but the objectives of the 1992 Agreement are more extensive, and include for instance provisions on environmental education, as well as measures to be taken in case of emergency (Articles 2 and 6). Economic, financial and legal issues arising will be resolved on the basis of negotiation between interested organizations in both Parties (Article 5).

In view of the above, it can be seen that the Joint Norwegian-Russian Commission is a more typical body of its kind, possessing, in the main, advisory powers in relation to various issues relating to watercourse co-operation within the general framework of ecological co-operation.[32]

---

[31] 1992 Agreement between the Kingdom of Norway and the Government of the Russian Federation on co-operation in the Field of Environmental Protection, signed on 13 September 1992, in force, text on file with authors.

[32] Mention should also be made of arrangements for less formal co-operation under the auspices of the OSPAR Commission, in respect of the area of the Barents Sea and the Murmansk region that are particularly vulnerable to pollution from the heavy industry in this area. This co-operation will be effected under the framework of the OSPAR surveillance system and will also extend invitations to Russian observers, despite the fact that Russia is not a Party to this Agreement. See <http://doksenter.svanhovd.no/engelsk/work_prog/northen_sea.html>.

4. Norway and Finland

A commission was set up in 1980 pursuant to an Agreement on a Finnish-Norwegian Transboundary Water Commission,[33] with the aim of preserving the environment along the frontier watercourses and with the intention of securing the interests of both parties, with special regard for the interests of the populations in the boundary areas regarding the use of the frontier watercourses. Russian representatives participate as observers in the work of this Commission. Pursuant to Article 1, the Commission is to serve as a co-ordination and collaboration committee between the governments of Norway and Finland on questions concerning shared watercourses. The commission is instructed to draw up proposals as necessary, and it is required to take the initiative regarding matters that affect the management of the boundary watercourses between Norway and Finland, such as the supervision and control of the quantity and quality of water, conditions for fishing, prevention of water pollution. The relevant authorities of the Contracting Parties shall notify the frontier watercourse commission about their plans which may in any discernible way affect of have influence on boundary watercourses or where realization of plans in any way will affect watercourses (Article 1).

The geographical area covered includes parts of river Inari and Tana river through which the demarcation line runs, as well as those lakes, rivers and brooks across which the demarcation line runs. The agreement will also apply to those watercourse areas of which these watercourses form a part (Article 2). The Governments of each Contracting Party appoints three members to the commission, of which one is required to have experience of the management of watercourses, and one shall be a person with sufficient knowledge of the conditions of the frontier (Article 3). The Commission can summon experts and also shall, as required, hear the points of views of representatives of local communities (Article 5).

[33] Set up on 5 November 1980; translation of the text on file with the authors. See further the internet site of the Lapland Regional Environment Centre, at <http://www.environment.fi/default.asp?node=9813&lan=en>. See further <http://www.environment.fi/default.asp?contentid=37001&lan=en> (where the observation is made that [t]ransboundary water commissions can promote a variety of cooperation between neighbouring countries".

The Commission has the right to communicate with relevant authorities in each of the Contracting Parties in order to assist with research and reporting.

5. Finland and Sweden

5.1 **Introduction**

The Finnish-Swedish Frontier River Commission (FSFRC) is the international body set up under the 1971 Agreement between Finland and Sweden Concerning Frontier Rivers (FSFRC Agreement) between Finland and Sweden (Chapter 2, Article 1).[34] The Agreement was signed on 16 September 1971 and it entered into force on 1 January 1972. The objective of the Agreement is to manage the watercourse system that both constitutes, and lies on either side of, the greater part of the border between these two countries.

5.1.1 *Geographical Scope*

The total geographical area covered by the jurisdiction of the FSFRC amounts to about 75,000 km^2. The area runs along the 546 km. border shared between Finland and Sweden. It comprises the following specific water areas: the Rivers Könkämä and Muonio as well as the part of River Torne and the lakes through which the Finnish-Swedish frontier runs (the frontier rivers), the lakes and watercourses which constitute side branches of tributaries of the frontier rivers, the special outflows formed by the separate arms of the mouth of the River Torne, and the part of the Gulf of Bothnia which lies within the Finnish and Swedish parishes of Nedertorneå (Chapter 1, Article 1). Thus, in global terms the jurisdiction of the Commission covers watercourses extending from the northern part of the Baltic Sea almost up to the Norwegian coast of the Atlantic.

[34] 825 *UNTS* 191.

5.1.2 *Scope of Activities*

The FSFRC Agreement covers hydraulic construction works and water regulation, including pollution caused by such uses; fishing; and timber floating (Chapter 1, Article 2).

5.1.3 *Structure and Composition of the FSFRC*

The FSFRC consists of six members (Chapter 2, Article 2). The Government of each state appoints three members. Each member is appointed for an unspecified period. One member of each state must be well versed in law and possess judicial experience; one must be a technician; and the third must be acquainted with the conditions of the borderland (the Finnish member should be appointed on the basis of a recommendation from Lappland County Administration and the Swedish member on the basis of a recommendation of the Norrbotten County Administration). The necessity of the broadening of the expert participation relating to the conditions of the area in the Aldval region was the subject of a Parliamentary question in Finland. The proposal was considered to be unnecessary and too expensive.[35] Both Governments alternately appoint one of the respective members for one year at a time to be a chairman and deputy chairman of the Commission, respectively. The Commission has secretarial staff at its disposal. The FSFRC may employ experts for special investigations (Chapter 2, Article 3).

Members and officials of the Commission, in the exercise of their duties, enjoy legal protection in accordance with the provisions of the law relating to persons employed in public service in the state where the duties are exercised. The responsibility of the members of the Commission for their official actions is governed by the municipal law of the state of the government by which he or she was appointed, not international law (Chapter 2, Article 5). The members of the FSFRC do not enjoy diplomatic immunities. On the other hand, the property of the FSFRC itself is

---

[35] Response to parliamentary question by the Minister of Agriculture of 18 June 1987, Esko-Juhani Tennila. It was considered that all the members of the Commission have the knowledge of the region. 1987, KK No. 86 (Finnish Parliamentary Reports).

exempt from customs formalities, and from import and export duties (Chapter 2, Article 7).

5.2 Scope of the FSFRC's Functions

Generally, the Commission's functions include virtually all matters, both judicial and administrative, which may affect the use and development of the watercourse, including matters relating to construction, the regulation of water flow, fishing, and protection of the watercourse from pollution.

5.2.1 *Hydraulic Construction Works*

The jurisdiction of the FSFRC covers the construction of installations in a watercourse, the regulation of the water level or flow, the diversion of water and any other measure that may result in a change in the water level or flow or in the depth or position of the water. In addition, it covers measures that may affect the groundwater conditions, the construction of a bridge or other installation over a watercourse, and the laying of pipes or the construction of other installations underwater (Chapter 3, Article 1). The works must be carried out without unreasonable cost, and with the least possible damage and inconvenience to other interests in either state (Chapter 3, Article 2).

If damage or inconvenience is caused as a result of the works, they may only be carried out if "they can be shown to bring public or private benefit that *substantially* outweighs the inconvenience" (emphasis added) (Chapter 3, Article 3, 1st paragraph). Thus, the permission of works is subject to the balancing of interests. This test is stricter if the works result in "a substantial deterioration in the living conditions of the population or cause a permanent change in natural conditions such as might entail substantially diminished comfort for people living in the vicinity or a significant nature conservancy loss or where significant public interests would be otherwise prejudiced". In such a case, permission may only be given if "it is of particular importance for the economy or for the locality or from some other public standpoint" (Chapter 3, Article 3, 2nd paragraph). If the works have a harmful effect on fishing, the person responsible for the works must take or pay for reasonable measures to protect the fish stock or maintain fishing of an equal standard (Chapter 3, Article 7) and to prevent inconvenience to traffic or timber floating (Chapter 3, Article 8). If the works cause a substantial change in water conditions, the person responsible for the works may be required to pay a specified annual charge (Chapter 3, Article 10).

5.2.2 *Fisheries*

The jurisdiction of the FSFRC with respect to fishing is limited to a special area. This special area is constituted by the frontier rivers with their branches and outflows as well as the parts of the Gulf of Bothnia situated within the Finnish and Swedish parishes of Nedertorneå north of latitude 65°35'N (River Torne fishing area) (Chapter 5, Article 1). The FSFRC's jurisdiction extends to the designation of fish ways (Chapter 5, Article 2). The Agreement establishes reserve zones in certain parts of the special area in or in the vicinity of the sea and confer responsibility on local authorities, namely the county authorities in Norrbotten county and Lappland county, to establish reserve zone in other areas (Chapter 5, Article 3). With the exception of permitted hydraulic construction works, the deployment of fishing gear or other devices that hinder fishing in fish ways or reserve zones is prohibited (Chapters 5, Articles 2 and 3). The FSFRC may, however, grant exceptions in fish ways provided that this will present a danger to fish conservation or cause substantial injury to any person who has not agreed to the measures in question (Chapter 5, Article 2). The competence of the FSFRC extends to the adoption of technical measures with respect to fishing (Chapter 5, Articles 4 to 7). The FSFRC is especially concerned with the conditions for fishing of salmon and trout population. Fishing in the fishery zone of the River Torne is regulated in an annex to the Agreement (Annex B) that sets out in great detail rules for fishery protection and exploitation in the designated by the Agreement areas, in particular fishing gear, open and closed seasons, as well as establishing liability for violations of the Agreement, with the FSFRC having significant discretion in implementing the abovementioned provisions and granting exceptions. (Annex B, Article 22).

5.2.3 *Pollution*

The Agreement provides general guidance as to the nature and extent of the prevention of pollution of the watercourses. Solid and liquid substances may not be discharged into the water area to a greater extent than is permitted under the Agreement if such discharge causes damage or inconvenience to public or private interests (Chapter 6, Article 1).

The Agreement provides for the application of national law of Finland and Sweden, namely legislation on public health, construction and nature conservation as well as legislation relating to protection against certain kinds of water pollution in the state where the discharge takes place or is intended to take place (Chapter 6, Article 2).

With the exception of hydraulic construction, the provisions relating to the prevention of pollution govern the use of land, building, or an installation in a manner which may result in pollution of a water area (Chapter 6, Article 3). Such use of land, building or installation may only take place if such precautions are taken as may reasonably be required in order to prevent or relieve inconvenience, taking into account available technical means as well as public and private interests (Chapter 6, Article 6). If in spite of precautions such use of land, building, or installation may cause "substantial inconvenience [...] the operations may be carried out only if special reasons exist for doing so" (Chapter 6, Article 7, paragraph 1). As is the case with hydraulic construction works, the operations may not be carried out if the inconvenience "entails a substantial deterioration in living conditions for a large number of people or a significant loss from the standpoint of nature conservancy or any similar substantial damage to the public interest" (Chapter 6, Article 7, paragraph 2).

The jurisdiction of the FSFRC in the field of pollution prevention extends to the granting of permissions in the areas of activities described above. The FSFRC may, if it deems necessary on account of the nature and effects of the activity or for another reason, submit to the examination of the Governments of Finland and Sweden the question of the permissibility of the activity and the conditions by which it should be governed, having regard to public interests. Such submission always takes place if either Government reserves the right of examination and notifies the FSFRC thereof before the Commission has decided the question of the permissibility of the activity. If the Commission has already decided the matter, the Governments have no right to investigate it. The FSFRC may also exercise its jurisdiction if the permit has not been granted. It may pass the decision to prohibit any activity or to enjoin a person who conducts or intends to conduct such activity to take preventive measures (Chapter 6, Article 4).

The environment in the FSFRC's area requires protection, because a large complex of metal industries is located close to the mouth of the River Torne in Finland. The FSFRC has issued very detailed regulations concerning the waste from these industries. The FSFRC Agreement describes special control measures relating to the protection of the fish. The owner of the industry complex has to pay a certain amount of money annually for the maintenance and control of fish stocks.

5.3 The Nature of the FSFRC's Functions

5.3.1 *Introduction*

The Commission acts as a national institution in Finland and Sweden in matters within its functional and geographical jurisdiction. The Commission acts both as a licensing board and a water court.[36] Both institutions are known to the legal systems of Finland and Sweden. For example, licensing boards grant permits for environmentally hazardous activities in Sweden (Section 9 Environmental Protection Act).[37] Water-rights courts

---

[36] Water Courts were abolished in Finland as of 1 March 2000 and replaced by regional environmental permit authorities. In Sweden, a new environmental code entered into force as of 1 January 1999 and a new system of environmental courts was established, replacing water courts. There are regional environmental courts established as the district courts, similar to the National Licensing Board for Environmental Protection. The regional Courts acts as appellate courts for decisions of state authorities in environmental questions. The decisions of municipal boards may be appealed to the Environmental Court of Appeal that is linked to the Svea Court of Appeal. Reviews of that court, however, are subject to leave of appeal being granted where the regional environmental court was not of the first instance in the matter. The Environmental Court of Appeal is the final instance in cases and matters that were initially adjudicated by municipalities or administrative authorities. Judgments and decision of the Environmental Court of Appeal that are eligible shall be appealed to the Supreme Court (<http://www.winge.se/pdf/miljbalk-eng.pdf>).

[37] Environmental Protection Act (1969:387).

have jurisdiction over activities relating to rivers, lakes, and other water areas.

The FSFRC replaces these courts in its jurisdictional area and exercises similar powers. The Commission is competent in the field of the following functions over matters within its jurisdiction: judicial functions, administrative functions, and supervisory functions.

Although the creation of the Commission and the application of a number of principles by it may originate in international law, the FSFRC is not an international organization that applies principles of international law between states or whose decisions are intended to be enforceable exclusively through the application of international law. The FSFRC exercises a mixture of international and domestic powers. The functions of the FSFRC were previously administered, with regard to the territory of each state, by that state's own water organs. The decision-making of the Commission is primarily based on the Agreement (Chapter 2, Article 3). In the second place, when the Agreement is silent on a matter and does not contain provisions to the contrary, the law prevailing in each state shall apply (Chapter 1, Article 8). Indirectly, the provisions contained in Chapter 1, Article 5, indicate the scope of municipal law sources, including judgments of courts, ancient custom, or other forms of special title that the FSFRC takes into consideration while taking decisions. This aspect distinguishes the Commission from other international bodies set up by an international agreement.

Apart from this general reference to the application of domestic law, the Agreement also includes specific instances of particular use of domestic law. For example, the Chapter on protection against water pollution provides that "[i]n addition to those of this Chapter, the provisions of the legislation concerning health, construction and nature conservancy of the state's special protective legislation against specific types of water pollution" shall apply (Article 2 of Chapter 6). As seen in sub-Section 5.3.3 below, the provision regarding payment of compensation provides yet another example of the use of domestic law.

5.3.2 *Administrative Functions*

Administrative functions – i.e. those functions that are not judicial or supervisory functions – are dealt with by the FSFRC in three ways: either on its own accord or at the request of the competent authority or an entitled party. All members of the Commission participate in administrative decision-making. The basic rule is to achieve unanimity. If unanimity is not achieved, decisions are to be adopted in accordance with a double majority voting rule. The adoption of a decision requires at least four out of six members, of whom two at least from each state. If no decision acquires the required number of votes, the question is considered to have lapsed (Chapter 8, Article 13).

Administrative decisions of the FSFRC are final. On certain matters, decisions of the FSFRC must be approved by the Governments of Finland and Sweden to acquire legal force. These matters are regulated in Article 6 and 7 of Chapter 5 dealing with fishing within the river are for salmon and sea trout with dragnets. These decisions are issued by the FSFRC on the request of one or more natural of legal persons possessing a fishing right, and remain in force for no more than ten years. The decision in question regulates joint fisheries, specifying the area concerned and the rules for the use and administration of the fisheries.

5.3.3 *Judicial Functions*

The judicial functions of the Commission are not as clear as its administrative and supervisory functions. There is a division between its procedural and substantive rules. Some guidance can be found in Article 17 of Chapter 8, which states that a question for examination by the FSFRC other than stated in Article 1 of Chapter 8 must be dealt with by the Commission as an administrative matter. This Article contains a list of matters within the judicial competence of the FSFRC, including permission for hydraulic construction, compensation, water regulation, protection against water pollution, and timber floating.

The most important matter falling within the judicial competence of the Commission is the payment of compensation. Compensation is due in cases in which a person who is entitled under the Agreement to make use of other person's property or to appropriate water powers belonging to another person or otherwise to take measures whereby another person's property suffers damage or encroachment, uses property or causes loss, damage or encroachment. Article 2 of Chapter 7 of the Agreement states that the amount of compensation is to be decided by the FSFRC in case of disagreement. The principle for payment of compensation, the right of the owner of the appropriated or damaged property to demand compulsory purchase, and the manner or time of compensation is governed by the law of the state where the appropriated property is situated or that in which the loss, damage, or encroachment arose (Article 3, Chapter 7).

The basic rule of the FSFRC proceedings is that all members participate in the examination of an application. In the event of differences of opinion, the prevailing view will be that in respect of which at least four members, including at least two from each state, are unanimous. If that fails, and if the question relates to compensation or for a loss, damage or encroachment, or for trial costs, the prevailing opinion will be that which is supported by a majority of members of the states where the property is situated, where the loss, damage, or encroachment occurred or to which the costs relate. In all other questions, disagreement is settled by reference to the Governments (Chapter 8, Article 13). This is one of the few cases, if not the only case, where governmental interference may occur. In practice, it has not happened.

There is the possibility of appeal against the decision of the Commission in matters of compensation for property appropriated or other loss, damage or encroachment. The appeal must be lodged with the Water Court of Appeal, which is to apply applicable rules of municipal law governing appeals in non-criminal water rights cases. The decisions of the Commission have immediate legal force, and may be put into effect notwithstanding the lodging of an appeal against the decision. Only appeals concerning compensation matters can result in a stay of execution. This suggests that the FSFRC is, to all intents and purposes, part of the national judicial system of both states.

5.3.4 *Supervisory Functions*

The FSFRC, in consultation with the proper authorities in each state, exercises supervisory functions over water use, water conditions, and fishing. The supervision is conducted by a specially appointed expert under the legislation of each state. Fishing supervision may be executed through the supervisory patrol common to both states. The FSFRC brings to the notice of the proper authority any observations made concerning conditions in the area of application in order that authority may take action as is incumbent upon it. The appointed expert and the Commission enjoy broad powers to enter premises and conduct an examination. The Commission maintains continuous supervision on the discharge in the outflow of the River Tärendö from the River Thorne.

Article 9 of the Agreement indicates the extent of powers of the Commission. For example, if a person takes a measure which manifestly cannot be implemented without the permission of the FSFRC, the proper authority in the state where the measure is taken may prohibit the continuation of the work until such permission has been granted. If reason exists, it may ordain executorial assistance as a remedy for what unlawfully has taken place. If work for which permission has been obtained is carried out contrary to the regulation prescribed for the work, such ordination may also be issued, unless it is manifest that neither a public nor a private right is violated through infringement. Contravention of certain rules concerning constructing in water or setting permanent fish traps without permission from the Commission, results for a person who realized or reasonably should have realized that permission was required under these provisions in sentencing to a fine, or to imprisonment of at the most one year. A person who had obtained the FSFRC's permission for an undertaking or measure which violates a public or private right is likewise subject to a fine or imprisonment of one year at the most. A fine and a prison sentence up to one year may also be imposed on a person who by intent or negligence infringes the provision of the FSFRC's decisions. The forum for such litigation is the court of first instance in the place where the violation took place.

The penalties for contravening the fishing regulations are contained in the Statute of the River Thorne Fishing Area. Paragraph 24 of the Statute sets the penalties of fine or imprisonment up to six months for certain acts in contravention of the Statute. Other penalties, for example for contravention of technical measures, result only in a fine.

5.4 Relationship between the FSFRC and Finland and Sweden

The main principle, as stated above, of the Commission's jurisdiction is its independent character. However, it appears from the Agreement that the Governments of Finland and Sweden become involved in certain cases. In such cases, the functions of the FSFRC are fulfilled by national organs.

According to the Agreement, one such special area relates to the protection against pollution. The interference of the Governments of Finland and Sweden is envisaged in three different ways. The FSFRC itself may, if it deems necessary, submit questions of permissibility of a potentially polluting activity to the Governments of Finland and Sweden. (Chapter 6, Article 4) Another instance arises when the FSFRC is required to submit questions concerning water related constructions that have particular importance for the population. Finally, the Governments of Finland and Sweden may retain the right to have questions related to both water constructions and protection against pollution, submitted to them for examination. In both instances, the Agreement provides that such submission will only take place if the governments' reservations are notified to the Commission before it has itself reached a decision. (Chapter 3, Article 13).

With respect to the settlement of disputes between Finland and Sweden concerning its interpretation or application, the Agreement refers to the 1924 Convention concerning the Establishment of a Permanent Commission for Investigation and Conciliation (Chapter 10, Article 1).

5.5 Conclusions

In Chapter 2, the main theoretical and practical problems relating to the doctrine of international watercourses were outlined, and it was pointed out that at present, the principle of "equitable utilization" and the duty to co-operate are the main principles on which the co-operation of states in relation to international watercourses is based. The purpose of this Section is to see whether and to what extent the FSFRC Agreement embodies the above-mentioned principles.

The Agreement recognises the "principle of equitable utilization" that is expressed in Article 5 of the 1997 UN Convention on the Law of the Non-Navigational Uses of International Watercourses. Article 1 of Chapter 1 of the Agreement provides that "[i]n the light of the considerations set out in detail in this agreement the waters covered by the agreement shall be used in such a manner that both countries derive benefit from the frontier watercourse and that the interests of the frontier areas are promoted as effectively as possible". The Agreement also seems to adhere to the principle of equitable participation. According to Article 3 of Chapter 1, "[p]articular importance shall be accorded to the interests of nature conservancy; the greatest possible attention shall be given to the preservation of fish stocks and the prevention of water pollution".

The balancing of interests principle, which plays an important role in environmental law, is expressed in the Agreement. The formulation, however, which refers to the fundamental principles governing the co-operation of the parties under the Agreement, is moulded according to the founding principles of the Commission. It relates thus to the potential conflicts and balancing of interests between interested parties, be they the states themselves or individuals, rather than to balancing international interests of the states in a more general way. An example of this may be found in Article 4 of Chapter 1 which states that "[i]n cases involving a number of different projects which affect the same waters or for some other reason cannot be carried out concurrently, preference is given to the project which may be assumed to be of greatest public and private benefit. Conflicting interests shall, in so far as possible, be adjusted in such a way that each may be satisfied without substantial injury to others".

This principle of balancing of interests is further developed in Articles pertaining to particular areas of activities. For example, Article 2 of Chapter 3 provides that "[h]ydraulic construction works shall be carried out in such a way that their purpose is achieved without unreasonable cost and with the least possible damage and inconvenience to other interests in either state. Due regard shall be given to proposed projects that may be affected by that installation". The same principle was embodied in part of Article 3 of Chapter 3 which provides that "[w]here any person would suffer damage or inconvenience as a result of hydraulic construction works, the works shall be carried out only if they can be shown to bring public or private benefits that substantially outweighs the inconvenience".

Similar concepts can be found in Chapter 6 which covers protection against water pollution. Article 6 provides that a person who conducts or intends to conduct a polluting activity must take such protective measures, endure such restrictions on the activity and observe such precautions as may be reasonably required to prevent or remedy a harm; and it further provided that this type of obligation is to be judged on the basis of what is technically feasible for the type of activity concerned and in the light of both public and private interests. This Article reflects Article 6 of the 1997 UN Convention on the Law of the Non-Navigational Uses of International Watercourses. It states that "[i]n weighing the validity of different interests, particular account shall be taken, on the one hand, of he nature of the area that may be exposed to pollution and the magnitude and, on the other hand, of the benefit derived from the operations and the costs of protective measures and other financial implications of the precautions which must be taken". Lammers states that a balanced solution requires observation of the relationship between the nature of the area which may be exposed to pollution and the significance of the pollution, on the one hand, and the usefulness of the activity and the cost of protective measures which may be required, on the other.[38] The embodiment of these concepts of balancing of interests provides a clear example of the extent to which the Agreement envisages the merging of interests of two states.

Another example is that of hydraulic construction. In Article 3 of Chapter 3, it is provided that "where the construction would result in substantial deterioration in living conditions of the population or cause a permanent change in natural conditions such as might entail substantially diminished comfort for people living in the vicinity or a significant nature conservancy loss or where significant public interest would be otherwise prejudiced, the construction shall be permitted only if it is of particular importance for the economy or the locality or from some public standpoint". It is noteworthy that reference is made to the population in general, not to the population of one of the Contracting Parties to the Agreement. Likewise, in balancing of public against private interests, the Agreement does not differentiate between the interests of one or the other of the Contracting Parties. This differentiation is expressly prohibited by the Agreement. According to Article 4 of Chapter 3, "[i]n deciding whether projected construction is to be carried out, conditions in both states shall be given equal weight". The balancing of interests clearly envisages the possibility of harm being allowed to some degree to certain

[38] J.G. Lammers, *Pollution of International Watercourses* (1984), p. 66.

interests, possibly even significant harm,[39] if it can be justified by the benefit derived by other interests.[40]

The above consideration brings us to the question of duty not to cause significant harm as embodied in the Agreement.[41] The treatment of harm as embodied in FSFRC Agreement derives from the special, transnational character of this body. The Agreement includes many provisions concerning the question of harm and compensation, not only in the field of pollution control but also in the fields of water constructions and regulation of diversion of water. The particular character of the Commission also conditions an application of certain international principles in the context of its work. In particular, the notion of one state causing or allowing harm to be caused to the other state is alien to the structure of the FSFRC Agreement and the institutional arrangements under it. Rather, the Agreement establishes a mechanism for the handling by the FSFRC of harm caused to the FSFRC area regardless of the side of the border on which the harm originates or is suffered, or by whom.

The premise on which the FSFRC was set up thus adopts an interesting approach to questions of sovereignty. The establishment of an international body fulfilling functions of a judicial organ as well as an administrative organ in both states to the exclusion of regular national courts (at least in the first instance) and administrative organs can only be possible if the judicial systems, organization of justice, and existing law are as close as they are in Finland and Sweden. This legal proximity allows for a "merged sovereignty" solution. As Lammers puts it, the FSFRC Agreement has set up "an extraordinary machinery whereby the

---

[39] Article 7(1) of Chapter 6 (Protection of Water Pollution) provides as follows: "When it is feared that the [polluting] operations [...] may cause substantial inconvenience even if [...] are taken, the operations may be carried out only if special reasons exist for so doing".

[40] There is, however, a degree of harm which is absolutely banned. For example, Article 7(2) of Chapter 6 continues: "When the anticipated inconvenience entails a substantial deterioration in living conditions for a large number of people of significant loss from the standpoint of nature conservancy or any substantial damage to the public interest, the operation may not be carried out".

[41] For the general consideration on theoretical problems relating to harm, see Chapter 2 above.

[two states] have eliminated many of the defects attaching to the domestic of intergovernmental approach".[42]

6. Concluding Remarks

The institutions considered in this chapter again underline the extent of co-operation with respect to the management and use of shared watercourses in the Nordic states and Russia. The institutions range from mere advisory bodies, such the Norwegian-Finnish Commission, to the more elaborate Finnish-Russian Commission, and then to the highly advanced FSFRC with its unique quasi-judicial nature and semi-international status. This range of institutions, when considered along with the various forms of co-operation described in the previous chapter, should provide a range of options to be considered for the establishment of other mechanisms and institutions for watercourse management in other parts of the world. As stated before, it is significant that such institutions exist between the Nordic countries on the one hand and Russia on the other, in spite of differences in the legal heritage and legal culture. It shows that, where the political will exists, the possibilities for establishing joint management abound, and that suitable institutions for this important aspect of the sustainable use of watercourses can be established with no more than a modest amount of creativity. Nevertheless, the note of caution sounded in the conclusion of the previous chapter concerning the gap between existing rules and procedures on the one hand and actual practice on the other holds; further work will need to be done to assess the use to which these rules and procedure are put in practice.

---

[42] J.G. Lammers, *supra* note 38, p. 67.

Chapter 6
NORDIC WATERCOURSE CO-OPERATION AND THE SUSTAINABLE USE OF WATER

1. Introduction

The sustainable management of water resources is one of the most pressing current global problems, despite a popular belief there is a sufficient supply of water in the world. While oceans cover 70% of the earth's surface, only 2.5% of the water supply on the earth is fresh. The ability of the natural process – the water cycle – to provide enough water to meet global needs is dependent on several factors, such as the limited quantity of fresh water and the fact that fresh water resources are distributed in an uneven manner over the earth's surface.[1] The distribution of water in the world ranges from 10,000 m^3 per capita in some areas to less than 1,000 m^3 in others. The regions of the world that are most affected by water scarcity are the Middle East, North Africa, Central Asia and Sub-Saharan Africa. In contrast, Nordic Europe is one of the regions of the world that has the most ample water supplies.[2]

The scarcity of water has severe consequences. Fresh water supplies are becoming increasingly expensive. People are turned away from their homes by floods, drought and erosion problems.[3] The growth of cities, particularly in developing states, leads to deterioration of water quality and puts strains on its purification system.[4] The sustainable use of water

---

[1] H.L.F. Saeijs and M.J. van Berkel, "The Global Water Crisis: The Major Issue of the Twenty-first Century, A Growing and Explosive Problem", in E.H.P. Brans, E.J. de Haan, A. Nollkaemper, J. Rinzema (eds.), *The Scarcity of Water, Emerging Legal and Policy Responses* (1997) (hereinafter *Scarcity of Water*), pp. 3-4.

[2] Finland has 22,700 m^3/person; Norway 98,100 m^3/person; Sweden 21,300 m^3/person; see P. Raskin, E. Hansen and R.M. Margolis, "Water and Sustainability; Global Patterns and Long-Range Problems", 20 *NRF* (1996), pp. 1-17.

[3] N. Myres, "Eco-refugees: A Crisis in the Making", Vol. 3, issue 4, *People & the Planet* (1994), pp. 6-9.

[4] *Ibid.*, pp. 11-14.

resources is thus affected by geographical, demographic, and economic factors; water may be scarce in rainy but heavily populated and industrialized areas, and the way water is used – for example in agriculture, also has consequences for sustainability.[5] Scarcity of water may of course also lead to international disputes and possibly conflicts, particularly where water resources – including surface water of rivers, lakes or ground water in aquifers – are shared between two or more states or entities.[6] Water disputes are not confined to the regions in which water is scarce or politically unstable regions, as demonstrated by the dispute between Hungary and Slovakia over a hydroelectric system on the River Danube.[7]

2. The Role of Law and the Concept of Sustainable Development

The sustainable use of water resources should be based on a basin-wide integrated planning and management approach,[8] which would require legal regulation. The role of law in this context is dual: it can ensure stability and facilitate the implementation of effective strategies to this end, and it can prevent and resolve disputes. The role of the concept of sustainable development is important in this context, and its legal implications, which have been the subject of considerable attention, need to be examined briefly.

As the name implies, the concept of sustainable development is concerned with the reconciliation of claims to development with environmental concerns. At the Stockholm Conference on the Human Environment in 1972, the growing awareness concerning environmental issues

[5] A. Kiss, "Legal Procedures Applicable to Interstate Conflicts on Water Scarcity: the Gabcíkovo Case", in *Scarcity of Water*, *supra* note 1, p. 60.

[6] H. Donkers, "Fresh Water as a Source of International Conflicts: the Water Conflicts between Israel, Jordan and the Palestinians", in *Scarcity of Water*, *supra* note 1, p. 136.

[7] See, e.g., E. Hoenderkamp, "The Danube: Damned or Dammed? The Dispute between Hungary and Slovakia Concerning the Gabcíkovo-Nagymaros Project", 8 *LJIL* (1995), pp. 287-311; A. Kiss, *supra* note 5, p. 59.

[8] S. McCaffrey, "Water Scarcity: Institutional and Legal Responses", in *Scarcity of Water*, *supra* note 1, pp. 52-54. See also 13 *RECIEL*, Issue 1 (2004).

was matched by the claims of developing states asserting their right to development. The Stockholm Declaration,[9] while recognising the obligation to preserve the environment, underlined the necessity of economic growth and advocated economic assistance to developing countries in order to enable them to meet obligations towards their environment and, at the same time, to secure their right to a clean environment.[10] The starting point in attempting to define the modern concept of sustainable development as such, however, is the 1987 Brundtland Report, where it was defined as development which meets the needs of future generations without compromising the ability of future generations to meet their own needs.[11] In other words, the core of the concept is to ensure living off nature's "income" rather than squandering its "capital".[12] The importance of the concept is palpable. It has been written that "not surprisingly it has turned out to be a notion around which legally significant expectations regarding environmental conduct have begun to crystallise. This concept might turn into a mandatory standard of international legal evaluation".[13] The concept of sustainable development was a guiding principle of the Rio Conference (Earth Summit in 1992).[14] It was considered in general, without assessing all the detailed considerations, as the key to solving the problems to be faced in the reconciliation of economic development and environmental protection, and is clearly reflected in modern treaties, such as the Climate Change Convention and the Biodiversity Convention, both of which were opened for signature in Rio.[15]

It has however been very widely noted that the concept of sustainable development does not easily provide *legal* guidance, as it is very general and imprecise.[16] It is in reality an "umbrella" concept. Although its for-

---

[9] A/Conf.48/14, 11 *ILM* (1972), p. 146.

[10] See, e.g., Principles 8, 9, and 11 of the Declaration.

[11] World Commission on Environment and Development, *Our Common Future* (Brundtland Report, 1987).

[12] G. Handl, "Environmental Security and Global Change", 1 *YIEL* (1990), p. 3 at 24.

[13] *Ibid.*, p. 33.

[14] United Nations Conference on Environment and Development (Rio), Declaration, UN Doc. A/Conf.151/26/Rev.1, Report of the UNCED, Vol. 1.

[15] 31 *ILM* (1992), p. 849, and 822 respectively.

[16] P. Malanczuk, "Sustainable Development: Some Critical Thoughts in the Light of the Rio Conference", in K. Ginther and E. Denters (eds.), *Sustainable Development and Good Governance* (1995), p. 25.

mulation attempts to link development and the environment, the linkage in itself has not resulted in agreement on fundamental issues arising from the concept; there is a lack of definition regarding key ideas such as poverty and degradation, sustainability and participation. Difficulties are also caused by the absence of complete scientific knowledge. It has accordingly been stated that "[t]he process of converting the broad concepts into a practical basis for analysis and decision-making is still in its infancy".[17]

Numerous suggestions have been made to elucidate the implications of the concept. An example, showing the all-embracing nature of the concept, is provided by the proposed Legal Principles and Recommendations on Environmental Protection and Sustainable Development, proposed by the Expert Group appointed by the WCED.[18] As a fundamental principle of sustainable development the Expert Group singled out the human right to a clean environment that is adequate for health and well-being. The Group also referred to the principle of conservation of nature and environment for the benefit of future generations. Other principles relate to specific areas of environmental protection, including the need to develop environmental standards, prior environmental assessment, the inclusion of civil society in environmental planning and the obligations of states to use transboundary or extraterritorial natural resources in reasonable and equitable manner. These principles confirm the duty to cease, and to provide compensation for, activities in breach of environmental obligations, and there are articles relating to peaceful settlement of environmental disputes. Others, also in an attempt to substantiate the legal implications of the concept, make a distinction between the "elements" underlying the notion of sustainable development and the "principles" relating to it.[19] "Elements" include concepts such as the principle of intergenerational equity, the principle of sustainable use, the principle of equitable use, and the principle of integration. "Principles" of sustainable development in-

[17] P. Raskin, et al., *supra* note 2, p. 6.

[18] Reprinted in R.D. Munro and J.G. Lammers (eds.), *Environmental Protection and Sustainable Development* (1987), p. 7.

[19] See, e.g., P. Sands, "International Law in the Field of Sustainable Development", 66 BYIL (1995), pp. 335-375; *id.*, "International Law in the Field of Sustainable Development: Emerging Legal Principles", in W. Lang (ed.), *Sustainable Development and International Law*, (1995), p. 53.

clude Principles 21 and 22 of the Stockholm Declaration (sovereignty over natural resources and the responsibility not to cause environmental harm), as do the principle of good neighbourliness and international co-operation, the principle of good governance (which includes participatory democracy), the principle of common but differentiated responsibility, the principle of preventive action, the precautionary principle and the polluter-pays-principle. Drawing partly from Principles listed in the 1992 Rio Declaration, Boyle and Freestone[20] include the following elements: sustainable utilisation as inferred from Principle 8 and closely connected with precautionary principle (Principle 15); integration of environmental protection and economic development, as embodied in Principle 4; and the right to development (Principle 4). These authors include the principles of inter- and intra-generational equity as well as procedural elements, such as environmental impact assessment and public participation in environmental decision-making, stating that the role of these principles "is not limited to the pursuit of sustainability, however, but has equal relevance to global and transboundary environmental law".[21] Increasingly, in recent years, the concept of sustainable development has also come to be seen as being integrated with human rights.[22] The role of a human rights approach in water agreements was stressed as a constraining factor in choices of possible outcomes. Ample supply of fresh water to both individuals and communities has to be secured as a necessary condition for human well-being and human dignity. The important role that is played

---

[20] A. Boyle and D. Freestone, "Introduction", in A. Boyle and D. Freestone (eds.), *International Law and Sustainable Development* (1999), pp. 9-16.

[21] *Ibid.*, p. 16.

[22] See D. McGoldrick, "Sustainable Development and Human Rights: An Integrated Conception", 45 *ICLQ* (1996), p. 796. The concept of sustainable development as expounded by McGoldrick is based on three pillars: international human rights law, international environmental law, international economic law: "[t]he integrated structure of sustainable development is such that it requires support from each of the pillars", at p. 797. Similar views were expressed by Madame Ksentini, in her Report on Human Rights and Environment, UN E/CN.4/Sub.2/1994/9, 6 July 1994. McCaffrey also argues that it is the duty of a state to safeguard human rights such as right to food, and thus secure clean potable water, which is a part of the right to food. He also argues that a state cannot refuse a co-riparian state water which is necessary for "survival of population on the ground that the water is needed for the economic development of the former"; S. McCaffrey, "A Human Right to Water: Domestic and International Implications", 5 *GIELR* (1992), p. 24.

by water in the culture and religion of indigenous people must also be remembered.[23]

What is apparent from the foregoing is the breadth of the concept of sustainable development, which makes it difficult to know exactly what legal content the concept itself adds to the existing body of principles of international environmental law.[24] Furthermore, if sustainable development is an international policy concept, it should as such imply some degree of accountability. Yet, as generally endorsed, it is accompanied by an express disclaimer of any intended encroachment upon state sovereignty.[25] Thus, it has been said that the concept is "inoperable" due to its inherent vagueness, but at the same time, that the emergence of a convenient definition that is agreeable to all players "would be an indication that the definition was inadequate, as the concept is too fundamental to be captured easily..."[26]

The ICJ made certain pronouncements to this effect in the 1997 *Gabcíkovo-Nagymaros* case[27] in which it acknowledged the existence and applicability of this principle in the context of international watercourses. The Court stated that

> "It is clear the Project's impact upon, and its implication for, the environment are of necessity a key issue. The numerous scientific reports which have been presented to the Court by the Parties – even if their conclusions are often contradictory – provide abundant evidence that this impact and these implications are considerable.
> In order to evaluate the environmental risks, current standards must be taken into consideration. This is not only allowed by the wording of Articles 15 and 19, but even prescribed, to the extent that these articles impose a continuing – and thus necessarily evolving – obligation on the parties to maintain the quality of the water of the Danube and to protect nature.

---

[23] E. Benevisti, "Collective Rights in the Utilisation of Shared Freshwater: The Challenges of International Resources Law", 90 *AJIL* (1996), p. 406. See Chapter 3 above.

[24] See, O. Elias, "Sustainable Development, War Reparations and Environmental Damage", in *Exploitation of Natural Resources in the 21st Century*, M. Fitzmaurice and M. Szuniewicz (eds.) 2003, p. 67, at pp. 76-90.

[25] G. Handl, *supra* note 12, pp. 25-26.

[26] *Ibid.*

[27] Judgment of 25 September 1997, *ICJ Rep* (1997), paragraph 140.

> The Court is mindful that, in the field of environmental protection, vigilance and prevention are required on account of the often irreversible character of damage to the environment and of the limitations inherent in the very mechanism of reparation of this type of damage. Throughout the ages, mankind has, for economic and other reasons, constantly interfered with nature. In the past, this was often done without consideration of the effects upon the environment. Owing to new scientific insights and to a growing awareness of the risks for mankind – for present and future generations – of pursuit of such interventions in a great number of instruments during the last two decades. Such new norms have to be taken into consideration, and such new standards given proper weight, not only when States contemplate new activities but also when continuing with activities begun in the past. This need to reconcile economic development with protection of the environment is aptly expressed in the concept of sustainable development".

For the purpose of the present case, this meant that the Parties together were to look afresh at the effects on the environment of the operation of the Gabcíkovo power plant. In particular, they were to find a satisfactory solution regarding the volume of water to be released into the old bed of the Danube and into the side-arms on both sides of the river.

It may be inferred from the Court's statement that prevention and vigilance are part and parcel of sustainable development and that it is not a static principle but an ongoing evolutionary process in which "current standards must be taken into consideration". However, the Court refrained from describing sustainable development as a "principle" and only referred to it as a "concept". In the Separate Opinion of Judge Weeramantry, however, the principle of sustainable development was viewed as being "more than a mere concept, but as a principle with normative value which is crucial to the determination of this case. Without benefits of its insights, the issues involved in this case would have been difficult to resolve".[28] He also stressed the evolutionary aspect of this principle and the importance of the applicability of the principle of contemporaneity to environmental standards since "environmental concerns are live and continuing concerns whenever the project under which they arise may have been inaugurated". Judge Weeramantry further stated that the normative value of this principle derives in part from its wide and

[28] *Ibid.*, at pp. 89-108.

general acceptance by the global community.[29] On the whole, the case may not be considered as being particularly illuminating as regards the crystallisation and development of the content and application of sustainable development in relation to international watercourses.

However, a different approach is proposed by Lowe, who, in discussing the case, argues persuasively that "the argument that the concept of sustainable development is now a binding norm of international law in the sense of 'normative logic' of traditional international law as reflected in Article 38(1) of the Statute of the International Court of Justice is not sustainable, but there is a sense in which the concept of sustainable development exemplifies another species of concepts of international environmental law".[30] He argues that all legal systems contain (primary) rules and principles that (potentially) overlap or conflict in relation to a specific set of facts (for example, "the right to development" and "environmental protection"), and there exist "modifying norms" that serve to enable a decision-maker to choose which rules or principles are to be given decisive force in a given situation. Sustainable development is of this character, and like other modifying norms (of which canons of interpretation in municipal law and the "Rule of Reason" and the "balancing of interests" test in disputes concerning extraterritorial jurisdiction are also examples), it does not depend upon state practice and *opinio juris*; nor does it necessarily carry a prescriptive charge. As Lowe puts it, "[w]hile the concept is insufficiently precise for it to be possible to say that it requires a state to do this or that, as a goal or policy it is perfectly adequate to offer some guidance to judges in their approach to establishing priorities and accommodations between primary norms". As such, sustainable development "can properly claim a normative status as an element of the process of judicial reasoning", exemplifying "another species of normativity which is of great potential value in the handling of concepts of international environmental law". The point is also made, however, that the concept of sustainable development may need to undergo further evolution before it

---

[29] See also Elias, *supra* n. 24, on the possible role of the concept in the work of the United Nations Compensation Commission

[30] V. Lowe, "Sustainable Development and Unsustainable Arguments," in A. Boyle and D. Freestone, *supra* note 20, p. 21.

becomes well suited for application by tribunals in this way.[31] Nevertheless, the concept, regardless of its status or normative force, can influence the decision-making of international courts and tribunals as well as negotiations.[32] It has also been argued that, even if international law as it stands cannot be said to require that development be sustainable, "it does require development decisions to be the outcome of a process which promotes sustainable development".[33]

Although the concept of sustainable development suffers from the drawbacks enumerated above, it has added a new dimension to international law and turned the attention of international lawyers in even more forceful manner than previously, to such problems as the conflict between North and South. On a more practical level it has added much to the debate concerning the expansion of financial and technical assistance to developing countries. In the words of Boyle and Freestone,

> "[w]hether or not sustainable development is a legal obligation, and as we have seen it seems unlikely, it does represent a goal which can influence the outcome of litigation and the practice of states and international organisations, and it may lead to significant changes and developments in the existing law. In that very important sense, international law does appear to require states and international bodies to take account of the objective of sustainable development, and to establish appropriate processes for doing so".[34]

3. International Legal Instruments on Sustainable Development and International Watercourses

A number of instruments address the question of the establishment of an international legal framework for the sustainable use of water resources. One such instrument is Agenda 21,[35] Chapter 18 of which is concerned

---

[31] As Lowe points out (*ibid.*), modifying norms also have a role to play even when states negotiate, and not only when third-party decision-makers are involved.

[32] *Ibid.*, p.32.

[33] P. Birnie and A. Boyle, *International Law and the Environment* (2nd edn. 2002), at p. 96.

[34] A. Boyle and D. Freestone, *supra* note 20, pp. 17-18.

[35] Agenda 21, Chapter 18, "Protection of the Quality and Supply of Fresh Water Resources: Application of Integrated Approaches to the Development, Management, and

with fresh water, and underscores the importance of sustainable use of shared water resources.[36] Three main objectives were identified: securing access to safe and sufficient water supplies or, at the lowest level, water supplies that meet basic drinking and food-growing requirements of peoples; enhancing public participation and management at the lowest level (subsidiarity); and attaining integrated development and management of water resources.[37] The other objectives of Agenda 21 in relation to water resources may be summarised as follows: the approach must be based on a premise that water is part of the ecosystem and a social and economic resource; special attention is to be paid to the rights of women, youths and indigenous people; water management must take into consideration the following fields: public health; the production, protection and distribution of food; environmental protection; conservation of natural resources; and reasonable charges for use of water to encourage the saving of water.[38]

Agenda 21 established a number of programmes to protect the quality and supply of water, two of which appear to be the most important with respect to the development of rules of international law relating to international watercourses. These are the programmes relating to integrated water resources development and management, and that relating to the protection of water resources, water quality and aquatic ecosystems.[39] The programme on integrated development and management of water resources establishes targets for states at the national and international level. At the national level, states, according to their capacities and availability of resources, are urged to establish their national action plans, institutional structures and legal instruments, and to create efficient water

---

Use of Water Resources". "Report of the United Nations Conference on Environment and Development", UN Doc. A/Conf.151/26, Annex II (1992).

[36] See E. Hey, "Sustainable Use of Shared Water Resources: The Need for a Paradigmatic Shift in International Watercourse Law", in G. Blake, W. Hildesley, M. Pratt, R.J. Ridley, C.H. Schofield (eds.), *The Peaceful Management of Transboundary Resources* (1995), pp. 127-152.

[37] *Ibid.*, p. 128.

[38] H.L.F. Saeijs and M.J. van Berkel, in *Scarcity of Water*, *supra* note 1, p. 15.

[39] The other programmes are: assessment of water resources; drinking water supply and sanitation; water and sustainable urban development; water and sustainable food production; and the impact of climate change on water resources.

programmes by the year 2000. States are urged to formulate water resources strategies and action programmes with regard to transboundary water resources management.

The programme for the protection of water resources supports "the holistic management of resources and a recognition of the interconnectedness of the elements related to freshwater and freshwater quality" (paragraph 18.35-36) and co-operation conducted for the mutual benefit of all states concerned, promoting the principle of balancing of interests. Aquatic ecosystems are to be preserved from any form of degradation on a "drainage basin" basis. Agenda 21 also emphasises the importance of the protection of groundwater. In order to achieve good water quality several actions have to be undertaken, such as the identification and preparation of outlines for the protection, conservation and rational use of all potential sources of water supply and water pollution prevention and control programmes. These programmes should be based on strategies to reduce pollution at source; environmental impact assessment; enforceable standards for major point source discharges and high risk non-point sources; and international water quality monitoring and management programmes. Agenda 21 also promotes other important general principles of environmental law in general such as the polluter-pays-principle, the precautionary principle and environment impact assessment.

It has been said that "Agenda 21 and Chapter 18 in particular is a blueprint for a legislative action in the field of the protection of and management of fresh water resources".[40] However, Agenda 21 is not a binding instrument. Nevertheless, it appears that states gradually implement postulates therein contained, not because it is a legally binding instrument "but because governments realise that it is in their own self-interest to do so".[41] The 2002 World Summit in Johannesburg followed up the route adopted in Rio.[42] It adopted a similar holistic integrated approach to the

[40] S. McCaffrey, *supra* note 8, p. 53.

[41] *Ibid.*

[42] See the Chapter IV of "Plan of Implementation of the World Summit on Sustainable Development", United Nations, *Report of the World Summit on Sustainable Development Johannesburg, South Africa*, 26 August-4 September 2002, A/Conf.199/20*, paragraphs 26-30.

problem of the management of water. The objectives of the World Summit have been summarised as follows:

> "halving, by the year 2015, the proportion of people who are unable to reach or to afford safe drinking water, and the proportion of people without access to basic sanitation; intensifying water prevention to reduce health hazards and protect ecosystems by introducing appropriate technologies and mitigating the effects of groundwater contamination, and establishing at the national level monitoring systems and effective legal frameworks; adopting prevention and protection measures to promote sustainable water use and to address water shortages; developing integrated water resource management and water efficiency plans by 2005; and developing and implementing national and regional strategies, plans and programmes on integrated river basin, watershed and groundwater management."[43]

Again, these objectives, and the aspirations do not impose binding legal obligations on states.

The 1997 UN Framework Convention on Non-Navigational Uses of International Watercourses, discussed in Chapter 2 above, is also important in this context. As discussed there, the fundamental principles underlying the Convention are the principles of equitable utilisation and prohibition of significant harm. Implementation of these principles is to be achieved through the general obligation to co-operate (Article 8) and imposes the procedural obligations of notification concerning planned activities that may have adverse effects (Article 12) and regular exchange of data and information (Article 9). The Convention also imposes on states the duty to protect and preserve ecosystems of international watercourses (Article 20). In order to facilitate this aim, watercourse states should establish joint management mechanisms, with a view to promoting the rational and optimal utilisation, protection and control of watercourses (Article 24).

The usefulness of the Convention for further development of the notion of sustainable use of international watercourses has been the subject of some discussion.[44] It has been said that the ILC's Draft Articles,[45]

---

[43] P. Sands, *Principles of International Environmental Law* (2nd edn., 2003), p. 496.
[44] E. Hey, *supra* note 36, p. 127.
[45] See Section 5 of Chapter 2 above.

which were adopted and became the Convention without significant modification, hamper rather than facilitate the objectives of Chapter 18 of Agenda 21. The main reason for this view is the considerable freedom accorded to states in implementing important principles of sustainable development. The wide discretion accorded to states appears to accord undue weight to state sovereignty, the effect of which is to limit the "capacity of international law to impose an obligation on a state without its consent and a lack of position for actors other than states in international law".[46] According to Agenda 21, states should facilitate the establishment of mechanisms that would assist implementation of Chapter 18, such as public participation, ensuring access to safe and sufficient water supplies and embracing the principle of subsidiarity. The Convention, in contrast, fails to confirm that the provision of safe and sufficient water supplies is a use which should have priority above other uses, and that vital human needs should prevail in case of conflict among uses in the absence of an agreement or custom establishing priority of uses.[47] The Convention also lacks provisions relating to transparency and is weak on guaranteeing the participation of individuals and collectives "in whose interest, ultimately, the management of international watercourses takes place".[48] The Draft Articles have also been criticized from the point of view of the interests of future generations, one of the main elements of the concept of sustainable use and development. This is because the Draft Articles and the Convention are not clear as to the relationship between the principles of equitable utilisation and prohibition of harm. The Convention does not prohibit unequivocally the occurrence of significant harm, but instead links it with the duty of due diligence, thus tolerating significant harm if the harm causing state was diligent. This solution is not strict enough to secure an environmentally sound environment for future generations.[49] All things considered, it does not appear that sustainability is sufficiently provided for in this the main international agreement on the use of inter-

[46] *Ibid.*, p. 19.

[47] *Ibid.*, p. 132.

[48] *Ibid.*, p. 133.

[49] M. Kroes, "The Protection of International Watercourses as Sources of Fresh Water in the Interest of Future Generations", in *The Scarcity of Water*, *supra* note 1, pp. 80-99 at p. 85.

national watercourses, particularly when compared to the provisions contained in the major non-binding instruments on the matter.

In October 2000, the Parliament and the Council of the European Union adopted a directive establishing a framework for Community action in the field of water policy.[50] The directive aims to establish a co-ordinated approach regarding all aspects of an integrated European water policy, and it adopts a model of management by river basin, the natural geographical and hydrological unit; Member States are required to set up river basin management districts which are the basic units of administration regarding the implementation of the directive.[51] The preamble is extensive and sets out the wide-ranging issues addressed in the directive. Article 1 sets out the purposes of the directive, which include: the establishment of a framework for the protection of inland surface waters, transitional waters, coastal waters and groundwater in order to prevent further deterioration and to protect and enhance the status of aquatic ecosystems and, with regard to their water needs, terrestrial ecosystems and wetlands directly depending on the aquatic ecosystems; the promotion of sustainable water use based on a long-term protection of available water resources; the progressive reduction of the discharge and emission of polluting substances; the mitigation of the effects of floods and droughts, thereby contributing to the provision of the sufficient supply of good quality surface water and groundwater as needed for sustainable, balanced and equitable water use. The directive sets out wide-ranging obligations to be implemented by Member States within established deadlines, based on their circumstances and according to the situation and condition of each river basin. The deadlines may be extended, and Member States may aim to achieve less stringent environmental objectives[52] than those set out in the directive, under specified conditions. The importance of public information and consultation is underlined (Article 14,

---

[50] Directive 2000/60/EC, *OJ* L327, 2000, pp. 1-73. See further, P. Sands, *Principles of International Environmental Law* (2nd edn. 1995), pp. 769-771.

[51] See, e.g., Articles 3, 5, 13 and 33 of the directive, and paragraphs 30, 33, 35 and 36 of the preamble.

[52] The "Environmental Objectives" of the directive are further laid out in Article 4. It has been said that the directive is rather ambiguous; see D. Grimeaud, "Reforming EU Water Law: Towards Sustainability?", 10 *RECIEL* (2001), p. 41.

and paragraphs 13, 18 and 46 of the Preamble). The directive also contains provisions governing international river basins, including both those entirely within the territory of the Community and those that extend beyond its boundaries; in the case of the latter, Member States are required to endeavour to produce and implement management plans governing the entire basin, and failing that, governing at least the part of the basin district within their territory (Article 13).

It is also stated that "as set out in Article 174 of the Treaty, the Community policy on the environment is to contribute to pursuit of the objectives of preserving, protecting and improving the quality of the environment, in prudent and rational utilisation of natural resources, and to be based on the precautionary principle and on the principles that preventive action should be taken, environmental damage should, as a priority, be rectified at source and that the polluter should pay" (Preamble, paragraph 11). Particularly significant for present purposes is the statement in paragraph 35 of the Preamble that the directive "is to contribute to the implementation of Community obligations under international conventions on water protection and management, notably the United Nations Convention on the protection and use of transboundary water courses and international lakes, approved by Council Decision 95/308/EC(15) and any succeeding agreements on its application".[53]

Regarding the Nordic states, much the co-operation discussed in Chapters 4 and 5 above will already be in line with the objectives of the directive. A new Finnish-Swedish transboundary water commission will be

[53] Paragraph 21 of the directive links the issue of the promotion of sustainable water use with the problem of pollution of the sea from land-based sources, and provides that the directive is to make a contribution towards enabling the Community and Member States to meet obligations "flowing from various international agreements containing important obligations on the protection of marine waters from pollution, in particular the Convention on the Protection of the Marine Environment of the Baltic Sea Area, signed in Helsinki on 9 April 1992 and approved by Council Decision 94/157/EC(11), the Convention for the Protection of the Marine Environment of the North-East Atlantic, signed in Paris on 22 September 1992 and approved by Council Decision 98/249/EC(12), and the Convention for the Protection of the Mediterranean Sea Against Pollution, signed in Barcelona on 16 February 1976 and approved by Council Decision 77/585/EEC(13), and its Protocol for the Protection of the Mediterranean Sea Against Pollution from Land-Based Sources, signed in Athens on 17 May 1980 and approved by Council Decision 83/101/EEC(14)". See also Article 1(e), to the same effect.

established to co-ordinate the implementation of the EU Water Framework Directive, in addition to the already considerable degree of co-operation between the two states.[54] Pursuant to the directive, two international river basin districts have been set up in the Lapland province in Finland, one shared with Sweden (the Tornio River) and the other shared jointly with Norway and Russia (consisting of catchments discharging into the Arctic Ocean).[55] While Finland and Sweden are Member States of the European Union, Norway is also bound to implement the Water Framework directive as it is a member of the European Economic Area. It is to be hoped that the machinery that exists for ensuring the effectiveness of European Community law in general could serve to enhance the implementation of the provisions of the Convention, and more generally the obligations set out in the directive promoting the sustainable use of water.

4. Nordic Watercourse Co-operation and Sustainable Development

In the light of the above, it may be asked whether the legal position in the regulation of the uses of Nordic watercourses is an improvement on the situation described in the previous section. The large network of treaties between Finland, Norway and Sweden, and between these states and Russia concerning the use of international watercourses will be examined to see how far they reflect the principles of sustainable use such as those expounded in Agenda 21.

Recognition of the need to co-operate and to balance the various uses of particular watercourses appears to be reflected in the treaty practice of these states. A good example of this is the regulation of Lake Inari by means of the Kaitakoski Hydroelectric Power Station and Dam. The agreement regarding the power station was concluded between Finland and the USSR on 24 April 1947 in relation to Lake Inari and Nikaskoski Dam.[56] This agreement included technical requirements such as those

---

[54] See Section 5 of Chapter 5 above.

[55] See <http://www.environment.fi/default.asp?node=9812&lan=en>.

[56] 1947 Agreement Between Finland and the USSR Concerning the Regulation of Lake Inari by means of the Niskakoski Control Dam, signed on 24 April 1947, *Suomen*

concerning the maintenance of water levels. Paragraph 2 of the Agreement (technical measures) was subsequently amended on 29 April 1954 by a Protocol. In 1956, Norway became a Party to the 1947 Agreement and the 1954 Protocol.[57] The technical Regulations appended to the 1956 Agreement provided for the possibility of future measures regarding conservation of fish stocks in Lake Inari. The governments of the USSR and Finland, as anticipated, concluded a Protocol on fish conservation, in particular on fish breeding activities in the Lake Inari aimed at guaranteeing the sustainability of fish stocks.[58]

In 1959, a new Agreement was concluded between the three Parties.[59] An additional Protocol to this Agreement was concluded between the USSR and Finland providing for compensation from the Government of the USSR in the event of any "loss or damage as have been or may have been caused to the lands, waters, structures or other property of any kind belonging to the State, communes and private persons and bodies of Finland under the Agreement of 24 April 1954..., and as payment for the works which has been and are to be carried out by the Finnish Ministry...". (Article 1)[60] This 1959 Agreement between Finland, the USSR and

---

Asetukokoelman 1947, No. 10 (on file with authors), superseded by Agreement of 1959. Text unpublished, the author's translation. Agreement between The Government of the Republic of Finland and the Government of the Union of Socialist Soviet Republics on Regulation of Lake Inari by means of the Dam Niskakoski and its Rules of Procedure (on file with authors).

[57] 1956 Protocol between Finland, Norway, and the Union of Soviet Socialist Republics concerning Amendments to the Regulation of 24 April 1947 for the Regulation of Lake Inari in Connection with the Use of the Niskakoski Dam and to the Protocol of 29 April 1954 concerning Amendments to Paragraph 2 of the Said Regulations, signed 24 February 1956, entered into force on the same day, 243 *UNTS* 147.

[58] 1983 Protocol between the Government of the Republic of Finland and the Government of the Union of Soviet Socialist Republics on the Participation of Soviet Organisation in Fish breeding Activities for the Conservation of Fish Stocks in Lake Inari, signed on 14 December 1983 entered into force on the same day, 1351 *UNTS* 142.

[59] 1959 Agreement between the Government of the Union of Soviet Socialist Republics, the Government of Norway and the Government of Finland concerning the Regulation of Lake Inari by Means of the Kaitakoski Hydroelectric Power Station and Dam, signed at Moscow on 29 April 1959, came into force on the same day, 346 *UNTS* 167.

[60] 1959 Additional Protocol between Finland and the USSR concerning Compensation for Loss or Damage and for Works to be Carried Out by Finland in Connection with the Agreement of 29 April 1959 Between Finland, Norway and the USSR Concerning the

Norway is also a good example of co-operation on exchange of information. Annex 3 of this agreement stipulates that the Finnish, Soviet and Norwegian Ministries will keep a daily log of the mean readings of water in different allocated parts of the watercourse and, that "...extracts from the logs and copies of the water level graphs shall be communicated to the other Parties on request" (Annex 3, Article 9).

Similar agreements were concluded by the governments of Finland and the USSR concerning the generation of hydroelectric power in the Vuoksi River and Lake Saimaa. The first of the agreements was concluded in 1972 and related to the production of electric power in the part of Vuoksi River by the Imatra and Svetogorsk hydroelectric stations.[61] This Agreement was supplemented by the Agreement of 1989, pursuant to which certain technical conditions were amended.[62] According to their preambles, both agreements were concluded by the two governments "desiring to regulate in a manner satisfactory to both Contracting Parties matters relating to the efficient operation of the Imatra hydroelectric station in the territory of the Republic of Finland and the Svetogorsk hydroelectric station in the territory of the Union of Soviet Socialist Republics..."[63] and "...taking into account the Agreement between the two countries concerning frontier watercourses... the principles generally recognised in international law for the use of watercourses which are of common interest to the States, and the good relations existing between the two countries".[64] Pursuant to this agreement, the USSR undertook to pay compensation for the losses of streamflow and energy amounting to 19,900 MWh per year.

Regulation of Lake Inari by means of the Kaitakoski Hydroelectric Power Station and Dam, signed on 29 April 1959, entered into force on 29 April 1959, 346 *UNTS* 209.

[61] 1972 Agreement between the Government of the Republic of Finland and the Government of the Union of Soviet Socialist Republics concerning the Production of Electric Power in the Part of the Vuoksi River bounded by the Imatra and Svetogorsk Hydroelectric Stations, signed on 12 July 1972, entered into force on 7 February 1973, 884 *UNTS* 64.

[62] 1989 Agreement between the Government of the Republic of Finland and the Government of the Union of Soviet Socialist Republics in relation to rules of regulation of the Lake Saima and the river Vuoksi, signed on 26 October 1989, entered into force on 8 September 1991, 1663 *UNTS* 325

[63] *Supra* note 61, p. 64; *supra* note 62, p. 336

[64] *Ibid.*

However, this trend is not always reflected in all treaties, as is illustrated by the agreements that were concluded between the USSR and Norway concerning the Pasvik River.[65] The agreement provides that the Soviet Union is not required to pay any compensation to Norway, Norwegian nationals or other persons for unavoidable damage caused to Norwegian territory or to Norwegian interests in general by flooding in connection with the construction and operation of water-power stations in the lower section. Likewise, Norway is not required to pay compensation to the Soviet Union, Soviet nationals or other persons for unavoidable damage caused under the same circumstances in the middle section of the river. However, as regards damage in the upper section of the river, the Soviet Union is required to pay a lump-sum in the amount of 1 million Nkr to Norway for any unavoidable damage caused to Norwegian territory or Norwegian interests, but not to physical or legal persons (Articles 10 and 11). The 1957 Agreement was supplemented by an agreement concluded in 1976[66] concerning compensation paid by Norway to the Soviet Union due to a decrease in power production, in the form of a transfer of the same amount of water to the Kola Peninsula (Article 3). These provisions do not seem to accord much weight to the concerns of sustainability, and the apparent eschewal of an unduly anthropomorphic approach (as may be suggested by the exclusions of compensation for damage caused to physical persons) cannot be considered to reflect environmental concerns in any meaningful sense.

Nevertheless, the importance attached to sustainability remains in evidence. As far back as 1928, Finland and Sweden concluded a Convention on joint exploitation and fisheries in the Tornio and Munio rivers.[67] This

---

[65] 1957 Agreement between Norway and the Union of Soviet Socialist Republics on the Utilisation of Water-Power on the Pasvik (Paatso) River, signed at Oslo, 18 December 1957, entered into force on 27 June 1958, 312 *UNTS* 274.

[66] 1976 Agreement between the Government of the Kingdom of Norway and the Government of the Union of Soviet Socialist Republics relating to Outlet of Water at the Norwegian Part of the River Pasvik (Patsjoki) above the Boris Gleb Power Plant, signed on 20 May 1976, entered into force on the same day (text on file with authors).

[67] 1927 Convention between the Republic of Finland and the Kingdom of Sweden Concerning the Joint Exploitation of the Salmon Fisheries in the Torneå (Tornio) and Munio Rivers, signed 10 May 1927, entered into force on 31 December 1927, LXX *LNTS* 201.

Convention provided for joint management of salmon exploitation and improvement of methods of salmon fishing, including regulations on maximum allowable catch during different seasons and also permissible nets. Norway and Russia also concluded an agreement concerning the management of fish stocks in the River Pasvik.[68] The Regulations annexed to the agreement contains typical provisions for these types of agreements, such as, licensing to fish, technical measures and closed seasons, all of which promote optimal exploitation of fish stocks.

Many articles in Chapter 7 of Agenda 21 provide for the full public participation of youth people, women, indigenous people, local communities, and delegate management of water resources to the lowest appropriate level (subsidiarity), "as keys to attaining the sustainable use of water resources".[69] This aspect of sustainable development and use has been implemented to quite a considerable extent in the Nordic co-operation. For example, we saw in Chapter 3[70] the extent to which the interests of the local population – the Saami – are taken into account in various ways in the management of watercourses in Lapland and Finnmark. Similarly, as seen in Chapter 4, the frontier river commissions consult the representatives of the Saami population in order to take decisions which may have effect on their rights.[71]

[68] 1971 Agreement between Norway and the Union of Soviet Socialist Republics on Fishing Regulation and Preservation of the Fish Stock in the Grense-Jacobs River (Voriema) and the Pasvik River (Patsjoki), text unpublished, signed on 7 December 1971, entered into force on the same day (text on file with authors).

[69] E. Hey, *supra* note 36, p. 133.

[70] See Sections 3 and 4 of Chapter 3 above.

[71] Another important field of common co-operation is timber-floating. At present this form of activity plays less crucial role. Nonetheless, timber floating formed an important part of the use of rivers. Agreements on timber floating usually provided for the participation of public representatives in the meetings of timber floating associations and of their governing bodies in order to safeguard public interest. See, e.g., 1949 Agreement between Sweden and Finland concerning Timber Floating in the Torne and Muonio Frontier Rivers, with Annexes, signed 17 February 1949, entered into force on 9 July 1949, 197 *UNTS* 123. If a public representative considers that a decision is contrary to the regulations in force or to the public interest and if the matter is not rectified after attention has been drawn to it, he reports the circumstances to the county administration which appointed him (Annex on Regulations, Article 13). Full compensation was provided for any damage

A more recent and important agreement in this context is the 1992 Helsinki Convention on the Protection and Use of Transboundary Watercourses and Lakes, to which all the Nordic countries and Russia are Parties.[72] This Convention adopts a modern approach to watercourse management, emphasizing the principle of sustainable use. It is based on three pillars: the precautionary principle, the polluter-pays-principle and the principle of intergenerational equity. This Convention may yet set a pattern for future multilateral co-operation in Nordic Europe and is currently used as the basis for the monitoring programme for minerals, phenols, nitrogen, total phosphorus and heavy metals in the river Vuoksi and Hiitolanjoki. Treaties such as the 1992 Treaty between the Republic of Finland and the Russian Federation on Co-operation in the Field of Environmental Protection[73] adhere to the principle of sustainable development, which is accorded a pivotal role in the regime established by the Convention. For example, Article 3 incorporates the precautionary principle and monitoring obligations, as well as provisions aimed at promoting ecological education.[74]

5. Concluding Remarks

From all the above it appears that co-operation in Nordic Europe and northern Russia does aim to achieve sustainability in the use of the watercourses in the area. Of course, as mentioned earlier, northern Europe has ample water resources, and it may be difficult to compare the situation

---

resulting from timber floating activity (Annex on Regulations, Article 21). If agreement cannot be reached as to liability or compensation, the matter is to be referred to arbitrators (Annex on Regulations, Article 24).

[72] 1992 UNECE Convention on the Protection and Use of Transboundary Watercourses and International Lakes, 31 *ILM* 1312 (1992). Finland signed on 18 March and ratified on 21 February 1996; Norway signed on 18 September and ratified on 1 April 1993; Russia signed on 18 March and ratified on 2 November 1993; Sweden signed on 18 March 1992 and ratified on 5 August 1993.

[73] 1992 Agreement Concerning Cooperation in the Field of the Environment, signed on 29 April 1992, entered into force on 14 January 1993, 1721 *UNTS* 362.

[74] Other illustrations of co-operation can be found at <http://www.environment.fi/default.asp?node=4080&lan=EN>.

here with that in more water-starved regions of the world. Nevertheless, it is submitted that the Nordic co-operation in the field of watercourses can serve as a blueprint for action in other areas. From the foregoing, perhaps the most important principle of sustainable water management introduced by Agenda 21, i.e. the need for a holistic, integrated approach, as well as the duty of riparian states to co-operate, based on the balancing of interests principle, have generally been implemented by riparian states of the region, and a successful attempt has been made to create a coherent system of watercourse co-operation which covers various uses of watercourses. Perhaps the best example of this is the solution adopted in the Agreement establishing the Finnish-Swedish Frontier River Commission.[75] The holistic approach adopted in the Agreement, the powers conferred on the Commission and the attention to the need for participation and transparency makes it a perfect example of sustainable approach to watercourses. Moreover, it may be noted that the majority of the agreements – even those preceding the emergence of the modern concept of sustainable development – between these states contain rules on compensation for harm, which indicates a rather sophisticated approach to the sustainable use of international watercourses, one promoted by the 1997 UN Convention. Finally, the broad approach taken by the European Union's Water Framework Directive could further enhance the realization of water policy in harmony with the dictates of sustainable development, even if Russia is not bound by its provisions.

[75] See Section 3 of Chapter 5 above.

Chapter 7
CONCLUDING REMARKS

The preceding chapters have attempted to describe and analyse aspects of the practice of Finland, Norway and Sweden, as well as their practice in co-operation with Russia, in respect of the management of international watercourses on their territory. Having sketched the general principles of international law regarding the use of watercourses, the nature and extent of co-operation between these countries was considered. This included an overview of the large network of treaties between these states, the institutions set up for the management and administration of watercourse issues, the extent to which the concerns of sustainability are addressed and the extent to which the rights and interests of the indigenous Saami populations, whose life is closely connected with the watercourses, are taken into account. On the whole, we can conclude that the watercourse management practice in these countries is quite advanced, and that, in general, it reflects various concerns and considerations that arise in the context of the equitable apportionment of water rights and the sustainable use of international watercourses. Some of the more important aspects of the practice of these states include: the adherence of all four states to the 1992 Helsinki Convention (considered to contain preferable provisions to those set out in, for example, the 1997 UN Convention); the great number of agreements on co-operation in respect of transboundary water issues; the various institutions set up to administer the co-operation (particularly the Finnish-Swedish Frontier River Commission); and the anticipated contribution of the EU Water Framework Directive. The existence of rules and principles do not necessarily guarantee their own effective implementation, but it is beyond question that the sheer expanse of mechanisms and institutions must provide a fertile ground for further studies on the subject.

As stated at the outset, the aim of this book is to examine this practice with a view to making a contribution to worldwide concern to achieve the sustainable use of water resources. It was noted that the position in the states under consideration might not offer easy solutions to the transboundary water resource problems that exist in other regions. There are vast expanses of freshwater in these states, and there is evidently a long history of co-operation in their use, and these are considerations that are not necessarily to be found in other parts of the world. However, it is considered that the more favourable situation in these states allows for a glimpse of the possibilities that exist in developing watercourse management strategies anywhere in the world; there will always be lessons to be drawn from the extensive practice of these states, and that is the basis upon which this study was undertaken. It should be noted that the co-operation includes the Soviet Union, and has been quite successful despite political and social differences. Nevertheless, even in these states, the earlier chapters show that the regulation of the use and management of watercourses is not without some difficulties.

International law regarding the use and management of watercourses has developed considerably in the course of the last century, and on the whole, the trend has been in favour of the principle of good neighbourliness. As indicated by the international Court in the *Gabcikovo-Nagymaros* case, in its most desirable form, this trend would also call for the establishment of joint institutions charged with the task of securing, as far as possible, exploitation for the mutual benefit of the states concerned on the one hand, and a more general environmental perspective on the other, taking into account the evolutionary character of international law as it relates to environmental protection. Together, these two aspects – bilateral interests coupled with protection of the environment – reflect to a certain degree the elements of the modern concept of sustainable development. The law of international watercourses must also share the evolutionary character of other areas of environmental law and the law relating to the exploitation of natural resources in taking account of the concept of sustainable development as being indispensable to the proper management of international watercourses. It is submitted that, on the basis of the preceding chapters, the practice of these states reflect concern for the concept of sustainable development, and that this further indicates that the nature and the extent of the co-operation between these states can serve at least as a testing ground, if not as a blueprint, for the development of watercourse management strategies in other parts of the world.

BIBLIOGRAPHY

A. Books and Articles

Åhren, I. – "Small Nations of the North in Constitutional and International Law", 64 *Nordic Journal of International Law* (1995), pp. 457-463

Alfredsson, G. – "The Right of Self-Determination and Indigenous Peoples", in C. Tomuschat (ed.), *Modern Law of Self-Determination* (1993), p. 50

Anaya, S.J. – *Indigenous Peoples in International Law* (Oxford University Press; New York/Oxford, 1996)

Baker Röben, B. – "Civil Liability as Control Mechanism for Environmental Protection at International Level", in F.L. Morrison and R. Wolfrum (eds.), *International, Regional and National Environmental Law* (Kluwer Law International; The Hague/ London/Boston, 2000), p. 821

Barsh, R.L. – "Indigenous Peoples in the 1990s: From Object to Subject of International Law", 7 *Harvard Human Rights Journal* (1994), pp. 33-86

Beach, H. – "The Saami of Lapland", in Minority Rights Group (ed.), *Polar Peoples: Self-Determination and Development* (Minority Rights Publications; London, 1994), pp. 149-150

Benevisti, E. – "Collective Right in the Utilisation of Shared Freshwater: The Challenges of International Resources Law", 90 *American Journal of International Law* (1996), p. 406

Birnie, P. and Boyle, A.E. – *International Law and the Environment* (Oxford University Press, 1st edn., 1992, 2nd edn., 2002)

Bohlin, J. – "Human Rights and Access to Natural Resources", 64 *Nordic Journal of International Law* (1995), pp. 495-499

Bourne, C. – "The International Law Association's Contribution to International Resources Law", 36 *Natural Resources Journal* (1996), pp. 156-216

—, "The *Case Concerning the Gabcíkovo-Nagymaros Project*: An Important Milestone in International Water Law", 8 *Yearbook of International Environmental Law* (1997), pp. 6-12

—, "Procedure in the Development of International Drainage Basin: The Duty to Consult and Negotiate", 10 *Canadian Yearbook of International Law* (1972), pp. 212-234

Boyle, A. – "*The Gabcíkovo-Nagymaros Case*: New law in Old Bottles", 8 *Yearbook of International Environmental Law* (1997), pp. 13-20

BOYLE, A. – "Making the Polluter Pay? Alternatives to State Responsibility in the Allocation of Transboundary Environmental Costs", in F. Francioni and T. Scovzzi (eds.), *International Responsibility for Environmental Harm* (Graham Trotman/Martinus Nijhoff Publishers; The Hague/Dordrecht/London, 1993), pp. 363-379.

BOYLE, A. AND FREESTONE, D. – *International Law and Sustainable Development* (Oxford University Press, 1999)

BRÖLMANN C. AND ZIECK, M. – "Indigenous Peoples", in C. Brölmann, R. Lefeber and M. Zieck (eds.), *Peoples and Minorities in International Law* (Martinus Nijhoff Publishers; Dordrecht/Boston/London, 1993), pp. 187-220

BRUCHACS, J. – *The Law of Non-navigational uses of International Watercourses* (Martinus Nijhoff Publishers; Boston/Dordrecht/Lancaster, 1993)

CAPONERA, D. – *The Law of International Watercourses, Some General Conventions, Declarations and Resolutions adopted by Governments, International Legal Institutions and International Organisations, on the Water Management of International Water Resources* (Food and Agriculture Organisation, 1980)

CAPOTORTI, F. – *Study on the Rights of Persons belonging to Ethnic, Religious and Linguistic Minorities*, Report to the UN Sub-Commission on the Prevention of Discrimination and Protection of Minorities UN Doc. E/CN.4/Sub.2/384/Rev. 1 (1979)

CAFLISCH, L. – "Règles Générales du droit des cours d'eau internationaux", 219 *RCADI* 1989, pp. 4-226

—, "The Law of International Watercourses in its Institutional Aspects", in W. Haller, A. Koltz and G. Muller (eds.), *Im Dienst an der Gemeinschaft, Festschrift für D. Schindler zum 65 Geburtstag* (Helbing u. Lichtenhahn; Basel, 1989), pp. 21-45

CASSESE, A. – *Self-Determination of Peoples: A Legal Reappraisal* (Cambridge University Press, 1995)

—, "Political Self-Determination, Old Concepts and New Developments", in A. Cassese (ed.), *UN Law/Fundamental Rights, Two Topics in International Law* (Sijthoff and Noordhoff; Alphen aan den Rijn, The Netherlands, 1979), p. 137

CEPELKA, C. – "The Dispute over Gabcíkovo-Nagymaros System of Locks is Drawing to a Close", 20 *Polish Yearbook of International Law* (1993), pp. 63-73

CHAUHAN, B.R. – *Settlement of International Water Law Disputes in International Drainage Basins* (E. Schmidt; Berlin, 1981)

CHURCHILL, R.R. – "Facilitating Transnational Civil Liability Litigation for Environmental Damage by Means of Treaties: Progress, Problems, and Prospects", 12 *Yearbook of International Environmental Law* (2001), pp. 3-41

CHURCHILL, R.R. AND LOWE, A.V. – *The Law of the Sea* (Manchester University Press, 2nd edn., 1999)

COBO, M. – *Study of the Problem of Discrimination against Indigenous Populations*, UN Doc. E/CN 4/Sub 2/1986/7 and Add. 1 to 4 (1986)

COLOMBOS, C.J. – *International Law of the Sea* (David McKay Company Inc; New York, 6th edn., 1967)

CRAWFORD, J. – "The Rights of Peoples: Some Conclusions", in J. Crawford (ed.), *The Rights of Peoples* (Clarendon Press; Oxford, 1988), pp. 160-175

—, "The Rights of Peoples' or Governments?", in J. Crawford (ed.), *The Rights of Peoples* (Clarendon Press; Oxford, 1988), p. 58

DANIEL, A. – "Civil Liability Regimes as a Complement to Multilateral Environmental Agreements: Sound International Policy or False Comfort?", 12 *Review of European Community and International Environmental Law*, Issue 3, (2003), p. 225

DAVIDSON, J.S. – "The Rights of Indigenous People in Early International Law", 5 *Canterbury Law Review* (1994), pp. 39-423

DICKSTEIN, H.L. – "International Lake and River Pollution Control: Question of Method", 12 *Columbia Journal of Transnational Law* (1973), p. 487-519

DIGEST of United States Practice in International Law (1978)

DIGEST of United States Practice in International Law (1979)

DONKERS, H. – "Fresh Water as a Source of International Conflicts: the Water Conflicts between Israel, Jordan and the Palestinians", in E.H.P. Brans, E.J. de Haan, J. Rinzema and A. Nolkaemper (eds.), *The Scarcity of Water. Emerging Legal and Policy Responses* (Kluwer Academic Publishers, London; The Hague, 1997), p. 136

EBBESSON, J. – "The Notion of Public Participation in International Environmental Law", 8 *Yearbook of International Environmental Law* (1997), pp. 51-98

ECONOMIST, THE, 5th October 2002, Comment by Alf Olsen

ELIAS, O. – "Sustainable Development, War Reparations and Environmental Damage", in *Exploitation of Natural Resources in the 21st Century: The Challenge of Sustainable Development*, M. Fitzmaurice and M. Szuniewicz (eds.) 2003, pp. 67-89

FAURE, M. AND HUI, W. – "The International Regimes for the Compensation of Oil-Pollution Damage: Are They Effective?", 12 *Review of European Community and International Environmental Law*, Issue 3, (2003), p. 242

FITZMAURICE, M. – "Environmental Protection and the International Court of Justice", in V. Lowe and M. Fitzmaurice (eds.), *Fifty years of the International Court of Justice, Essays in Honour of Sir R. Jennings* (Cambridge University Press, 1995), pp. 308-315

—, "Some Reflections on Public Participation in Environmental Matters as a Human Right in International Law", 2 *Non-State Actors and International Law* (2002), pp. 1-22

FITZMAURICE, M. – "Expression of Consent to be Bound by a Treaty as Developed in Certain Environmental Treaties", in J. Klabbers and R. Lefeber (eds.), *Essays on the Law of Treaties, A Collection of Essays in Honour of Bert Vierdag* (Martinus Nijhoff Publishers; The Hague, 1998), pp. 59-80

FRANCK, T. – "The Emerging Right to Democratic Governance", 86 *American Journal of International Law* (1992), pp. 46-91

GRIMEAUD, D. – "Reforming EU Water Law: Towards Sustainability?", 10 *Review of International and European Community Environmental Law* (2001), p. 41

HANDL, G. – "National Uses of Transboundary Air Resources: The International Entitlement Issue Reconsidered", 26 *Natural Resources Journal* (1986), pp. 405-467

—, "Territorial Sovereignty and the Problem of Transnational Pollution", 69 *American Journal of International Law* (1975), pp. 50-77

—, "Environmental Security and Global Change", 1 *Yearbook of International Environmental Law* (1990), pp. 3-31

HANNIKAINEN, L. – "The State of Minorities, Indigenous Peoples and Immigrant and Refugee in Four Nordic States", 65 *Nordic Journal of International Law* (1996), pp. 1-71

HANNNUM, H. – "Rethinking Self-Determination", 34 *Virginia Journal of International Law* (1993), pp. 1-69

—, *Autonomy, Sovereignty and Self-Determination, The Accommodation of Conflicting Rights* (University of Pennsylvania Press, 1990)

HARHOFF, F. – "The Status of Indigenous Peoples under International Law: Greenland and the Right to Self-Determination", 32 *Canadian Yearbook of International Law* (1994), pp. 243-258

HARMON, J. – US Attorney-General, Opinion, 21 Official Opinions of the Attorneys General of the United States (1895), p. 274

HERTSLET, L. (ed.) – *A collection of treaties and conventions between Great Britain and Foreign Powers* (Butterworths; London, 1827-1924)

HEY, E. – "Sustainable Use of Shared Water Resources: The Need for a Paradigmatic Shift in International Watercourse Law", in G. Blake, W. Hildesley, M. Pratt, R.J. Ridley and C.H. Schofield (eds.), *The Peaceful Management of Transboundary Resources* (Graham & Trotman/Nijhoff; The Hague/London/Boston, 1995), pp. 127-152

HIGGINS, R. – *Problems and Process; International Law and How We Use It* (Clarendon Press; Oxford, 1995)

HOENDERKAMP, E. – "The Danube: Damned or Dammed? The Dispute between Hungary and Slovakia Concerning the Gabcíkovo-Nagymaros Project", 8 *Leiden Journal of International Law* (1995), pp. 287-309

IFTENE, P – *Voisinage et bon voisinage en droit international* (Editions A. Pedone; Paris, 1980)

IORNS, C.J. – "Indigenous Peoples and Self Determination: Challenging State Sovereignty", 24 *Case Western Reserve Journal of International Law* (1992), pp. 199-348

IUCN/Inter-Commission Task Force on Indigenous People, *Indigenous Peoples and Sustainability: Cases and Actions* (International Books; Utrecht, 1997)

JAATINEN, S. – "Joint Finnish-Russian Commission on the Utilization of Frontier Watercourses-Cooperation at its Best", in *Cooperation on the Frontier Watercourses During Thirty Years* (published by Joint Finnish-Russian Commission on the Utilization of Frontier Watercourses, 1995), pp. 11-15

KAPASHESIT, R. AND KLIPPENSTEIN, M. – "Indigenous Group Rights and Environmental Protection", 36 *McGill Law Journal* (1991), pp. 934-936

KAUPPI, L., TSIKUREJEVA, L.S., ANTIKAINEN, S., AND KORHONEN, M. – "Protection and Monitoring of the Frontier Watercourses" in *Cooperation on the Frontier Watercourses During Thirty Years* (published by Joint Finnish-Russian Commission on the Utilization of Frontier Watercourses, 1995), pp. 29-37

KISS, A. – "Legal procedures Applicable to Interstate Conflicts on Water Scarcity: the Gabcíkovo Case", in E.H.P. Brans, E.J. de Haan, J. Rinzema and A. Nolkaemper (eds.), *The Scarcity of Water. Emerging Legal and Policy Responses* (Kluwer Academic Publishers; London/The Hague, 1997), pp. 59-79

KROES, M. – "The Protection of International Watercourses as Sources of Fresh Water in the Interest of Future Generations" in E.H.P. Brans, E.J. de Haan, J. Rinzema and A. Nolkaemper (eds.), *The Scarcity of Water. Emerging Legal and Policy Responses* (Kluwer Academic Publishers, London/The Hague, 1997), pp. 80-99

KSENTINI, F.Z – "Report on Human Rights and Environment", 6 July 1994, UN Doc. E/CN.4/Sub.2/1994/9

KLABBERS, J. AND LEFEBER, R. – "Africa: Lost Between Self-Determination and *Uti Possidetis*", in C. Brölmann, R. Lefeber and M. Zieck (eds.), *Peoples and Minorities in International Law* (Martinus Nijhoff Publishers; Dordrecht/Boston/London, 1993), pp. 37-76

KOSKENNIEMI, M. – "National Self-Determination Today: Problems of Theory and Practice", 43 *International and Comparative Law Quarterly* (1994), pp. 241-269

LAMMERS, J. – *Pollution of International Watercourses* (Martinus Nijhoff Publishers; Boston/Dordrecht/London/Lancaster, 1984)

—, "The Gabcíkovo-Nagymaros case Seen in Particular from the Perspective of the Law of International Watercourses and the Protection of the Environment", 11 *Leiden Journal of International Law* (1998), pp. 287-320

LEFEBER, R. – *Transboundary Environmental Interference and the Origin of State Liability* (Kluwer Law International; The Hague, 1996)

LERNER, N. – "The Evolution of Minority Rights in International Law", in C. Brölmann, R. Lefeber and M. Zieck (eds.), *Peoples and Minorities in International Law* (Martinus Nijhoff Publishers; Dordrecht/Boston/London, 1993), pp. 73-101

LIPPER, J. – "Equitable Utilization", in A.H. Garretson and C.J. Olmstead (eds.), *The Law of International Drainage Basins* (Oceana Publications; New York, 1967), pp. 15-88

LOIBL, G. – "Groundwater Resources - A Need for International Regulation", 5 *Austrian Review for International and European Law* (2000), pp. 81-120

LOWE, V. – "Sustainable Development and Unsustainable Arguments", in A. Boyle, and D. Freestone (eds.), *International Law and Sustainable Development* (Oxford University Press, 1999), pp. 19-37

LUSO-AMERICAN DEVELOPMENT FOUNDATION, *Shared Water Systems and Transboundary Issues with Special Emphasis on the Iberian Peninsula*, Proceedings of the Conference held at the Luso-American Development Foundation, Lisbon, 2000

MALANCZUK, P. – "Sustainable Development: Some Critical Thoughts in the Light of Rio Conference", in K. Ginther, E. Denters (eds.), *Sustainable Development and Good Governance* (M. Nijhoff; Dordrecht/Boston, 1995), pp. 23-38

MARKS, G.C. – "Indigenous People in International Law. The Significance of Francisco Vittoria and Banolome di Casa", 13 *Australian Yearbook of International Law* (1992), pp. 1-51

McCAFFREY, S. – *The Law of International Watercourses: Non-Navigational Uses* (Oxford University Press, 2001)

—, "The International Law Commission Adopts Draft Articles on International Watercourses", 89 *American Journal of International Law* (1995), pp. 395-404

—, "Non-Navigational Uses of International Watercourses", in R. Lefeber (ed.), *Contemporary International Legal Issues: Opportunities at a Time of Momentous Change* (Martinus Nijhoff; Dordrecht, 1994), p. 380

—, "A Human Right to Water: Domestic and International Implications", 5 *Georgetown International Environmental Law Review* (1992), pp. 1-20

—, "Water Scarcity: Institutional and Legal Responses", in E.H.P. Brans, E.J. de Haan, J. Rinzema and A. Nolkaemper (eds.), *The Scarcity of Water. Emerging Legal and Policy Responses* (Kluwer Academic Publishers; London/The Hague, 1997), pp. 52-54

McCAFFREY, S. AND SINJELA, M. – "The 1997 United Nations Convention on International Watercourses", 92 *American Journal of International Law* (1998), pp. 97-107

McGOLDRICK, D. – "Sustainable Development and Human Rights: An Integrated Conception", 45 *International and Comparative Law Quarterly* (1996), p. 796

MENON, P.K. – "Institutional Mechanism for the Development of International Water Resources", 8 *Revue Belge de Droit International* (1972), p. 81

MERRILS, J.G. – *International Dispute Settlement* (Cambridge University Press, 3rd edn., 1998)

MINDE, H. – "A Century of Norwegian Research into Sámi Rights", in A. Victorin (ed.), 31 *Scandinavian Studies in Law* (Juristförlaget; Stockholm, 1995), pp. 109-140

MOODY, R. – *The Indigenous Voice, Visions and Realities* (International Books; Utrecht, 1988)

MORRIS, G.T. – "In Support of the Right of Self-Determination for Indigenous People under International Law", 29 *German Yearbook of International Law* (1986), pp. 277-316

MÜLLERSON, R. – *International Law, Rights and Politics* (Routledge; London, 1994)

—, *Human Rights Diplomacy* (Routledge; London, 1997)

MYERS, N. – "Eco-refugees: a crisis in the making", Vol. 3, 4 *People & the Planet* (1994), pp. 6-9

NETTHEIM, G. – "'Peoples and 'Population' - Indigenous Peoples and the Rights of Peoples", in J. Crawford (ed.), *The Rights of Peoples* (Clarendon Press; Oxford, 1988), p. 188

NOLLKAEMPER, A. – *The Legal Regime for Transboundary Water Pollution: between Discretion and Constraint* (Martinus Nijhoff/Graham Trotman; Dordrecht/Boston/London, 1994)

NOWAK, M. – "The Evolution of Minority Rights in International Law", in C. Brölmann, R. Lefeber and M. Zieck (eds.), *Peoples and Minorities in International Law* (Martinus Nijhoff Publishers; Dordrecht/Boston/London, 1993), pp. 103-118

NYYSSONEN, J. – "The Environmental Sustainability of the Property Rights Regimes in Inari: The Performance of the Forest Government and Reindeer Herding Co-operatives", in S. Jentoft, H. Minde and R. Nilsen (eds.), *Indigenous Peoples* (Eburon Academic Publishers; The Netherlands, 2003), pp. 249-274

OKOWA, P. – *State Responsibility for Transboundary Air Pollution in International Law* (Oxford University Press, 2000)

OLLILA, M. AND ROZKOV, N. – "Regulation of the Lake Saimaa and the River Vuoksi Watercourses", in *Cooperation on the Frontier Watercourses during Thirty Years* (published by the Joint Finnish-Russian Commission on the Utilization of Frontier Watercourses, 1995), p. 21

PERRIN, C. – "Approaching Anxiety: The Insistence of the Postcolonial in the Declaration on the Rights of Indigenous Peoples", 7 *Law and Critique* (1995), pp. 55-74

POMERANCE, M. – *Self-Determination in Law and Practice, The New Doctrine in the United Nations* (M. Nijhoff; Boston, 1982), pp. 37-42

Raić, D. – *Statehood and the Law of Self-Determination* (Kluwer Law International; The Hague/London, 2002)

Raskin, P., Hansen, E., Margolis, R.M – "Water and Sustainability; Global patterns and long-range problems", 20 *Natural Resources Forum* (1996) pp. 1-15

Riseth, Age J. – "Sami Reindeer Management in Norway: Mondernization Challenges and Conflictong Strategies", in S. Jentoft, H. Minde and R. Nilsen (eds.), *Indigenous Peoples* (Eburon Academic Publishers; The Netherlands, 2003), pp. 229-248

Saeijs, H.I.F. and van Berkel, M.J. – "The Global Water Crisis: The Major Issue of the Twenty-first Century, A Growing and Explosive Problem", in E.H.P. Brans, E.J. de Haan, J. Rinzema and A. Nolkaemper (eds.), *The Scarcity of Water. Emerging Legal and Policy Responses* (Kluwer Academic Publishers; London/ The Hague, 1997), pp. 3-20

Sands, P. – *Principles of International Environmental Law*, Cambridge University Press, 2003)

—, "International Law in the Field of Sustainable Development", 66 *British Yearbook of International Law* (1995), pp. 335-375

—, "International Law in the Field of Sustainable Development: Emerging Legal Principles", in W. Lang (ed.), *Sustainable Development and International Law* (Graham & Trotman; London, 1995), pp. 53-66

Sanders, D. – "Collective Rights", 13 *Human Rights Quarterly* (1991), p. 369

—, "Self-Determination and Indigenous Peoples", in C. Tomuschat (ed.), *Modern Law of Self-Determination* (M. Nijhoff Publishers; Boston, 1993), pp. 55-81

Schreuder, J.P. – "Minority Protection within the Concept of Self-Determination", 8 *Leiden Journal of International Law* (1995), pp. 53-80

Schrijver, N. – *Sovereignty over Natural Resources: Balancing Rights and Duties in an Interdependent World* (Cambridge University Press, 1997), pp. 336-339

Sette-Camara, J. – "Pollution of International Rivers", 186 *Recueil des Cours* (1984-III), pp. 117-218

Shutkin, W.A. – "International Human Rights Law and the Earth: The Protection of Indigenous People and The Environment", 31 *Virginia Journal of International Law* (1991), p. 484

Sillanpää, L. – Political and Administrative Responses to Saami Self-Determination (University of Helsinki, Finland, 1994)

Silva Soares, G.F. – "The Basel Liability and Compensation for Damage Resulting from Transboundary Movements of Hazardous Wastes and Their Disposal", 12 *Yearbook of International Environmental Law* (2001), pp. 69-105

Simmonds, K.R. (ed.) – *New Directions in the Law of the Sea*, Vol. V, (Oceana Publications; London/Rome/New York, 1995)

SPIRY, E. – "From 'Self-Determination' to a Right to 'Self-Development' for Indigenous Groups", 38 *German Yearbook of International Law* (1995), p. 129

SUTHERLAND, J. (with assistance of D. Craig and D. Posey) – "Emerging New legal Standards for Comprehensive Rights", 27 *Environmental Policy and Law* (1997), p. 13-30

TANZI, A. – "The UN Convention on International Watercourses as a Framework for the Avoidance and Settlement of Waterlaw Disputes", 11 *Leiden Journal of International Law* (1998), pp. 441-472

TANZI, A. AND ARCARI, M. – *The United Nations Convention on the Law of International Watercourses* (Kluwer Law International; London/The Hague/ Boston, 2001)

TECLAFF, L.A. – "Fiat or Custom: The Checkered Development of International Water Law", 31 *Natural Resources Journal* (1991), pp. 45-73

THORNBERRY, P. – *International Law and the Rights of Minorities* (Clarendon Press, Oxford 1991)

TOMUSCHAT, C. (ed.) – *Modern Law of Self-Determination* (M. Nijhoff Publishers; Boston, 1993)

TUULENTIE, S. – "For and Against the Rights of Sami Peoples: The Argumentation of the Finnish Majority in the Debate on the Sami Rights", in S. Jentoft, H. Minde and R. Nilsen (eds.), *Indigenous Peoples* (Eburon Academic Publishers; The Netherlands, 2003), pp. 275-296

TUUNAINEN, P., KUTIZOV, A.M., AUVINEN, H. AND NIEMELÄ, A. – "Fish Studies in Joint Finnish-Russian Frontier Water-Courses", in *Cooperation on the Frontier Watercourses During Thirty Years* (published by Joint Finnish-Russian Commission on the Utilization of Frontier Watercourses, 1995), pp. 39-51

VALLO, O. AND KLEEMOLA, E. – "Nearby Area Cooperation with St. Petersburg and the Leningrad District to Improve Protection of Watercourses", in *Cooperation on the Frontier Watercourses During Thirty Years* (published by Joint Finnish-Russian Commission on the Utilization of Frontier Watercourses, 1995), pp. 57-59

VAN DER VYVER, J.D. – "State Sovereignty and the Environment in International Law", 109 *South African Law Journal* (1992), p. 472

VON MARTENS, G.F. – *Nouveau Recueil Général des Traités*, (Dieterich; Goettingue, 1843-1875)

WILMER, F. – *The Indigenous Voice World Politics* (Sage Publications, 1993)

WIRKKALA, R.S. AND KETTUNEN, I. – "Water Quality of the River Vuoksi on the Finnish and Russian Sides", in *Cooperation on the Frontier Watercourses During Thirty Years* (published by Joint Finnish-Russian Commission on the Utilization of Frontier Watercourses, 1995), pp. 61-68

YLI-KUHA, KARI – "The Sami", at <http://www.lysator.liu.se/nordic/scn/faq23 .html#2.3.1>

B. Documents of the International Law Commission

Report of the ILC on the work of its thirty-fifth session, UN Doc. A/38/10, *YBILC* (1983) Vol. II (Part Two), p. 62

Report of the ILC on the Work of its fortieth session, UN Doc. A/43/10, *YBILC* (1988), Vol. II (Part Two), p. 22

Report of the ILC on the work of its forty-third session, UN Doc. A/46/10, *YBILC* (1991), Vol. II (Part Two), p. 63

1991 Draft Articles on the Law of the Non-Navigational Uses of International Watercourses, in *Report of the ILC on the work of its forty-third session*, UN Doc. A/46/10, *YBILC* (1991), Vol. II (Part Two), p. 67

1994 Draft Articles on the Law of the Non-Navigational Uses of International Watercourses, UN Doc. A/49/10, *YBILC* (1994), Vol. II (Part Two), p. 89

Resolution on Confined Transboundary Groundwater, UN Doc. A/49/10, *YBILC* (1994), Vol. II (Part Two), p. 135

Report of the International Law Commission on the work of its forty-sixth session, UN Doc. A/49/10, *YBILC* (1994), Vol. II (Part Two), p. 89

Report of the ILC on the Work of its fifty-third session, UN Doc. A/56/10 available at <http://www.un.org/law/ilc/reports/2001/english/cover.htm>

Reports by S. McCaffrey

Second Report on the Law of Non-navigational Watercourses, UN Doc. A/CN.4/399 and Add.1-2, *YBILC* (1986), Vol. II (Part One), p. 130

Sixth Report on the Law of the Non-Navigational Uses of International Watercourses, UN Doc. A/CN.4/427, *YBILC* (1990), Vol. II (Part I), p. 41

Reports by S. Schwebel

Third Report on the Non-Navigational Uses of International Watercourses, UN Doc. A/CN.4/348 and Corr.1, *YBILC* (1982), Vol. II (Part One), p. 76

Reports by J. Barboza

Sixth Report on International Liability for Injurious Consequences Arising out of Acts not Prohibited by International Law, UN Doc. A/CN.4/428, *YBILC* (1990), Vol. II (Part One), p. 83

Reports by R. Rosenstock

First Report on the Law of Non-Navigational Uses of International Watercourses, UN Doc. A/CN.4/451, *YBILC* (1993), Vol. II (Part One), p. 179

C. Documents of the United Nations

Legal aspects of Hydro-Electric Development of Rivers and Lakes of Common Interest, UN Doc. E.ECE/136 (1952)

General Assembly, 1970 Declaration on Principles of International Law concerning Friendly Relations and Co-operation among States in accordance with the United Nations Charter, UN Doc. A/Res/2625 (XXV)

—, Resolution on Co-operation between States in the Field of the Environment, UN Doc. A/Res/2995 (1972)

—, Resolution on co-operation in the Field of Environment concerning Natural Resources Shared by Two or More States, UN Doc. A/Res/3129 (1973)

—, Resolution on the Charter of Economic Rights and Duties, UN Doc. A/Res/3281 (1974)

—, 1992 Declaration on the Rights of Persons Belonging to National or Ethnic, Religious and Linguistic Minorities, UN Doc. A/RES/47/135, adopted on 18 December 1992

Economic Commission for Europe, 1990 *UN/ECE Guidelines on Responsibility and Liability Regarding Transboundary Water Pollution*

1972 UN Declaration on the Human Environment, Stockholm 16 June 1972, 11 *ILM* 416

1992 Rio Declaration on Environment and Development, 13 June 1992, 31 *ILM* 874

UN Subcommittee on Prevention of Discrimination and Protection of Minorities, Study of the Problems of Discrimination against indigenous Population, UN Doc. E/CN.4/sub.2/1986/7 and Adds.1-4 (1986), p. 28

—, UN Doc. E/CN.4/sub.2476 and Add.1-6

—, UN Doc. E/CN.4/Sub.2/1982/2 and Add.1-7

—, UN Doc. E/CN.4/sub.2/1983/21 and Add.1-8

Agenda 21, "Report of the United Nations Conference on Environment and Development", UN Doc. A/Conf.51/26, Annex II (1992)

Committee on Economic, Social and Cultural Rights, General Comment No. 15, *The right to water (Arts. 11 and 12 of the International Covenant on Economic, Social and Cultural Rights)*, UN Doc. E/C.12/2002/11 (Twenty-ninth session, 2002) at <http://www1.umn.edu/humanrts/gencomm/escgencom15.htm>

Sub-Commission on Prevention of Discrimination and Protection of Minorities (at present Sub-Commission on the Protection and Promotion of Human Rights), *Draft Declaration on the Rights of Indigenous Peoples,* UN Doc. E/CN.4/Sub.2/1994/2/Add.1 (1994)

Working Group on Indigenous Populations, *Declaration on Principles on the Rights of Indigenous Peoples,* Geneva (1985), reaffirmed and amended by representatives of indigenous peoples and organisations meeting in Geneva (1987), reprinted in UN Doc. E/CN.4/Sub.2/1987.22, Annex 5 (1987)

Human Rights Committee, General Comment No. 23 (Article 27) UN Doc. HRI\GEN\1\Rev.1 (1994), (Fiftieth session, 1994)

—, *Lubicon Lake Band* case (Bernard Ominayak et al. v. Canada), Communication No. 167/1984. Text of the decision of the Human Rights Committee of 1990 in 11 *Human Rights Law Journal* (1990), pp. 305-311

—, *Kitok* case, Communication No. 197/1985, Report of the Human Rights Committee, UN Doc. A/43/40, pp. 221-230

—, *Ilmari Länsman case* (Ilmari Lansman et al. v. Finland), Communication No. 511/1992, Human Rights Committee, Final Decisions, 74, CCPR/C57/1 (1996)

UNESCO, Intergovernmental Committee for the Protection of the World Cultural and Natural Heritage, *Operational Guidelines for the Implementation of the World Heritage Convention*, WHC/2Revised, February 1995

UNEP, 1978 Principles of Conduct on Shared Natural Resources, Official Records of the General Assembly, Thirty-Third Session, Supplement No. 25, (A/33/25), pp. 154-155

D. Other Reports and Documents

Arctic Council, Project on Co-Management of Marine Resources in Arctic Areas with Respect to Indigenous Peoples and Traditional Ecological Knowledge at < http://www.arctic-council.org/sdwg_projects.asp>

—, *2002 Report from the Sustainable Development Working Group*, "Project on Sustainable Reindeer Husbandry", at <http://www.arctic-council.org/files/inari2002sao/sdwg_report.pdf>

Convention on Biological Diversity (1992), *First National Report of Sweden*, at <http://www.biodiv.org/doc/world/se/se-nr-01-en.pdf>.

—, National Action Plan for Biodiversity in Finland for 1997-2005 at <http://www.biodiv.org./doc/world/fi/fi-nr-01-en.pdf>

—, Norway's National Report on Implementation of the Convention on Biological Diversity, at <http://www.biodiv.org/doc/world/no/no-nr-01-en.pdf>

Directive 2000/60/EC of the European Parliament and of the Council of 23 October 2000 establishing a framework for Community action in the field of water policy, *Official Journal* L 327 , 22/12/2000, p. 0001-0073).

Framework Convention for the Protection of National Minorities, "Report submitted by the Government of Norway to the Council of Europe pursuant to Article 25 of the Convention", 2 March 2001, at <http://www.coe.int/T/e/human_rights/Minorities/2._FRAMEWORK_CONVENTION_(MONITORING)/2._Monitoring_mechanism/3._State_reports/ACFC_SR(2001)001%20E%20state%20report%20Norway.asp#TopOfPage>

—, "Report submitted by the Government of Finland to the Council of Europe pursuant to Article 25 of the Convention", 16 February 1999, at <http://www.coe.int/T/e/human_rights/Minorities/2._FRAMEWORK_CONVENTION_(MONITORING)/2._Monitoring_mechanism/3._State_reports/ACFC_SR(1999)003%20%20E%20state%20report%20Finland.asp#TopOfPage>

—, "Report submitted by the Government of Sweden to the Council of Europe pursuant to Article 25 of the Convention", 2001, at <http://www.coe.int/T/e/human_rights/Minorities/2._FRAMEWORK_CONVENTION_(MONITORING)/2._Monitoring_mechanism/3._State_reports/ACFC_SR(2001)003%20E%20state%20report%20Sweden.asp#TopOfPage>

Institut de Droit International, "Heidelberg Regulation on River Navigation", *Annuaire de l'Institute de Droit International*, Session de Heidelberg 1887, also at: <http://www.idi-iil.org/idiF/resolutionsF/1887_hei_01_fr.pdf>

—, "Resolution on the Pollution of Rivers and Lakes and International Law of 12 September 1979", *Annuaire de l'Institute de Droit International,* Session of Athens, Vol. 58 (1980), p. 197

International Law Association, "1966 Helsinki Rules on the Uses of the Waters of International Rivers", *Report of the Fifty-Second Conference*, Helsinki, (1966), p. 484

—, "Montreal Rules of International Law Applicable to Transfrontier Pollution", *Report of the Sixtieth Conference*, Montreal, 1982, pp. 531-552

International Labour Organization, "Report of the Committee on Convention 107", *International Labour Conference*, Provisional Record 25, 76th Session.

International Council for International Law, *1995 Report of the Expert Group Meeting on Identification of Principles of International Law for Sustainable Development*, Geneva, Switzerland, 26-28 September 1995, at <http://www.un.org/gopher-data/esc/cn17/1996/backgrnd/law.txt>

Joint Finnish-Russian Commission on the Utilization of Frontier Watercourses, "Frontier Guards Assist the Commission", in *Cooperation on the Frontier Watercourses during Thirty Years* (published by the Joint Finnish-Russian Commission on the Utilization of Frontier Watercourses 1995), p. 53

Non-Governmental Organisation Conference on Discrimination against Indigenous Populations, *Draft Declaration on Principles for the Defence of Indigenous Nations and Peoples of the Western Hemisphere*, Geneva (1977), UN Doc. E/CN.4/Sub.2/476/Add.5, Annex 4 (1981)

Organisation for Economic Co-operation and Development, 1974 OECD Principles Concerning Transfrontier Pollution

Organisation for Economic Co-operation and Development, 1976 OECD Recommendation on Equal Right of Access in Relation to Transfrontier Pollution

—, 1977 OECD Recommendation for the Implementation of a Regime of Equal

Right of Access and Non-Discrimination in relation to Transfrontier Pollution

13th Saami Conference, *The Saami Programme for the Environment,* at <http://www.dkik.gl/komp/saami_programme_4_the.html>

United Nations Conference on Environment and Development (Rio), Declaration, UN Doc. A/CONF.151/26/Rev.1, Report of the UNCED, Vol. 1

United Nations Conference on the Human Environment, Declaration (Stockholm), UN Doc. A/CONF/48/14/REV.1

World Bank, *Tribal Peoples in Bank-Funded Projects*, World Bank Operational Manual, (1982)

—, *Indigenous Peoples*, World Bank Operational Directive 4.20 (1991), at <http://wbln0018.worldbank.org/Institutional/Manuals/OpManual.nsf/toc2/0F7D6F3F04DD70398525672C007D08ED?OpenDocument>

World Commission on Environment and Development

—, Legal Principles and recommendations on Environmental Protection and Sustainable Development", reprinted in R.D. Munro and J.G. Lammers (eds.), *Environmental Protection and Sustainable Development* (1987)

—, *Our Common Future* (Brundtland Report), (Oxford University Press, 1987)

World Council of Indigenous Peoples, *Declaration on Principles of Indigenous Rights*, adopted at Fourth General Assembly of the Council, Panama (1984), reprinted in UN Doc.E/CN.4/1985/22, Annex 2 (1985)

TABLE OF TREATIES

A. Multilateral Agreements

1997 UN Convention on the Law of Non-Navigable Uses of International Watercourses, signed 21 May 1997, not yet in force, 36 *ILM* 700

1999 Basel Convention on the Transport of Transboundary Hazardous Waste adopted the Protocol on Liability and Compensation for damage Resulting from Transboundary Movement of Hazardous Wastes and Their Disposal, signed 22 March 1989, in force on May 1992, available at <http://www.unep.ch./basel/COP5/liabilityJ172000.html>

2003 Protocol on Civil Liability and Compensation for Damage Caused by the Transboundary Effects of Industrial Accidents on Transboundary Water, signed 21 May 2003, not yet in force, available at <http://www.unece.org/env/civil-liability/documents/protocol_e.pdf>

B. Agreements between Denmark, Finland, Norway and Sweden

1962 Agreement between Finland, Denmark, Iceland, Norway and Sweden Concerning Cooperation. Signed 23 March 1962, in force 1 July 1962, 434 *UNTS* 145

1962 Agreement between Finland, Denmark, Norway and Sweden Concerning uniform rules for the marking of navigable waters, signed 18 September 1962, entered into force 18 October 1962, 442 *UNTS* 228 (terminated on 1 July 1978) 1122 *UNTS* 378

1974 Convention between Denmark, Finland, Norway and Sweden on the Protection of the Environment, signed 19 February 1974, in force 5 October 1976 for all participants, 13 *ILM* 592

1989 Agreement between Denmark, Finland, Norway and Sweden on Cooperation over National Territorial Borders with the Aim of Preventing or Limiting Damage to Man or Property or the Environment in the Event of Accidents, signed 20 January 1989, in force 9 August 1989, 1777 *UNTS* 250

C. Agreements between Norway and Sweden

1929 Agreement on Certain Questions Relating to the Law of Watercourses, signed 11 May 1929, in force 1 August 1931, CXX *LNTS* 279

1969 Exchange of Letters Constituting an Agreement Concerning the Free Passage of Salmon in Vanern Lake, signed at Stockholm on 22 July 1969, in force the same day, 968 *UNTS* 253

1971 Protocol on the Construction and Maintenance of reindeer fences along certain sections of the International Frontier (Jamtland county and Nord-Trondelag and Sor-Trondelang counties) (with annexes and maps), signed 13 December 1971, in force 16 June 1972, 968 *UNTS* 326

1991 Agreement Concerning Fishing of Salmon and Trout in Svinesund, Iddefjorden and Enningsdalelva, signed 5 December 1991,in force 1 January 1992, on file with authors

D. Agreements between Finland and Norway

1924 Convention Concerning the Passage of Travelers over the Pasvik (Patsjoki) and the Jakobselv (Vuoremajoki) and Final Protocol, signed 28 April 1924, in force 26 September 1924, XXX *LNTS* 35 No. 757

1924 Convention Concerning the Frontier between the Province of Finnmark and the Territory of Petsamo, and Final Protocol, signed 28 April 1924, in force 26 September 1924, XXX *LNTS* 49

1925 Agreement between Norway and Finland concerning the international legal regime of the waters of the Pasvik (Patjoki) and Jakobselv (Vuoremaloki) signed 14 February 1925, in force the same day, on file with authors

1925 Navigation Convention between Finland and Norway, signed 19 December 1925, in force 20 September 1926, LVI *LNTS* 183

1951 Agreement Concerning the Transmission from the Neiden Watercourse, of Water from Garsjoen, Kjerringvatn and Forestevannene, to the Gandvik Watercourse, signed 25 April 1951, in force the same day, 1257 *UNTS* 70

1953 Agreement between Norway and Finland Regarding Fishing Regulations for the Fishing Area of the Tana River, signed at Helsinki on 20 May 1953, in force 20 May 1953, 173 *UNTS* 163

1957 Agreement between Norway and Finland concerning the construction and maintenance of a bridge across the Anarjokka (Inarijoki) River, signed on 28 June 1957, in force the same day, 272 *UNTS* 196

1959 Exchange of Notes Constituting an Additional Agreement to the 1953 Agreement between Norway and Finland Regarding Fishing for the Fishing Area of the Tana River (signed at Helsinki on 20 May 1953), signed at Oslo on 2 June 1959, in force 1 June 1959, 338 *UNTS* 373

1960 Agreement between the Kingdom of Norway and Finland Regarding New Fishing Regulations for the Fishing Area of the Tana River, signed at Oslo on 15 November 1960, in force 1 January 1961, 383 *UNTS* 178 (terminated by Agreement of 1972 Concerning Common Regulations for Fishing in the Fishing Area of the Tana River)

1964 Agreement between the Republic of Finland and the Kingdom of Norway Regarding Fishing in the Fishing Area of the Naatamo (Neiden) Watercourse, signed at Oslo on 9 June 1964, in force 9 June 1964, 503 *UNTS* 205

1972 Agreement Concerning Common Regulations for Fishing in the Fishing Area of the Tana River, signed 12 May 1972, in force 1 January 1973, 1289 *UNTS*

105 (terminated by the Agreement of 1989 Concerning Common Regulations for Fishing in the Fishing Area of the Tana River)

1976 Agreement Concerning Fisheries, signed 29 December 1976, entered into force 11 May 1977, 1051 *UNTS* 292

1977 Agreement Concerning Fishing in the Fishing Area of Naatamo (Neiden) River, signed 14 December 1977, in force 1 June 1984, 1215 *UNTS* 121, as amended by the Agreement of 3 May 1984, in force 1 June 1984, 1372 *UNTS* 213

1980 Agreement Concerning a Norwegian-Finnish Commission for Transboundary Watercourses, signed 5 March 1980, in force 1 May 1981, *Suomen Saadosko-koelman* 1981, No. 32 (translation on file with authors)

1989 Agreement Concerning Common Regulations for Fishing in the Fishing Area of the Tana River, signed 1 March 1989, in force 1 January 1990, 1588 *UNTS* 195

E. Agreements between Norway and Russia and its Predecessors

1947 Final Protocol of the Mixed Soviet-Norwegian Commission, Descriptive Protocol with Annexes, 415 Protocols describing the frontier marks and an album of maps and triangulation diagrams constituting an agreement for the demarcation of the State Frontier between the two countries, signed 18 December 1947, in force 23 May 1949, 52 *UNTS* 3

1949 Agreement between the Royal Norwegian Government and the Government of the Union of the Soviet Socialist Republics Concerning the Regime of the Norwegian-Soviet Frontier and Procedure for the Settlement of Frontier Disputes and Incidents, signed 29 December 1949, in force 30 October 1950, 83 *UNTS* 342

1957 Agreement Between Norway and Union of the Soviet Socialist Republics on the Utilization of Water-Power on the Pasvik (Paatso) River, signed 18 December 1957, in force 27 June 1958, 312 *UNTS* 274

1971 Agreement Concerning the Regulation of Fishing and the Preservation of Fish Stocks in the Grense-Jacobs River (Voriema) and the Pasvik River (Patsojoki), signed 7 December 1971, in force the same day, on file with authors

1976 Agreement Concerning the Outlet of Water at the Norwegian Part of the Pasvik River (Paatsojoki) above the Boris Gleb Power Plant, signed 20 May 1976, in force the same day, on file with authors

1988 Agreement between the Kingdom of Norway and the Government of the USSR on Co-operation in the Field of Environmental Protection, signed 15 January 1988, in force same day, on file with authors

1992 Agreement between the Kingdom of Norway and the Government of the Russian Federation on co-operation in the Field of Environmental Protection, signed 13 September 1992, in force the same day, on file with authors

F. Agreements between Finland, Norway, and Russia or its Predecessors concerning Lake Inari

1947 Agreement Between Finland and the USSR Concerning the Regulation of Lake Inari by means of the Niskakoski Control Dam, signed 24 April 1947, *Suomen Asetukokoelman* 1947, No. 10, on file with authors (superseded by Agreement of 1959)

1954 Protocol for the Implementation of the Agreement of 24 April 1947 between Finland and the USSR concerning the Regulation of Lake Inari by means of the Niskakoski Control Dam, signed 29 April 1954, in force, on file with authors, on file with authors (superseded by Agreement of 1959)

1956 Protocol Between Finland and the USSR Concerning Amendments to the Regulations of 24 April 1947 for the Regulation of Lake Inari in connection with the Use of the Niskakoski Dam and to the Protocol of 29 April 1954 concerning Amendments to paragraph 2 of the Said Regulations, signed 24 February 1956, in force the same day, 243 *UNTS* 147 (superseded by the Agreement of 1959 Concerning the Regulation of Lake Inari by means of the Kaitakoski Hydroelectric Power Station and Dam)

1959 Agreement (with Annexes) Between the Union of Soviet Socialist Republics, Norway and Finland, Concerning the Regulation of Lake Inari by means of the Kaitakoski Hydroelectric Power Station and Dam, signed 29 April 1959, in force the same day, 346 *UNTS* 167

1959 Additional Protocol Between Finland and the USSR Concerning Compensation for Loss or Damage and for Works to be Carried Out by Finland in Connection with the Agreement of 29 April 1959 Between Finland, Norway and the USSR Concerning the Regulation of Lake Inari By means of the Kaitakoski Hydroelectric Power Station and Dam, signed 29 April 1959, in force the same day, 346 *UNTS* 209

1983 Protocol between Finland and the USSR on the Participation of Soviet Organizations in Fish Breeding Activities for the Conservation of the Fish Stocks in Lake Inari, signed 14 December 1983, in force the same day, 1351 *UNTS* 142

G. Agreements between Finland and Russia or its predecessors

1920 Treaty of Peace, signed 14 October 1920, in force 31 December 1920, III *LNTS* 6

1922 Convention Regarding Fishing and Sealing in the Territorial Waters of the Arctic Ocean, signed 21 October 1922, in force 2 July 1924, XXIX *LNTS* 197

1922 Convention Regarding Fishing and Sealing in Lake Ladoga, signed 28 October 1922, in force 2 July 1924, XXIX *LNTS* 211

1922 Convention Concerning the Maintenance of Rivers, Channels and the Regulation of Fishing on Watercourses forming part of the Frontier Between Finland and Russia signed 28 October 1922, in force the same day, XIX *LNTS* 183 and 67 *UNTS* 157 (terminated by the Agreement of 1964)

1922 Convention Regarding the Floating of Timber in Watercourses flowing from Finland to Russia or vice versa, signed 28 October 1922, in force the same day, XIX *LNTS* 153 and 67 *UNTS* 153, as amended by the Agreement of 15 October 1933 that entered into force 7 February 1934, CXLIX *LNTS* 243 and 67 *UNTS* 153 (terminated by the Agreement of 1964)

1923 Convention Regarding the Navigation of Finnish Merchant and Cargo Vessels on the Neva between Lake Ladoga and the Gulf of Finland, signed 5 June 1923, in force 20 August 1923, XVIII *LNTS* 217

1928 Protocol Modifying the Article VII of the Convention of 5 June 1923 regarding the Navigation of Finnish Merchant and Vessels on the Neva between Lake Ladoga and the Gulf of Finland, signed 17 March 1928, in force 31 July 1928, LXXX *LNTS* 151

1932 Convention of Conciliation, signed 22 April 1932, in force 9 August 1932, CLVII *LNTS* 401

1947 Treaty between the USSR and Finland on the Transfer to the Territory of the USSR of part of the State Territory of Finland in the Region of the Janiskoski Hydroelectric Power Station and the Niskakoski Control Dam, signed 3 February 1947, in force 18 April 1947, 216 *UNTS* 231

1960 Agreement Concerning the Regime of the Finnish-Soviet State Frontier and the Procedure for the Settlement of Frontier Incidents, signed 23 June 1960, in force 5 October 1960, 379 *UNTS* 277

1962 Agreement on the Transfer for Rent of the Saimaa Canal and Part of the Island of Maly Vysotsky, signed 27 September 1962, in force 30 September 1963, 479 *UNTS* 122

1964 Agreement Concerning Frontier Watercourses, signed 24 April 1964, in force 6 May 1965, 537 *UNTS* 231

1964 Agreement between Finland and the USSR concerning Frontier Watercourses, signed 24 April 1964, in force 6 May 1965, 573 *UNTS* 231

1964 Protocol to the Agreement of 27 September 1962 on the Transfer for Rent of the Saimaa Canal and Part of the Island of Maly Vysotsky, signed 11 August 1964, in force 12 September 1964, *Suomen Asetuskokoelman* 1964 No. 47, translation on file with authors

1965 Agreement between the Government of Russia (former Soviet Union) and Finland concerning Reindeer, signed 4 June 1965, in force 12 March 1966, 560 *UNTS* 180

1965 Agreements concerning the boundaries of sea areas and the continental shelf in the Gulf of Finland, signed 20 May 1965, in force 25 May 1966, 566 *UNTS* 38

1965 Agreement between Finland and Russia on the Frontier Water Systems, signed 24 April 1964, *Suomen Asetuskokoelman* 1965 No. 26, translation on file with authors

1965 Agreement between Finland and Russia on the delimitation of the leased Territory of the Saimaa Canal and Maly Visotsky island, signed 17 December 1965, *Suomen Asetuskokoelman* 1966, No. 3, translation on file with authors

1972 Agreement Concerning the Production of Electric Power in the Part of the Vuokski River bounded by the Imatra and Svetogorsk Hydroelectric Stations, signed 12 July 1972, in force 7 February 1973, 884 *UNTS* 64

1985 Agreement between Finland and Russia concerning Co-operation in the Field of Environmental Protection, signed 5 July 1985, in force 10 January 1986, 1419 *UNTS* 166

1989 Agreement of Co-operation between Finland and Russia for Adoption of Measures to Diminish Substances Polluting the Atmosphere, signed 26 October 1989, *Suomen Asetuskokoelman* 1990, No. 35, translation on file with authors

1989 Agreement in Relation to Rules of Regulating Lake Saimaa and River Vuoksi, signed 26 October 1989, in force 9 October 1991, 1663 *UNTS* 325

1992 Agreement concerning Co-operation in the field of the Environment, signed 29 April 1992, in force 14 January 1993, 1721 *UNTS* 362

1992 Agreement between Finland and Russian on Co-operation between the regions of Murmansk, the Republic of Karelia and the St. Petersburg and Leningrad regions, signed 20 January 1992, *Suomen Asetuskokoelman* 1992, No. 61-62, translation on file with authors

1992 Agreement between Finland and Russian on Water Pollution Action Programme in the basin of the Baltic Sea and other territories adjacent to the frontier between Finland and Russia, signed 26 May 1992, *Suomen Asetuskokoelman* 1992, No. 77, translation on file with authors

H. Agreements between Finland and Sweden

1810 Treaty on Frontier Regulation, signed 20 November 1810

1923 Navigation Convention between Finland and Sweden and Final Protocol, signed 26 May 1923, in force 21 June 1923, XVIII *LNTS* 57

1924 Convention Concerning the Establishment on a Permanent Commission for Investigation and Conciliation, signed 27 June 1924, in force 13 September 1924, XXIX *LNTS* 19

1927 Convention Concerning the Joint Exploitation of the Salmon Fisheries in the Tornea and Muonio Rivers, signed 10 May 1927, in force 31 December 1927, LXX *LNTS* 201, and Declaration of 10 May 1927 Concerning the Adoption of Regulation for Fishing in the Fishery Zone of the Tornea River and of 8 September 1966 Concerning the Application of the Convention of 10 May 1927; terminated by Agreement of 1971

1949 Agreement Concerning Timber Floating in the Torne and Muonio Frontier Rivers, signed 17 February 1949, in force 9 July 1949, 197 *UNTS* 123

1971 Agreement Concerning Frontier Rivers (with Annexes), signed 16 September 1971, in force 1 January 1972, 825 *UNTS* 191

I. Other Conventions

1804 Convention between France and Elector of Mainz, in G.F. von Martens, *Nouveau Receuil General des Traités*, (1843-1875), Vol. VII, p. 261

1815 Final Act of the Congress of Vienna, L. Hertslet (ed.), A collection of treaties and conventions between Great Britain and Foreign Powers, Vol. I, p. 3

1885 Act of Berlin, *Australian Treaty Series* (1920) No. 17

1926 Persia-Russia Convention regarding the Mutual Use of Frontier Rivers and Waters, signed 20 February 1926, in force the same day, in L. Shapiro, *Soviet Treaty Series 1917-1928* (Vol. I, 1950), p. 314

1927 Turkey-USSR Convention regarding the Use of Frontier Waters, signed 8 January 1927, in force the same day, in L. Shapiro, *Soviet Treaty Series 1917-1928* (Vol. I, 1950), p. 324

1934 USSR-Manchukuo Agreement regarding the Improvement of Navigation on Frontier Rivers, signed 4 September 1934, in force the same day, in L. Shapiro, *Soviet Treaty Series 1929-1935* (Vol. II, 1955), p. 110

1932 Poland-USSR Convention regarding Juridical Relations on the Frontier, Article IX, signed 10 April 1932, in force 4 October 1934, CXLI *LNTS* 349, in L. Shapiro, *Soviet Treaty Series 1929-1935* (Vol. II, 1955), p. 48.

1976 Frigg Field Agreement made by Norway and the United Kingdom, 1977 *UKTS* 113

INDEX

GPSR Compliance

The European Union's (EU) General Product Safety Regulation (GPSR) is a set of rules that requires consumer products to be safe and our obligations to ensure this.

If you have any concerns about our products, you can contact us on ProductSafety@springernature.com

In case Publisher is established outside the EU, the EU authorized representative is:

Springer Nature Customer Service Center GmbH
Europaplatz 3
69115 Heidelberg, Germany

Batch number: 10854423

Printed by Printforce, the Netherlands